By John Carver:

Board Leadership: A Bimonthly Workshop with John Carver
The CarverGuide Series on Effective Board Governance
John Carver on Board Governance (video)
Empowering Boards for Leadership (audio)

Other books in the Jossey-Bass Nonprofit and Public Management Series:

Achieving Excellence in Fund Raising, *Henry A. Rosso and Associates*
The Board Member's Guide to Fund Raising, *Fisher Howe*
The Board Member's Guide to Strategic Planning, *Fisher Howe*
Board Overboard, *Brian O'Connell*
Building an Effective Nonprofit Board (audio), *National Center for Nonprofit Boards*
The Drucker Foundation Self-Assessment Tool for Nonprofit Organizations, *The Peter F. Drucker Foundation for Nonprofit Management*
Executive Leadership in Nonprofit Organizations, *Robert D. Herman, Richard D. Heimovics*
Governing Boards, Revised Edition, *Cyril O. Houle*
The Jossey-Bass Handbook of Nonprofit Leadership and Management, *Robert D. Herman and Associates*
The Leader of the Future, *Frances Hesselbein, Marshall Goldsmith, Richard Beckhard, Editors*
Leader to Leader (quarterly), *The Peter F. Drucker Foundation for Nonprofit Management*
Making Boards Effective, *Alvin Zander*
Managing for Accountability, *Kevin Kearns*
Marketing Nonprofit Programs and Services, *Douglas B. Herron*
Nonprofit Boards and Leadership, *Miriam M. Wood, Editor*
Nonprofit Management and Leadership (quarterly)
The Organization of the Future, *Frances Hesselbein, Marshall Goldsmith, Richard Beckhard, Editors*
Pathways to Leadership, *James Lawrence Powell*
Welcome to the Board, *Fisher Howe*

Boards That Make a Difference

Boards That Make a Difference

A New Design for Leadership in Nonprofit and Public Organizations

Second Edition

John Carver

JOSSEY-BASS
A Wiley Company
www.josseybass.com

Published by

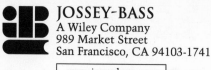

JOSSEY-BASS
A Wiley Company
989 Market Street
San Francisco, CA 94103-1741

www.josseybass.com

Copyright © 1997 by John Wiley & Sons, Inc.

Jossey-Bass is a registered trademark of John Wiley & Sons, Inc.

Jossey-Bass books and products are available through most bookstores. To contact
Jossey-Bass directly, call (888) 378-2537, fax to (800) 605-2665, or visit our website at
www.josseybass.com.

Substantial discounts on bulk quantities of Jossey-Bass books are available to
corporations, professional associations, and other organizations. For details and
discount information, contact the special sales department at Jossey-Bass.

We at Jossey-Bass strive to use the most environmentally sensitive paper stocks available
to us. Our publications are printed on acid-free recycled stock whenever possible, and
our paper always meets or exceeds minimum GPO and EPA requirements.

Policy Governance[SM] is a service mark of John Carver.

Library of Congress Cataloging-in-Publication Data

Carver, John.
    Boards that make a difference : a new design for leadership in
nonprofit and public organizations / John Carver. — 2nd ed.
        p.   cm. — (The Jossey-Bass nonprofit series) (The Jossey-
Bass public administration series)
    Includes bibliographical references and index.
    ISBN 0-7879-0811-8
    1. Directors of corporations.   2. Associations, institutions,
etc.—Management.   3. Nonprofit organizations—Management.
I. Title.   II. Series.   III. Series: The Jossey-Bass public
administration series.
    HD2745.C37   1997
    658.4'22—dc21   97–4694

HB Printing   10 9 8   SECOND EDITION

The Jossey-Bass Nonprofit and
Public Management Series

Contents

Preface to the Second Edition

When the first edition of *Boards That Make a Difference* came out in 1990, the Policy Governance^{SM} model was already in use all across the United States and Canada. Traditional approaches to the board role were so prevalent, however, that this radically new idea was still not very visible. In the intervening years, the Policy Governance model of board leadership has become known from coast to coast. It has even gone beyond North America to Europe and Australia and, if book sales are an indication, to Japan as well. Personal presentations around the world and global Web access (www.carvergovernance.com) promise to accelerate the model's influence still further.

There is also increasing attention to Policy Governance from those whose interest is not in nonprofit and public organizations but in the befuddled state of corporate governance. Boards of business corporations have come increasingly under the spotlight of stockholder groups, regulators, and academics alike. Thus far, however, none of the various proposals to improve the corporate boardroom have the conceptual integrity offered by Policy Governance. In 1996, the board of British Petroleum (BP), the third largest corporation in Europe, adopted a detailed Policy Governance–based plan. Other business corporations in the United States and Canada have been using adaptations of Policy Governance for up to a decade. There may be light at the end of the tunnel.

Consultants are adding Policy Governance to their bag of tricks. I have personally trained dozens of consultants in the fine points of theory and implementation. As widespread experience with the model accumulates (Gregory, 1996a, 1996b; Royer, 1996a, 1996b), we can see that we've learned much and still have much to learn. Organized, credible research is still lagging. We can point to research that enhances our understanding of theory and implementation issues and that which is too flawed to be useful, but most strikingly, we cannot find much research at all.

Admittedly, research on the effectiveness of Policy Governance is difficult. Is a board to be counted as using the model simply because it claims to be doing so, or worse, because its CEO says it is? Or do we count it only if it has in place all, or a significant amount, of the model's principles and concepts? Such judgment calls require researchers who are skilled not only in experimental design and analysis but in Policy Governance as well, or else how will they know it when they see it? There are striking examples of those who possess research skills but who have a flawed understanding of the model (Murray, 1994; Brudney and Murray, 1996). On the other hand, there also is a growing body of useful research by those who do understand the model (C. J. Smith, 1996). Good criticism should push us toward a greater conceptual integrity. Governance deserves the best that competent criticism has to offer.

As printings of the first edition moved into the double digits, the time came for this second edition. I have updated most of the policy samples used in 1990 and added a chapter to display the process of policy development. Further, to describe step-by-step implementation, my wife, Miriam Mayhew Carver, and I have authored *Reinventing Your Board: A Step-by-Step Guide to Implementing Policy Governance,* to be released as a companion text a little later in 1997.

This second edition—proof in itself that a more sophisticated understanding of board leadership is lighting up the darkness—is dedicated to the board members, CEOs, and other leaders who have higher ideals of leadership than traditional governance structures and processes can ever support. Thanks for being bold, thanks for being conceptually flexible, and thanks for fine-tuning the mechanisms that make a better world.

Atlanta, Georgia   John Carver
March 1997

Preface

This is a book about boards, particularly boards of nonprofit and public organizations. But rather than describe nonprofit and public boards, councils, and commissions as they are, *Boards That Make a Difference* prescribes how they can be.

This is a hopeful book. Boards can be the forward-thinking, value-oriented, leading bodies we claim them to be. In my consulting work with a multitude of boards and chief executives, I have found a great deal of cynicism and resignation. Knowledgeable skeptics think boards can never get beyond being spoon-fed by their executives and that, because of their nature, boards must remain fundamentally reactive. With good evidence, many people believe that boards will always stumble from rubber-stamping to meddling and back again. They believe the realities of group decision making forever destine boards to be incompetent groups of competent people. My impressions, too, are just as dismal, but I believe the cynicism is justified *only so long as boards continue to be trapped in an inadequate design of their jobs.*

Board members are as conscientious and as giving a group as one could ever hope to find. Members of volunteer boards and underpaid public boards interrupt their personal and occupational lives to support something in which they believe. There is not adequate space to give sufficient credit to the works wrought by board members in any given community in one year. The personal drive of board members has accomplished formidable tasks. The perseverance of board members has surmounted seemingly intractable barriers. The patience of board members has outlasted drudgery. The generosity of board members has made the impossible possible.

Board members arrive at the table with dreams. They have vision and values. In many cases, their fervently held beliefs and sincere desire to make a difference impel them to board membership in the first place. Symphony board members want to improve community culture. City councilpersons want to increase the benefits of citizenship. A trade association board wants to augment business opportunities. School board members want to prepare children for life. Boards of hospitals, port authorities, social agencies, chambers of commerce, credit unions, and other organizations want to offer their constituents a better life.

Yet, by and large, board members do not spend their time exploring, debating, and defining these dreams. Instead, they expend their energy on a host of demonstrably less important, even trivial, items. Rather than having impassioned discussions about the changes they can produce in their world, board members are ordinarily found listening passively to staff reports or dealing with personnel procedures and the budget line for out-of-state travel. Committee agendas are likely to be filled with staff material masquerading as board work. Even when programs and services are on the agenda, discussion almost always focuses on activities rather than intended results. Boards are less incisive, goal directed, and farsighted than their average members.

Much as board members and executives unintentionally conspire to water down the powerful work of genuine governance, they often have a nagging awareness that something is not quite right. Usually, however, their recognition is focused on a specific aspect of board folly. It is rarely the basic design, the system of thought. Concern is often expressed as complaints about time spent on trivial items, time spent reading reams of documents, meetings that run for hours and accomplish little, committees that are window dressing for what staff members want to do, meddling in administration, staff members who are more in control of board agendas than is the board, reactivity rather than proactivity, an executive committee's becoming the de facto board, confusion about what is going on, a rubber-stamping of staff recommendations, and the lack of an incisive way to evaluate the executive.

Some of the preceding complaints apply to all nonprofit and public boards. In my experience, *most* of what the majority of boards do either does not need to be done or is a waste of time when done by the board. Conversely, most of what boards need to do for strategic leadership is not done. This sweeping indictment is not true of all boards all the time, of course, but I contend that it is startlingly true enough of the time to signal a major dysfunction in what we accept as normal.

In these pages I argue for dissatisfaction with what we now accept as ordinary and outline a path that boards can follow to become extraordinary. The failures of governance are not a problem of people, but of *process*. The problems lie squarely in our widely accepted approach to governance, including its treatment of board job design, board-staff relationships, the chief executive role, performance monitoring, and virtually all aspects of the board-management partnership. This book is a strong indictment of what is, but it is intended to make a compelling case for what can be.

The model presented here originated in the mid-1970s. Like many managers, I had training in a professional discipline rather than in management. As a CEO, or chief executive officer, I worked for years learning how to do what I was already paid to do. Those who worked for this manager-in-training endured that travesty far beyond what I can even now appreciate. As my skills as a manager grew, I became increasingly aware of the shaky foundation upon which management rests—the determination of purpose, which is largely a product of governance. Increasingly schooled as administrators, we worked toward haphazardly established ends as if we were introducing computer guidance into a Conestoga wagon. I was driven to discover what could bring governance into the modern age. Out of that quest, I developed an approach to governance that severely departed from much of conventional wisdom. Boards here and there wanted to hear more about it, so a consulting practice grew that subsequently made regular employment impossible.

I have worked with boards and their executives around the world, particularly in the United States and Canada. I meet with them twice in the average week. These clients have assets ranging from near zero to over $25 billion. In the course of this work, I have written articles on governance and executive management for such organizations as the U.S. Department of Health and Human Services (1979b), the Canadian Hospital Association (1989a), the Association of Mental Health Administrators (1979a, 1981b), the Human Interaction Research Institute (1984a), the National Association of Corporate Directors (1980a), the Non-Profit Administrator's Guide (1982), the University of Wisconsin (1981a), the Florida League of Cities (1984c), the Nonprofit Management Association (1984b), the

Indiana Library Association (1981c), the National Association of Community Leadership Organizations (1983), the Center for Community Futures (1986b), and others (1988a, 1988b). My work has been featured in audiotapes for the Public Management Institute (1985a) and Family Service America (1985b) and in videotapes for the Georgia Power Company (1986c), the National Recreation and Park Association (1987), and the University of Georgia (1989b). Quite a few other unpublished writings of mine have been circulated (1980b, 1985c, 1986a; Carver and Clemow, 1990).

I have run hundreds of governance and chief executive workshops for communitywide groups, state and national conferences, trade associations, and political bodies. The attraction for these clients was a model or framework that enabled them to see their roles and gifts in a new light. They were not always able to implement the model in full, but they had a new standard to shoot for.

So the past couple of decades have provided me with rich relationships with members and chief executives of literally thousands of boards located in every American state and in every Canadian province. The probing and challenging of these insightful clients contributed to the widespread applicability of my governance model. The model that emerged is generic, capable of whatever tailoring is necessary to fit any type of organization. And while I do adapt the model to business board settings, particularly to parent-subsidiary systems, the exclusive focus of this text is on nonprofit and public organizations. This extensive dialogue in which I forged a generic application of the model for nonprofit and public governance included a wide array of organizations.

public schools	city councils
private schools	county commissioners
liquid waste disposal	libraries
Third World development	architects' societies
YWCA	real estate boards
hospitals	sports facilities
mental health centers	industrial associations
poverty agencies	local churches
mental retardation	family services
junior league	family planning
airport authorities	adult learning

parks and recreation
women's centers
national church bodies
housing authorities
art guilds
pest control districts
chambers of commerce
dental societies
county fairs
community theaters
agriculture cooperatives
wilderness programs
alcoholism treatment
private industry councils
League of Women Voters
child protective services
health departments
Hispanic leadership
holding companies

credit unions
regional planning
zoos
postrelease programs
economic development
women's shelters
retirement funds
rehabilitation centers
national associations
state boards of education
state mental health systems
medical specialty societies
planning and zoning commissions
health maintenance organizations
community leadership training
golf course superintendents
employment services
vocational centers
extension services

I cannot begin to describe the personal and professional sustenance that these many boards and their executives continue to give me. Working routinely with organizations whose pursuits exceed my understanding and dedication is humbling even to a consultant's robust ego. Their boards have educated me about topics such as waste disposal, international relief, public housing, and the ravages of racism. Their work and their determination have awed me time and time again. Not infrequently have I been literally moved to tears by their perseverance and commitment to make a difference in the world. Their contribution to me is not only one of the mind, in helping forge an approach to governance, but one of the spirit as well.

Out of that profound appreciation and respect, my counsel to boards minces few words. I am hard on boards simply because *I know how good they can be.* Out of what is, frankly, a love affair with boards, I have written this book for board members who want to make a difference. I have written it for board leaders who wish to guide deliberation toward the big questions. I have written it for executives who want a strong rather than a weak board, one that demands a strong executive as well. I have written for executives who know that management can be only as good as its governing foundation. I have written for the long-term benefit of taxpayers and donors, as well as the clients, patients, students, and other beneficiaries whose needs are to be served.

So come with me on an adventure into what strategic board leadership might be. Let us consider how a board can do in the boardroom what it sought to do in the first place: project a vision, infuse an organization with mission, bid a staff to be all it can be, and make itself grow a little in the process.

Organization of the Book

Chapter One recounts the varieties of boards, their predictable difficulties, and the need for more precise principles of governance. I seek to establish not only that individual boards need to function better, but that our idea of what "better" means is sorely in need of revision.

Chapter Two makes a case for a new approach to policymaking and what types of policies boards should make. Even though there is more to the board job than policymaking, I argue that reconceiving the nature of policy allows a new level of leadership to be born. Rather than use the traditional categories of board policies borrowed from administration, I develop four new categories tailored for the governing role.

In Chapter Three, I deal with the depth and breadth of board policy in a way that frees boards from staff details and even from the endless stream of approvals.

Chapter Four deals with policies about organizational results and initiates the next five chapters, which explain the four categories of board policy. These policies engage the board in governing outcomes rather than activities and resolve such issues as mission, priorities, and target recipient groups.

Chapter Five covers those policies that give the board control over administrative and programmatic action. These policies enable the board to fulfill its fiduciary responsibilities and to control the prudence and ethics of organizational practice without resorting to "meddling."

Chapter Six deals with policies that establish an effective relationship between board and staff through a CEO. We explore the meaning of the CEO's role and the board's approach to delegating and to evaluating the performance of this important person.

Chapter Seven addresses the board's relationship to its stockholder equivalents and its primary accountability to that trust. Policies covered in this chapter address the board's governing process and its job description.

Chapter Eight extends the discussion of board roles to subgroups of the board. I explore ways to minimize committees and officers and ensure that they do not interfere with either CEO or whole board roles.

In Chapter Nine, I demonstrate how to make board policies "grow" by adding depth to initially very broad policy statements.

Chapter Ten focuses on keeping the board on track by building structured discipline and agendas into the long view.

Finally, in Chapter Eleven, I discuss the importance of thinking big, keeping the dream in front, and including other ingredients of strategic leadership.

I promise readers that they will never see governance in quite the same way again. In the midst of the great quality revolution in American management, I submit a new standard of what quality means in a board's work. This book redefines excellence in governance. And because we have so far to go, it is an urgent argument for revolution in the boardroom.

Consequently, however gentle my intent, *Boards That Make a Difference* is a presumptuous book. It is presumptuous in broadly lumping together such apparently different organizations as governmental bodies, social agencies, quasi-public entities, private clubs, and foundations. It is presumptuous in claiming that virtually all such boards, councils, and commissions, *even those that are not perceived to be in trouble,* are currently performing at a distressingly low percentage of their leadership potential. It is presumptuous in depreciating finance and personnel committees; in belittling financial reports, budget approvals, and the office of the treasurer; and in exhorting boards to get out of long-range planning. And it is presumptuous in claiming that time-honored, virtually unquestioned beliefs and practices of nonprofit and public

boards are the major impediments to their being the strategic leaders they could be. "The whole industry," to borrow an unidentified
observer from Waterman (1988, p. 9), "seems trapped in a disas-
trous set of habits."

I propose a sweeping revision, a new conceptual framework, so
that we can conduct ourselves with purpose and performance. This
is not a book of helpful hints, nor is it written to suggest incremental improvements in current board operation. The need I see
is not so much to make boards better at the work they are doing,
but to reinvent that work and its fundamental precepts, to design
from the ground up a general theory—or at least a technology—
of governance. My commitment is that boards and managers, impelled by a new comprehension of what governance is all about,
will do no less than transform how we conceive and proclaim leadership in the boardroom.

Acknowledgments

For the intellectual spark that led me to question the conventional wisdom and thereby to create a new model, I am indebted
to Wolfgang S. (Bill) Price. When I discovered his work in program
policy planning in 1975 (it was later published in 1977), I thought
it the most refreshing approach to governance I had ever come
across. Bill's acceptance of me as co-consultant changed the direction of my career.

In addition, the board members of Quinco Consulting Center
in Columbus, Indiana, boldly accepted the challenge to adopt an
untested governance method in 1976. In my eight-year association
with that board, it remained faithful to its commitment. In doing
so, it helped fine-tune a new approach, a contribution for which
tens of thousands of nonprofit and public boards are unknowingly
in Quinco's debt.

Furthermore, the extensive support I have received from those
close to me had much to do with my completing this work. Ronald
P. Myers brought my board model to the attention of Jossey-Bass
Publishers. Ken and Melanie Campbell, Rob and Kathy Kenner,
Tom Lane, and Mary D. Shahan made their homes available for
getaway writing. Sandra Meicher, Ronald and Sue Myers, David
Mueller, and Sally Jo Vasicko offered commentary on the manu-

script. My former secretary, Virginia Haag, chased references and made the painstaking transfers from one word processor to another. Lynn D. W. Luckow and Alan Shrader, my long-suffering editors at Jossey-Bass, offered more support and patience with my intermittent writing schedule than I had any right to expect. I am also grateful to the many former clients who allowed me to use their policies for illustration and to quote their words to make my points.

Carmel, Indiana   John Carver
February 1990

The Author

John Carver is a theorist, consultant, and the world's most published author on the design of governance. His consulting and public presentations are conducted as Carver Governance Design, Inc. He received his B.S. degree (1964) in business and economics and his M.Ed. degree (1965) in educational psychology from the University of Tennessee at Chattanooga, and his Ph.D. degree (1968) in clinical psychology from Emory University. He served four years of active duty with the U.S. Air Force Electronic Security Command (1956–1960).

After working several years in the administration of a small manufacturing company, Carver spent the bulk of his time first in managing public mental health and mental retardation services, then in developing and applying governance and executive management concepts. Although most of his model building and consulting have been with nonprofit, governmental, and other public boards, councils, and commissions in the United States and Canada, he has consulted on every continent except Antarctica. An increasing amount of his current interest is in business boards, particularly roles and controls for the parent-subsidiary relationship.

Carver incorporated the National Council of Community Mental Health Centers in 1970 and served as its first chairperson. He presented testimony to U.S. House and Joint Conference committees in 1969, 1970, and 1971. He has served as adjunct and visiting faculty member with the University of Tennessee Space Institute, Tulane University, the University of Texas, and the University of Minnesota.

He and his wife, Miriam Mayhew Carver, coauthored *A New Vision of Board Leadership* (Carver and Mayhew, 1994), *Reinventing Your Board: A Step-by-Step Guide to Implementing Policy Governance* (Carver and Carver, 1997), and The CarverGuide Series on Effective Board

Governance (Carver, 1996b, 1996c, 1996f, 1996i; Carver and Carver, 1996a, 1996b). He is featured in the audiotape set *Empowering Boards for Leadership* (1992b) and the videotapes *John Carver on Board Governance* (1993c) and *Reinventing Governance* (1993d). Carver is author of the periodical *Board Leadership: A Bimonthly Workshop with John Carver* and has published in scores of other periodicals in Canada, the United States, and the United Kingdom, including the London *Times* (1994a), *Solicitors' Journal* (1995a), the *Chronicle of Philanthropy* (1992h), *Nonprofit World* (1991a, 1992e, 1992i), *Hospital Trustee* (1989a), and *Nation's Cities Weekly* (1996g). John Carver and his wife live in and operate independent consulting practices in Atlanta.

Boards That Make a Difference

Chapter One

A New Vision for Governing Boards

It is virtually impossible to escape contact with boards. We either are on boards, work for them, or are affected by their decisions. Boards sit atop almost all corporate forms of organization—profit and nonprofit—and often over governmental agencies as well. The elected forums of our political jurisdictions are boardlike structures: Congress, state legislatures, city councils, and county commissions. In all kinds of human activity, we find formally constituted, empowered groups deciding courses of action and future conditions toward which some body of people will aspire.

This chapter claims that great opportunities exist for leadership because of the sheer number of boards and their relative ineffectiveness. First, I look at ways of classifying boards and then limit the scope of the book to *governing* boards. Next, I describe the peculiar market circumstances that justify grouping nonprofit and public organizations together. I then step back to view the difficulty all boards—business, nonprofit, and public boards—have in fulfilling their opportunities. I summarize the normal prescriptions for board ills along with reasons that the existing answers are insufficient. Next, I make the case that governance deserves special attention apart from other elements of management. The chapter concludes with an argument for a new model of governance and the contributions this model should make to strategic leadership by boards.

Varieties of Boards

At one end of the scale, decisions are made by individuals and by small groups such as families or associates. At the other end, decisions are made in plebiscites and elections. In between, decisions are made by empowered bodies called boards.

Houle (1989, p. 195) cites the existence of approximately 4.5 million boards in this country. This number includes non-profit, governmental (including local legislative), and business boards. The argument in these pages for new principles of governance is not directed to every entity that calls itself a board. But it is meant for almost 1.4 million of them in the United States alone. Drucker estimated that nonprofit organizations "may now employ more people than federal, state and local government put together" (1978) and that "half the personal income of the United States (and of most other developed countries) is spent on public service institutions (including those operated by government)" (1977, p. 17). Two considerations delineate those bodies to whom my commentary directly applies: (1) the organizational position of the board and (2) the economic nature of the organization.

Boards Considered by Organizational Position

Governing board. The most important kind of board is that of ultimate corporate accountability—the governing board. The governing board is always positioned at the top of the organization. "Corporate board," "board of directors," "board of trustees," "board of regents," and similar titles denote groups that have authority exceeded only by owners and the state. The governing board is as high in the structure as one can go and still be within the organizational framework. Its total authority is matched by its total accountability for all corporate activity.

Advisory board. There are also boards whose function is to give counsel, not to govern. Advisory boards can advise the governing board, the CEO, or other staff. They can be positioned anywhere in the organization as long as they formally attach to some "proper" organizational element. Advisory boards are optional and have only as much authority as the authorizing point within the legitimate organization chooses to grant. In some fields it is common to find advisory boards that have been given extensive authority and whose advice is virtually certain to have an effect. As long as some position within the organization can, even potentially, retract the group's authority, it is not a governing board. Its authority can be curtailed only by the governing board itself, by law, or—in the case of membership organizations—by the membership.

Line board. Considerably more rare is the line board. "Line" describes a heretofore unlabeled board type. I know of no treatment of this category in the literature except the modified form discussed by Ackoff (1981). The line board is not advisory, for it wields definite authority over subordinate positions. But it is not at the top of the organization and does not, therefore, qualify as a governing board. It is merely a group inserted where a single manager might have served.

Workgroup board. Sometimes people speak of a "working board" when they simply mean a board that stays busy. Hence, a governing, advisory, or line board might be a working board rather than a figurehead. My term *workgroup,* however, denotes a governing board with little or no staff. It must govern and be the workforce as well.

Very small organizations, such as civic clubs, are often in this dual position. The group is incorporated, so a corporate governing board exists. Yet, absent enough funds to pay a staff, board members become the only workforce in sight. This kind of board is not a true type in the way that governing, advisory, and line boards are. It is merely a governing board with another set of responsibilities. The organizational position of a workgroup board is not only at the top, but everywhere else as well. It is most important that such boards remember that they have two different, simultaneous roles and they can best perform those roles by keeping them clearly separated.

Boards Considered by Economic Nature of the Organization

The power and responsibilities of advisory and line boards are determined by the specific organization rather than by a commanding generic principle. The foregoing discussion serves only to distinguish governing boards as the sole subject of this text. Throughout this book I deal only with *governing* boards.

It has long been common practice to differentiate the vast and disparate array of organizations governed by boards into three groups: profit ("business"), nonprofit, and governmental. Further characteristics distinguish subgroups of each. For example, businesses are grouped as "public" (publicly traded equity) and "private" (no public trading). Nonprofits are also divided into "public" (directly related to government) and "private" (not as related). "Governmental" includes the jurisdictional governance of cities, townships, counties, and states, but it also covers districts for water supply, schools, pollution control, and a host of other authorities. I ignore the subgroups and concentrate on the three major types: profit, nonprofit, and governmental.

1. *Profit boards.* Business corporations engage in trade in order to produce a return for stockholders. These companies ordinarily compete in a market that is more or less free. Governing boards in business range from the obligatory, figurehead board of an entrepreneurial business to a highly formalized, paid group representing diverse stockholders.

2. *Nonprofit boards.* Corporations chartered for charitable purposes have no stock ownership, though state statutes may require a formal membership as a stockholder-equivalent. Abroad, such organizations are often referred to as nongovernmental organizations (NGOs). In the United States, the term *private voluntary organization* (PVO) is frequently used to describe international nonprofits. NGOs and PVOs, though not terms used in this text, are included among nonprofit agencies.

Although nonprofit corporations may accumulate surpluses, their accounting systems have no place for profit. They differ from other corporations in that they are exempt from certain taxes and are unable to distribute their surpluses to holders of equity. Nonprofit corporations ordinarily receive a large proportion of their revenues from "funding" and donations rather than from sales of a product. Nonprofit governing board obligations under the law, however, are similar to those for other corporations.

3. *Governmental boards.* Governmental boards, elected or appointed, are more bound by legal requirements on both composition and process than are the foregoing types. They are like nonprofit boards with respect to profit and distribution of earnings. Governmental boards may be quasi-governmental (such as water systems or airport authorities) or fully governmental (such as city councils). They may or may not have taxing authority. Governmental boards, like nonprofit boards, ordinarily do not derive their revenues from sales but from taxation and user fees.

Profit, nonprofit, and governmental governing boards have much in common. They are alike in that they all bear ultimate accountability for organizational activity and accomplishment. They are unlike in how they are situated in the larger context of political-economic life. They differ in how much public scrutiny they receive, a factor that produces differences in the amount of posturing involved in board dynamics. They vary in the degree to which the procedures of governance are prescribed by law. They differ greatly in the strength of the traditions that drive their methods. Many governmental boards have traditions that were established long before twentieth-century management appeared on the scene. Powerful precedents make it difficult for state legislatures and county commissioners, for example, to behave as though modern management principles were ever developed.

This book focuses specifically on governmental and nonprofit governing boards. From here on I use the word *public* to refer to the various types of governmental entities, because in common perception, *public* bridges the gray area between special-purpose governmental groups and quasi-public nonprofits. This focus is useful as we explore governance, even though there is nothing inherent in the nonprofit or public organization per se that causes governance to be different than in profit companies. Then why address public and nonprofit governance, particularly in view of the extremely disparate array of organization types included under that rubric? After all, are they not more different than they are alike? The Ford Foundation, a community arts guild, and a credit union may little appreciate membership in this mixed club. The justification for classifying them together is that the boards of most nonprofit and public organizations share a compelling factor: the peculiar nature of their markets.

Life in the Muted Market

Companies organized for profit receive money through sales. Sales revenues are the result of a free exchange between the company and consumers. Consumers judge whether the good or service is worth the exchange demanded. If it is not, they do not buy; if it is, they do.

Nonprofit and governmental organizations ordinarily receive money from sources other than from those who buy their products.

Direct consumers may pay a discounted price or even nothing. The organization receives a subsidy from donors and tax sources to make up the deficit. There is no consumer judgment of the product's rightful price, because the consumer is not confronted with that choice. Consequently, although nonprofit and public organizations may be buffeted about by budget pressures and funding squeezes, there is no direct market force bearing on the relationship between product and price.

The relevant variable that separates the governance of *most* public and nonprofit enterprises from *most* profit organizations is the automatic market test of product worth. I define a market test as consumers' free decisions about whether a given product, among alternatives, is worth the cost of its production. If alternatives are unavailable because of artificially blocked competition, there is no clean market test. If the consumer does not pay the entire price, there is no clean market test. This definition focuses on the *automatic consumer judgment* aspect of market. The absence of this automatic judgment does not mean that the word *market* cannot be used in other ways. For example, public schools and family planning centers operate in some identifiable *market* and may fare better if their staffs do a good job of *marketing*. This use of market and marketing, however, is unrelated to the integrity of the market test I have described.

Without a market to summarize consumer judgment, an organization literally does not know what its product is worth. It may know what the product costs to make and what the staff thinks about product quality. It may know that consumers are raving with delight. It may even know precisely how effective the product is. But the organization still does not know what its product is worth.

From a governance perspective, then, the relevant factor that sets most nonprofit and public organizations apart from profit organizations is not in the essence of managing, for the principles of management are the same in each setting. The difference is not in distribution of earnings, for this is a matter of accounting rather than substance. What is different—with profound effects—is that most nonprofit and public organizations lack a behavioral process to aggregate the many individual evaluations of product and cost. The organization is missing the foundation that would enable it to define success and failure, to know what is worth doing, and, in the largest sense, even to recognize good performance.

So the typical public or nonprofit board is faced with a challenge business boards never have to confront. "In the nonprofit organization," observed Anthony (1977), "the objectives are difficult to define and there is no automatic danger signal comparable to the profit measure." In the absence of a market test, *the board must perform that function.* The board must bear this peculiar, additional burden if it is to act responsibly. It is not enough to be efficient, nor is it enough even to produce fine products. Any reasonable definition of productive excellence must relate chiefly to whether a good or service is worth the full economic cost of its production.

From this point on, I refer to public and nonprofit organizations as if they all lack a rigorous market test. That will prove sufficiently true to justify the simplification, though exceptions exist. Nonprofit hospitals, for example, operate in a harsh market environment, albeit one of great artificiality imposed by regulation and insurers. For those nonprofit and public organizations that are truly subject to an unsubsidized market judgment, the peculiarity discussed here is not true. In these cases, the board's task is easier, though the concepts and principles in the model presented here will still contribute to their governance. Among the vast array of public and nonprofit organizations, however, such truly market-tested instances are in the minority. With this proviso, I consider public and nonprofit boards to be, by and large, engaged in serving a muted market.

The Flaws of Governance

Yet, even boards that are free of this added "market surrogate" burden have shown that the challenges of governing are almost too great. Governing boards have not been vessels of exemplary efficiency in the best of situations. Writing of corporate boards, Drucker (1974, p. 628) said "there is one thing all boards have in common, regardless of their legal position. *They do not function.* The decline of the board is a universal phenomenon of this century" (emphasis added). Neu and Sumek (1983) found it "evident that the governance process is not working well. . . . New approaches need to be developed."

Geneen (1984) of ITT complained that boards are unable to protect the interests of stockholders whom they represent: "Among the boards of directors of Fortune 500 companies, I estimate that

95 percent are not fully doing what they are legally, morally, and ethically supposed to do. And they couldn't, even if they wanted to" (p. 28). Worried that hospital board effectiveness is "getting critical," John A. Witt (1987, p. xiii) decried "untrained boards instructing, or at least controlling, untrained subordinate boards. . . . Ineffectualness of boards and their members permeates several layers and often multiplies itself."

Smith (1958, p. 52) found it to be "ironic . . . that we in the United States have so neglected this most vital area." While every other management function has been exhaustively studied and analyzed, "the responsibilities of the board and the distinction between board and management have been sorely neglected. Management literature on the subject is pitifully brief and strikingly devoid of any real depth or new ideas."

Juran and Louden (1966, p. 7) pointed to the same root for the problem: "It is an astonishing fact that the job of the board of directors is, in proportion to its intrinsic importance, one of the least studied in the entire spectrum of industrial activities. . . . As a consequence, the job of the board of directors has received neither the benefit of the broad exchange of practical experience nor the intensity of study which has been available to other corporate activities."

Though possessed of ultimate organizational power, the governing board is understudied and underdeveloped. Here we confront a flagrant irony in management literature: *where opportunity for leadership is greatest, job design for leadership is poorest.*

It is against this uninspiring backdrop of governing boards in general that we deal here specifically with boards of public and nonprofit organizations. It is little wonder that such boards have difficulty, for their faults include those of profit boards, plus those peculiarly contributed by their artificial market situation. If the governing of supposedly rational, modern business corporations is not without underlying weaknesses, it should not be surprising that governance of nonprofit and public enterprise presents an extensive array of blemishes.

What Goes Wrong

It takes no scholar to find the problems. Simple, random observation of a few nonprofit and public boards will expose many of the normal shortcomings. Nonprofit and public boards stumble regularly and visibly. Individual board members and executives have often felt that one specific act or another is silly or empty. They rarely say so, however, for the charade has a commanding history, eliciting an almost conspiratorial agreement not to notice organizational fatuousness. Robert Gale, president of the Association of Governing Boards of Universities and Colleges, reported that "of the some thirty-five nonprofit boards I have served on, only one was truly effective" (personal communication, 1989).

The problem is not that a group or an individual *occasionally* slips into poor practice, but that intelligent, caring individuals regularly exhibit procedures of governance that are deeply flawed. Certain common practices are such obvious drains on board effectiveness that one does not need a sophisticated model to recognize them. Although some boards may avoid a few of the following conditions, rarely does any one board avoid them all.

Time on the trivial. Items of trivial scope or import receive disproportionate attention compared with matters of greater scope or importance. Richard J. Peckham of Kansas, on joining a major public board, found it so lost in trivia that "I thought I'd been banished to outer darkness" (personal communication). Major program issues go unresolved while boards conscientiously grapple with some small detail. An Illinois school board proudly proclaimed the "active role the members of our board take in purchasing decisions. . . . The administration [to replace desks in two classrooms] was directed to select three chairs from different companies and have them available for the next board meeting. The board then made the decision on warranty, durability, price and color." A national survey found that almost half of America's school boards made the purchasing decisions for tape recorders, cameras, and television sets (National School Boards Association, n.d.).

Short-term bias. The "time horizon" about which a board should make decisions is more distant at the governing level than anywhere else in the organization. Yet we find boards dealing mainly with the near term and, even more dysfunctionally, with the past. Last month's financial statement gets more attention than an agency's strategic position.

Reactive stance. Boards consistently find themselves reacting to staff initiatives rather than acting proactively. Proposals for staff action and recommendations for board action so often come from staff that some boards would cease to function if called upon to create their own agendas.

Reviewing, rehashing, redoing. Some boards spend most of their time going over what their staffs have already done. "Eighty-five percent of our time was spent monitoring staff work," says Glendora Putnam, Boston, of a prominent national board. "We can't afford that. We have too much wisdom to be put to use" to be wasted in that way (personal communication). Just keeping up with a large staff can take prodigious hours and even then can never be done fully. But the salient point is that reviewing, rehashing, and redoing staff work—no matter how well accomplished—do not constitute leadership.

Leaky accountability. Boards often allow accountability to "leak" around the chief executive. Having established a CEO position, the board members continue to relate in their official capacities with other staff, either giving them directions or judging their performance.

Diffuse authority. It is rare to find a board-executive partnership wherein each party's authority has been clarified. A vast gray area exists. When a matter lies in this uncertain area, the safe executive response is to take it to the board. Instead of using this opportunity to clarify to whom the decision belongs, the board simply approves or disapproves. The event has been settled, but authority remains as unclear as it was before.

Moving Toward Solutions

Many board flaws are cosmetic blemishes, indicative of more fundamental errors. "These are just symptoms of a problem," says Barry Romanko of the Alberta Ministry of Parks and Recreation, St. Paul, Alberta. "The problem is that we are giving boards the wrong job" (personal communication). Attacking the superficial flaws would in itself be a worthy undertaking. Similarly, it might be useful to invoke the usual admonitions: "Stick to policy!" "Let your CEO manage!" "Don't rubber-stamp!" But it would be even more instructive to build a healthier infrastructure of governance concepts. Framing the governance challenge more effectively can go far beyond merely eliminating common problems; it can provide a clearing in which boards can be strategic leaders.

Inadequate Prescriptions

At some level, boards and executives are well aware of the historical deficiencies. An explosion of popular interest in management issues beginning in the 1970s sharpened the perception that governance is not all it can be. Board training has received more attention because of this awareness. Many board members, executives, and observers have offered counsel for ailing board practices all along. But somehow the prescriptions, quite rational in themselves, have fallen short. At best, they have cleaned up some of the clutter and the more striking inefficiencies in board operation. But because few previous efforts have been based in a complete conceptual model, prescriptions have largely been piecemeal, anecdotal wisdom. Most prescriptions have concerned the level of board activity, the board-staff relationship, or the nature of board work. The appeal of each is that it accurately assesses one part of the elephant.

Prescriptions About Activity and Involvement

More involvement. One solution to the problems of governance is that boards should be more involved. They should participate directly in the work of the organization, volunteering time and energy to become physically involved in doing things. A board operating at a distance is a board too detached to understand, much less to make a difference. Board membership means having access to the good works of an organization without having to go through the hiring process to get there. Those who espouse greater board activity greatly need to "know what is going on" in the organization. Reflecting the hyperinvolvement, the board agenda is likely to be drawn out and committee work may be heavy.

Less involvement. Boards should be less involved. By participating directly in the work of the organization, the board tends to become lost in the trees and to lose sight of the forest. Board members are better as governors around a board table than as a prestigious auxiliary staff. The board's job is "to choose a CEO, then stay out of the way," confided a hospital trustee in Wisconsin. Persons who call for less involvement often propose keeping up with relevant facts through reports, particularly financial ones. Agendas are likely to be crisp and "businesslike." Committee work may be light.

Prescriptions About Board-Staff Relations

Board as watchdog. The board, as the ultimately accountable agent, should keep a sharp eye on staff activities. This close oversight limits the degree of power delegated, requiring many board approvals and close questioning of staff. A utility commissioner in Minnesota claimed that the commission's main function is to "keep a wary eye on the staff." Boards acting as watchdogs become heavily involved in administration, often in busy committees related to staff activities. Tight control is seen as the road to accountability or, at least, to safety. Some boards take the watchdog posture so far that they develop an adversarial relationship with staff; anything brought before the board becomes a trial. In an alternate watchdog role, the board allies itself with lower-echelon staff members and perceives issues—as stated by a poverty agency board member in Ohio—in terms of protecting staff from administrators. At their best, such boards are constructive skeptics.

Board as cheerleader. Staff members are basically honest and capable, so the best board role is to be supportive and cheer them on. The hallmark is trust. After all, the key to governing well is choosing a chief executive in whom you can believe and then standing behind him or her. Cheerleader boards stay out of administration because it is none of their business. They may even refrain from asking the hard questions, because to do so would show a lack of faith. Rubber-stamping executive requests is an expression of gratitude that things are going so smoothly. Often, the governing board role is seen as advisory after a CEO is installed. Loose control is the best approach ("After all, we are *just* volunteers"). A part-time board should not get in the way; its role is not so much to govern staff as to be its apologist and champion.

Prescriptions About Board Work and Skills

Board as manager. Boards, though one step removed from daily operation, should become more proficient in management skills so as to act as managers. Board members are chosen in part because of their skills in personnel, finance, program leadership, and so forth. The board is likely to pore over financial statements, staffing patterns, and maintenance reports. It engages staff in the intricacies of management. Committees are structured along the lines of staff departments, such as personnel and public relations. The board, more or less autocratic, is seen as the supermanager or at least as sharing management responsibilities with its top staff.

Board as planner. As planning is an integral part of managing, boards should predominantly plan. Boards plan the elements of personnel, finance, and so forth, rather than engaging in current implementation. Boards develop long-range plans and, with their committees, spend long hours to create a plan document.

Board as communicator. The board should communicate better among its members and with staff. If board and staff could only hear each other better, the organization would have a more satisfying process and, hence, a more satisfactory product. Particularly in multiethnic community boards, barriers to communication lend great support to this approach. The path to better governance lies in better human relations.

Why the Prescriptions Disappoint

These are not the only prescriptions, nor are they really distinct types. They illustrate the range and divergence of solutions to board ineffectiveness. And, from the standpoint of slight improvements, they do not all fail. What is confusing is that each prescription contains just enough truth to be on track. At one time or another, they are all good approaches.

The problem with anecdotal wisdom, however, is its spotty applicability. A formerly rubber-stamp-type board that has been duped by its CEO will surely improve with greater involvement, tighter control, or the board's acting as supermanager. A board fatigued by interminably long meetings may be wise to move toward shorter meetings with more "businesslike" agendas. In slightly different circumstances, however, these solutions would themselves be the problems.

Problem-based prescriptions sow the seed for the next difficulty, because the solution often outlives the problem that justified it. Soon the board that shifted to shorter meetings finds it cannot keep up as well as it desired. Or a good CEO is lost because he or she will not tolerate the tight control and suspiciousness left over from the previous pendulum swing.

Prescriptions for board improvement are often based on current problems or problems that board members have experienced elsewhere. Problem-based improvements may be absolutely sensible and still miss the mark. They may cure the present difficulties, yet not prevent a wide range of potential future problems. Correcting insufficiencies by looking backward at what they have been simply invites the next, perhaps opposite, error.

Governance as Unique Management

A paradigm tailored to the special circumstances of governance would enable us to apply wisdom more coherently. When a function has been *assembled* from bits of historical practice more than it has been *designed,* it cannot so gracefully incorporate wisdom, but must patch it on here and there. Tailoring management principles for governance, however, assumes that boards call for special treatment. This section argues that governance certainly is special, though not for the reason most frequently cited.

The Red Herring of Voluntarism

Boards of nonprofit and some public organizations think of themselves primarily as volunteers. This identity adds little and potentially costs a great deal. Responsibility, authority, job design, and demands of a board are not affected by being paid or unpaid. Beyond strengthening the sense of public service, being a *voluntary* board is irrelevant to governance and its attendant burden of accountability. On the other hand, some connotations of voluntarism can *detract* from the board's job, severely reducing its ability to lead.

Volunteers are a tradition of American life, offering many skills, insights, and hours in a commendable expression of helpfulness. Volunteers help get a job done without compensation. For an existing organization, that usually means helping the staff, inasmuch as staff is engaged in the actual work. Governing boards, however, do not exist to help staff, but to own the business—often in trust for some larger ownership. If anyone is helping, it is the staff. Volunteers on governing boards are expressing an *ownership interest* rather than a *helpfulness interest.* Owning the business conveys a power that cannot be responsibly grasped so long as board members think they are there to help. Power not used is power defaulted on and, ultimately, power irresponsibly used. It is destructive to confuse helpfulness with ownership. By emphasizing their volunteer status, boards risk weakening their effectiveness.

Because the same person can wear two different hats, board members may also be volunteers at a staff level. It is important that the hats be kept distinct in everyone's mind. The board as an official body (as opposed to individual members) is well advised to limit its role to owner only.

Boards as Trustees

Unlike other managers who work for a well-defined superior, boards ordinarily work for either a vaguely defined group or a well-defined but difficult-to-communicate-with group. The former is illustrated by a public radio station board, the latter by a city council. There is someone out there for whom the board acts in trust, but it is difficult to tell who that someone is. Consequently, boards have more difficulty than other managers in getting their marching orders and their evaluations.

This book promotes the concept of "moral ownership" to isolate the various stakeholders to whom the board owes its primary allegiance. For community boards, this ownership is the community at large. A board cannot carry out its responsibilities without determining exactly whom the ownership includes and how those owners can be heard.

Boards as Special Managers

Governing boards would do better to think of themselves as a special kind of management, not as volunteers. Consequently, what is known about the managing process, particularly "general" management, is relevant to boards. Boards need some of the same skills a CEO needs. These skills involve "overview" management as opposed to specialized management, such as purchasing, marketing, and personnel administration. In fact, some would strongly argue that sufficient information about governing is already available in management texts, workshops, academic degree programs, and journals. To these persons, governance is simply management at the board level and, indeed, for them the word *governance* serves no useful conceptual distinction.

This point of view is that management is management is management, even when it is governance. But the governance task *is* different from other management positions. In dealing with thousands of board members, I find that structural and interpersonal factors cause governance to be a unique kind of management. Certainly, the same basic management principles apply, but the form must be adjusted to deal with several features found in no other manager but the governing body:

- Boards are at the extreme end of the accountability chain. Other managers must deal with persons both above and below their stations. The buck stops with the board. It has no supervisor to carve out what portion of a given topic it is to oversee.
- The board acts, in a moral sense and sometimes a legal one, as agent of a largely unseen and often undecided principal, an entity that expresses itself in curious ways if at all.
- The board is a set of individuals operating as a single entity. Melding multiple peer viewpoints and values into a single resolution is peculiar to a group acting collectively as a manager.
- Individuals' discipline tends to suffer when they belong to groups. A board is likely to have less discipline than any one of its members operating alone.
- Boards are ordinarily more than the usual managerial arm's length from the next lower organizational level. They are not only part-time, but also physically removed.

Mueller (1981) argued that governance in its essence differs from management. It is, he claims, an unfolding, always incomplete phenomenon driven by "soft realms of thought and deportment. They are value-laden, subjective, intuitive and characteristic of the art forms dealing with social interaction" (p. xii).

For all these reasons, I have translated principles of modern management to address the peculiar circumstance of governing boards. The adaptation goes beyond a collection of helpful suggestions; it is a fundamentally reordered paradigm for governance.

Toward a New Governance

A model of governance is a framework within which to organize the thoughts, activities, structure, and relationships of governing boards. A designed model yields a new nature of governance, quite unlike a collection of even wise responses to specific governance problems. What should we expect from a model? What conditions should be better if there were a better framework within which to build governance actions? I think we have a right to expect a good model of governance to

1. *"Cradle" vision:* A useful framework for governance must hold and support vision in the primary position. Administrative systems cause us to devote great attention to the specifics. Such rigor, itself commendable, can overshadow the broader matter of purpose. There must be systematic encouragement to think the unthinkable and to dream.
2. *Explicitly address fundamental values:* The governing board is a guardian of organizational values. The framework must ensure that the board focuses on values. Endless decisions about events cannot substitute for deliberations and explicit pronouncements on values.
3. *Force an external focus:* Because organizations tend to focus inward, a governance model must intervene to guarantee a marketlike, external responsiveness. A board would thus be more concerned with needs and markets than with the internal issues of organizational mechanics.
4. *Enable an outcome-driven organizing system:* All functions and decisions are to be rigorously weighed against the standard of purpose. A powerful model would have the board not only establish a mission in terms of an outcome, but procedurally enforce a mission as the central organizing focus.
5. *Separate large issues from small ones:* Board members usually agree that large issues deserve first claim on their time, but they have no common way to discern a big item. A model should help differentiate sizes of issues.
6. *Force forward thinking:* A governance scheme should help a board thrust the majority of its thinking into the future. Strategic leadership demands the long-term viewpoint.

7. *Enable proactivity:* So that boards do not merely preside over momentum, a model of governance should press boards toward leading and away from reacting. Such a model would engage boards more in *creating* than in *approving.*

8. *Facilitate diversity and unity:* It is important to optimize the richness of diversity in board composition and opinion, yet still assimilate the variety into one voice. A model must address the need to speak with one voice without squelching dissent or feigning unanimity.

9. *Describe relationships to relevant constituencies:* In either a legal or a moral sense, boards are usually trustees. They are also, to some extent, accountable to consumers, neighbors, and staff. A model of governance should define where these various constituencies fit into the scheme.

10. *Define a common basis for discipline:* Boards have a tough time sticking to a job description, being decisive without being impulsive, and keeping discussion to the point. A model of governance should provide a rational basis for a board's self-discipline.

11. *Delineate the board's role in common topics:* A model of governance should enable a board to articulate roles without isolating roles from each other, so the board's specific contribution on any topic is clear.

12. *Determine what information is needed:* A model of governance would introduce more precise distinctions about the nature of information needed to govern, avoiding too much, too little, too late, and simply wrong information.

13. *Balance overcontrol and undercontrol:* It is easy to control too much or too little and, ironically, to do both at the same time. The same board can simultaneously be a "rubber-stamper" and a "meddler." A model of governance would clarify those aspects of management that need tight versus loose control.

14. *Use board time efficiently:* Members of nonprofit and public boards receive token pay or none in exchange for their time. Though they willingly make this contribution, few have time to waste. By sorting out what really needs to be done, a model should enable boards to use the precious gift of time more productively.

A conceptually coherent way to approach governance would be strong medicine for nonprofit and public organizations. It would also apply in business corporations. In fact, McConkey (1975, p. 1) foreshadowed a business breakthrough originating in the nonprofit sector when he predicted that "the next major breakthrough in management will not occur . . . in the world of business. The breakthrough will, and must, take place in the so-called nonprofit sector."

Whether, as he indicates, the breakthrough "must" take place, it certainly *should* take place, given the serious flaws that exist. The most significant management breakthrough that could occur would be in the highest-leverage element of organization—the governing board. Both the leverage and the room for improvement scream urgently for attention.

But boards have been around so long that it is hard to see that the emperor has no clothes. We have grown accustomed to mediocrity in nonprofit and public board process, in the empty rituals and often meaningless words of conventional practice. We have watched intelligent people tied up in trivia so long that neither we nor they notice the discrepancy. We have observed the ostensible strategic leaders consumed by the exigencies of next month. Mindful people regularly carry out mindless activity and appear to be, as Phillip T. Jenkins of Bryn Mawr Associates in Birmingham, Michigan, put it, "the well intentioned in full pursuit of the irrelevant" (personal communication). Inexplicably, effective people have a different standard of excellence for public and nonprofit boards than for other pursuits, "often [tossing] aside the principles of good management, and sometimes even common sense, when they put on trustee hats" (Chait and Taylor, 1989). The forum in which *vision* could be the chief order of business is mired so chronically in details that, growing weary, we come to see nothing amiss. Boards, after all, will be boards!

We need strong boards and we need strong executives as well. "One of the key problems," observed Robert Gale, "is that many boards are either too weak to accomplish anything or so strong they wind up managing the organization" (personal communication, 1989). When increased strength is dysfunctional, the solution is not, of course, to weaken the strong. It is better that the blessing of a strong engine be augmented by an improved chassis, not "solved" by shorting out a few spark plugs. When their strength causes boards not to do their job better but to intrude into the jobs of others, something is awry in the design. We must take a fresh look at governance concepts and the board-management partnership. The stark truth of Gale's comment is reason enough for a new model of governance.

It need not bespeak paranoia to observe along with Louden (1975, p. 117) that "if we do not concern ourselves with how we can rule organizations, the organizations will rule us." But the paradigm with which we traditionally "rule" is worthy neither of the people who give their time and talent nor of the missions they serve. Governance is overdue for a rebirth. Though much has been written over the past several decades about governing boards, with rare exceptions the efforts offer incremental improvement to an inadequate vehicle via new paint and tires. The purpose of this book is not to indict previous efforts or current performance so much as to prescribe a better way. Its message is that strategic leadership is exciting and accessible.

Next Chapter

The chapters that follow lay out a new vehicle for governing, a model whose premise is not incremental improvement in the capacity to govern, but transformation. Seeing policies in a more exacting light is the first step toward creating a new model of governance. Therefore, I begin in Chapter Two by arguing that the opportunity for greater strategic leadership lies first in the redefinition of policy and policymaking.

| Policy as a Leadership Tool

Public and nonprofit managers have incorporated much of modern management into their operations. Boards that would provide strategic leadership to increasingly sophisticated management require an equally modern governance. Modern governance is not simply modern management practiced by a governing board. To be sure, the principles of management and governance are closely related. But governance is more than management writ large. And it is more than a quality-control board of expert managers and technicians running inspections and approvals to maintain order.

The pressure toward better management has created an awkward gap between the sophistication of management and the sophistication of the board. Although public and nonprofit management is not known for its rigor, it has advanced considerably in the past two decades. Governance, on the other hand, has scarcely moved at all. When chief executives are increasingly skilled as managers while their boards are not increasingly skilled as governors, leadership becomes a brittle commodity or, at worst, a mockery. Executives may end up patronizing the board in order to manage well. Boards can be led to busy pursuits that interfere as little as possible with management. The resulting scenario is not unlike that of a very mature child dealing skillfully with an immature parent. Most public and nonprofit CEOs expect, as part of their job obligation, to "stage-manage" board meetings so their boards will not wander aimlessly or go out of control. Such a game of seemingly necessary manipulation carries a cost that the fragile balance of leadership can ill afford. For this reason alone, governing boards must modernize the process of governance.

A modern approach to governing will enable a part-time, possibly inexpert group of persons *to lead*. They have neither the time nor the ability to control every action, circumstance, goal, and decision. And if perchance they did have both time and ability, the organization would slow to a halt as they carried out their task. The most expensive resource of public and nonprofit organizations, the staff, would be significantly wasted as the official second-guessing process ground on. Boards caught in the trap of being better staff than staff, and boards bewildered by unending details or confused by technical complexities, cannot lead. A modern approach to governance must enable a board to cut quickly to the heart of an organization, being neither seduced into action nor paralyzed into inaction by trappings along the way.

This chapter argues that the secret to the new governance lies in policymaking, but policymaking of a finely crafted sort. I begin by defining *policy* as it is used throughout this text. After making a case that policy clarification is the central feature of board leadership, I consider how a board might get a handle on policy in real board life. I end the chapter by describing the four new categories of board policy to be used throughout the text.

Policies as Values and Perspectives

The essence of any organization lies in what it believes, what it stands for, and what and how it values. An organization's works, rather than its words, are the telling assessment of its beliefs. Studies of corporate culture (such as Davis, 1984) look at the way people deal with problems, differences, customers, decision making, and each other as a way to penetrate the essence of an organization. These values and perspectives form the bedrock on which the more mechanical and visible aspects of an organization are based.

I use the word *value* in its common meaning of "belief" or "relative importance," as when we speak of right and wrong, prudent and imprudent, ethical and unethical, proper and improper, worthy and worthless, acceptable and unacceptable, tolerable and intolerable, and so forth. I use the word *perspective* to mean "way of looking at," "guiding principle," "approach," or "conceptual point of view." A board value might be: "Cost-of-living raises should be consistent with those in other organizations in our county." But what do we call the board position: "CEO evaluation will be based on total agency performance"? Though there is surely valuing to be found in the latter, we would be strained to call the statement a value. It can easily be called an "approach" to CEO performance, a "way of looking at" the nature of delegation, or a "perspective" on the CEO role.

Consider an organization's goals, compensation, inventory procedures, cash management, plant maintenance, paint scheme, promotion practices, market penetration plans, and innumerable other factors. With enough patience and inference, we could construct from these concrete realities a picture of the organization's values and perspectives. The organization likely was not designed by stating explicitly considered values and perspectives at the core, then continuing outward to the event-specific and concrete. Consequently, values and perspectives across the organization may be inconsistent. In this case we have uncovered a value—always unwritten—that the organization does not place great importance on consistency of values and perspectives!

As individuals, we apply certain perspectives and values whenever we confront external realities. Under a certain condition, our values or perspectives lead us to act in a certain manner. We are valuing, conceptualizing beings who constantly seek to make sense of our world and ourselves by linking sense data with frameworks. The sense data are our more or less reliable measures of "reality"; the frameworks are our values and perspectives. Moreover, our sense data (what we think are "facts") are affected by the conceptual frameworks we have adopted. Even if the "facts" were wholly objective, our frameworks would lead us to say that a certain phenomenon is best looked at in this way, or that this result is more important than that. External realities vary beyond our control, but ostensibly we are captains of our perspectives and values. And those values and perspectives compel us to develop certain competencies, to make certain choices, and, generally, to behave with some measure of continuity.

Organizations are similar to individuals in these respects. Their frameworks of values and perspectives determine specific decisions and behaviors in the face of specific facts. And the same frameworks determine what they regard as relevant facts about the environment. So subtle is this effect that boards often do not regard their selection of facts as choices; after all, facts are facts. Organizations, like individual persons, are caught in a self-perpetuating, circular phenomenon that does untold damage to vision and to thinking about possibilities. Values and perspectives are thus powerful, often invisible forces that determine not only organizational circumstances, activities, and goals, but even the data that organizations admit into their assessment of reality.

Excellence in governance begins when boards recognize this central, determining feature of organizations. Setting goals, deploying staff, writing procedures, formulating plans, developing strategy, establishing budgets, and *all other board and staff activity* depend on values and perspectives, whether those result from debate or default. Decisions of all sorts, as Drucker so clearly argued (1967, pp. 113–141), rest on principles and generic understandings. Unrecognized, this dependence can produce pernicious disparities, difficulties, and unfulfilled potential. For leaders may develop goals and plans without being mindful of their underlying meaning, the binding glue that transforms disjointed parts into a whole. But when recognized and properly used, these values and perspectives offer leaders the key to effectiveness.

It has been my experience with boards that a simple shift away from detailed and event-specific governance and toward values and valuing produces a powerful shift in board leadership. In focusing *directly* on perspectives and values, a board moves closer to the underpinnings of organizational behavior.

In the language of this text, *values* and *perspectives* are blended with the concept of *policy,* so in most contexts henceforth I refer to them in undifferentiated fashion simply as policies. Values dominate policies that are instructive to staff—that is, policies that tell staff what to do or not to do. Perspectives dominate the policies that codify the board's own process and relationships. I have found no utility in belaboring the distinction between values and perspectives, so any differences between them are of no significant interest in subsequent discussion. It is only important to remember that *policy* as used here can express values, perspectives, or both.

Policy is an apt and familiar word for us to employ when referring to organizational values and perspectives, but the strength of familiarity is also a weakness. We must avoid the looser definitions currently attached to the word *policy* if we are to build a more exacting framework for policy-based governance. Conventionally, policy has referred to any board utterance. Policy sometimes means procedures, as in personnel "policies." Policy can refer to unstated as well as explicit values and perspectives. If this same word is to be used for more precise governance, we will have to keep in mind that what once passed for policy may not any longer.

To get to the core of organizational meaning, governing boards must concern themselves with policies. But because the central challenge is to lead rather than to analyze, governance must pronounce rather than merely educe policies. Inasmuch as sophisticated management processes use board policies as the point of departure, these documents must be conceived with care.

Leadership Through Policies

Because policies permeate and dominate all aspects of organizational life, they present the most powerful lever for the exercise of leadership. Peters and Waterman (1982, p. 291) wrote, "Clarifying the value system and breathing life into it are the greatest contributions a leader can make." Leadership through explicit policies offers the opportunity to think big and to lead others to think big. Leaders acutely aware of the value aspect of life's events continually link day-to-day exigencies with the underlying important elements of life. They tap into something deeper, perhaps more uniquely human, than the accountant, supervisor, or technician in all of us. Work becomes not so much a series of structured mechanical activities as a process of creating and becoming. Policy leadership clarifies, inspires, and sets a tone of discourse that stimulates leadership in followers.

There are four reasons that policy-focused leadership is a hallmark of governance.

1. *Leverage and efficiency:* By grasping the most fundamental elements of an organization, the board can affect many issues with less effort. However high-flown their intentions, boards have only so much time available, often measurable in hours per year.
2. *Expertise:* Board members do not ordinarily have all the skills required to operate their organization. To compensate, some

boards focus their recruiting more on skills that match those of staff than those of governance. Governing by policies requires none of the specialties and can often be done better without them.

3. *Fundamentals:* When a board sifts through and sorts all the material it might deal with, the real heart of the matter is the body of politics those materials represent. Boards that govern by attending directly to policies are more certain to address that which has enduring importance. Dealing so directly with the fundamentals has a compelling legitimacy.

4. *Vision and inspiration:* Dreaming is not only permissible for leaders—it is obligatory. Dealing meticulously with the trees rather than the forest can be satisfying, but it neither fuels vision nor inspires.

Directing an organization can be like rearing a child. Controlling every behavior is a fatiguing and ultimately impossible charge. Inculcating the policies of life is far more effective and, even if some slippage occurs on individual behaviors, it is the only serviceable approach in the long run. So whether a board wishes to control narrowly or to lead more expansively, governing through policies is the efficient way to operate.

To the extent that a board wishes to provide strategic leadership, it must clarify policies and expect organizational activities to give them life. Making policies explicit and consistent, consciously choosing policies from among alternatives, and obsessively keeping the spotlight on the chosen policies never allows the governing focus to waiver from policies and the organization's fidelity to them.

Getting a Handle on Policies

Boards have not been well equipped with language or useful conceptual categories to discuss policies. Even though we are all accustomed to speaking of policies, and even though boards claim to be "policy boards," the promising idea of Policy Governance is handicapped by our nascent skill in managing policies. Which policies must be addressed? What does a board policy look like? Are there inherent differences among types of policies? If a board addresses policies, what are the nonpolicy issues that it stops addressing? In preparation for proposing a classification system for board policies, I look at the relationship between policy and the unending stream of organizational decisions.

Let us consider how boards ordinarily see their reality. Organizations present themselves to boards as a collection or sequence of concrete decisions, documents, arrangements (for example, staffing patterns or plans), and persons. Boards are accustomed to dealing with specific decisions and with resolving specific problems about this unending list. In fact, they pride themselves on being decision makers and problem solvers. They gauge their performance by such decisions and solutions, *not by the clarity of the policies that led to them.*

A board decision to increase a specific staff member's salary by $500 might really represent a board policy that would allow any salary to be adjusted up to 15 percent so long as budget balance is maintained. A board decision to establish mileage reimbursement at twenty-four cents might flow from the board's belief that the rate should be consistent with that of local governments. A board presented with a staff plan for clinic hours might approve the extension of operating time to 8 P.M. if its own value is merely that service hours not penalize patients who hold daytime jobs. A board's only policy concern, when asked to approve purchase of certain insurance coverage, may be that equipment is insured to 80 percent of replacement cost.

A board would do well to examine the policy implications of any initiative it is asked to approve. It can rise above the technical complexities by being a guardian of values rather than a superstaff. "What policies are represented here?" should be a constant board query. "How do these actions relate to previous policies adopted by the board?" "What resolution of competing policies does this program, budget, or plan embody?"

For example, in many service agencies, a "sliding fee" schedule adjusts the price of services or products on the basis of recipients' financial condition. Such schedules are ordinarily developed by staff, then inspected and approved by the board with great attention to form and content. Not uncommonly, the policies that the fee schedule represents receive no systematic—much less rigorous—airing at all. Above all, fee markdowns in a public agency are implicitly based on how the organization's economic nature is conceived. If, to put it simply, the agency is to plug holes in the market mechanism (meaning, provide for those whom the market price system would leave behind), there are many value choices to be made about which holes are plugged and which are not. In other words, if we are to subsidize some persons or some needs more than others, on what basis will we establish differential subsidy? These values will, at some level, be decided within the bounds drawn by a mission statement. In fact, the policies relevant to this issue could be seen as "subsidiary" to the mission. If these policies were clearly stated, administrative writing of the specifics of a fee adjustment schedule could proceed without board involvement.

To use another example, budgets are adopted with exhaustive attention to detail but with only cursory review of the important policies inherent in the array of numbers. Zero-based budgeting (ZBB) arose primarily in response to the unstated value in conventional budgeting that ongoing activity has the benefit of the doubt over marginal additions. That value had gone largely unnoticed in millions of annual budget approvals. Budgets make powerful, albeit nonverbal, commentary on policies regarding fiscal risk, conservatism in projection of revenues, and apportionment of resources among competing intentions. Budgets are often cited as the most important policy statement. And so they may be, but they are poorly conceived policies. The policies represented are buried so well in numbers that few boards get past the numbers to any rigorous debate about the underlying policies. If anything, the numbers seduce board members into a myriad of interesting but peripheral details.

We pore over the many pages of personnel "policies" (a misnomer), even though there are a mere handful of important policies underlying—and usually hidden in—the ample specifics. Similarly, boards often overinvolve themselves in the many aspects of a long-range plan, rather than isolate and resolutely deal with the very small number of large value issues on which a staff planning process can focus.

In other words, because of the allure and handy concreteness of specifics, boards are no more accustomed to dealing directly with policies than are their staffs. Individual board members do hold values, of course, and sometimes state them clearly. The problem is that the board job design and process do not focus on the policy aspect of organization; nor do they provide a systematic way of collecting, deliberating, and enunciating those policies. Indeed, boards occasionally make a clear value pronouncement about an encompassing issue, only to "lose" the statement by burying it in a far longer document or in the minutes. Wisdom expressed but uncodified slips away.

By attending to policy content, a board can gain far more control over what matters in the organization and be at less risk of getting lost in the details. Even then, the board will be trapped into reactivity if its policy deliberation is limited to what it receives from the staff. James P. Weeks, member of the park commission in Naperville, Illinois, captured this thought when he said, "My *philosophy* will affect a process rather than react to a function already underway" (personal communication). There is no proactivity in inspecting what is already developed. Moreover, by that time the organization already has a sizable investment in the document or the staff recommendation. Beyond being reactive, this after-the-fact value inspection is shaped by staff interests, initiative, pace, and categories of work. Further, there is a great deal of executive prerogative about what to bring to the board and what not to bring. Inasmuch as boards often answer only what they have been asked, the resulting board response is hardly leadership.

To lead instead of follow, boards must get to the other end of the parade. Rather than following agendas driven by what the staff wants approved, boards should initiate the agendas. Of course, no board knows what is going on in the staff domain well enough to do this. I am not suggesting that boards try to connect in a real-time sense to staff activity. I am saying that boards can know what is going on—and what should go on next—*in the board job*. The board is not responsible for managing, but it can surely be responsible for governing.

The objective is not to bring the board more knowledgeably into an ongoing administrative process, as if staff operations is the train to be caught. The point is to establish the board's policymaking process as both preliminary and predominant. If boards are truly governing, then board members are not obliged to tag along behind management. And they need not become superstaff in a conscientious attempt to tag along more professionally. They need only tend to their job of proactively establishing organizational policies.

Categories of Board Policy

Boards can scarcely lead the parade if their categories of work are derived from staff work. Normally, when a board addresses matters of policy, it is likely to do so within categories that mimic the administrative realm. Administrators are accustomed to breaking their domains down into certain areas: financial, personnel, service, data processing, and so on. Our tradition of board work encourages boards to derive their agendas from staff-based divisions of work. That these are sensible divisions of labor within a paid staff does not make them optimal divisions of thought at the board level.

This common board practice is tantamount to classifying a manager's functions on the basis of his or her secretary's job areas. Consider a new manager who asks his or her secretary just what categories of work have been successful in the clerical position. The manager finds that the secretary divides the job into typing, filing, telephone answering, and scheduling. So informed, the manager proceeds to divide the managerial job into managing about typing, managing about filing, managing about telephone answering, and managing about scheduling. Such a course of action would be ludicrous. We would think that such a manager had given little thought to the design of his or her own job, preferring thoughtlessly to mimic the concrete, handily available arrangement of a subordinate's duties. In fact, it is hard to conceive of any manager behaving in this way, *unless the "manager" is a board!* This error is so routine that we fail to see another way. Thus, conventional governance is subtly managed by management, a far cry from management governed by governance.

In constructing a new wisdom of governance, I begin by creating categories to guide a board's debate and pronouncements, *groupings not derived from administration but from an inquiry into governance.* These categories also serve as vessels to contain board policies as they accumulate, and thereby become divisions of the board policy manual. The categories embrace board policies about (1) ends to be achieved, (2) means to those ends, (3) the board-staff relationship, and (4) the process of governance itself. Policymaking is not all of a board's job; linkage with the external environment, assessment of executive performance, and, in many cases, fundraising must be mastered as well. Policymaking, however, is the *central* role and one that verbally contains board positions and intentions about the other activities. Well-considered and well-ordered policymaking fashions all other board tasks into a coherent whole. Let us consider each of the four categories.

Ends to Be Achieved

What should the results be? How will our being in business affect the world? Our choices range from the broad (effects on whole populations) to the specific (outcomes for a particular client, student, patient, or other beneficiary). They relate to both the long and the short term. This set of values about an intended impact on the world is at the root of an organization's reason for existence.

Both the cost and the benefit to the world must be taken into account when a board considers an organization's transaction with its environment. This most critical of all policy areas concerns itself with what human needs are satisfied, for whom, and at what cost. The governing board's highest calling is to ensure that the organization produces economically justifiable, properly chosen, well-targeted results.

Strategic leadership is proclaimed more through wisely developed organizational ends than through any other aspect of governance. This policy category could be called results, impacts, goals, or outcomes as well as ends, each title having its connotations. Governance of ends is specifically addressed in Chapter Four.

Means to the Ends

If we isolate all values about organizational ends, the only remaining values concern means. When we have dealt with where we want to go, we are left with how we can get there. Speaking for myself, keeping ends and means separate is important, particularly because I have a pernicious habit of confusing means for ends. But suppose I supervise a team and delegate portions of the intended results to the members of that team. To maintain clarity in our communications, it is even more important that I differentiate the activities from the results to which the activities lead.

Beyond the need for clear communication, however, there is another important reason to keep ends and means separate. As a delegator, I am dealing not only with my own means but with those of others as well. And what we know about managing people draws a sharp distinction between my means and theirs. I must tell myself how to do my part, but telling my subordinates how to do their jobs (rather than simply what results I expect) has unintended effects. Unless they are unable or unwilling to make decisions, people do not like to be told how to do things. Their creativity is thwarted; they feel more like machines. If left free to choose the methods and to be held accountable only for results, people make the best of their hierarchical burden.

When this phenomenon is applied to an organization larger than a team, controlling methods at the top becomes a major source of organizational stress and even pathology. Bottlenecks develop because the part-time board cannot keep up with staff activities fast enough to prescribe them. The CEO cannot empower staff by decentralizing decision making because the board has withheld the power to make decisions. Having chosen to control a wide range of methods, boards look like amateurs trying in vain to play a professional game. Moreover, when organizational dialogue is so heavily invested in the "how," the "why" receives less attention. And issues of "why" are those most in need of board involvement.

Because policies concerning one's own means and policies concerning subordinates' means are such different topics, they must be kept separate. Policies about board means are addressed in the two categories yet to be introduced. Policies about staff means represent board values about the methods employed to achieve organizational ends. What expression is proper for board values in the domain of staff means? As we examine this question, remember that the most effective governing controls what needs to be controlled, yet sets free what can be free.

At the outset, the board's only interest in staff means is that they be effective, prudent, and ethical. I have never found any other legitimate reason to interfere with a subordinate's means. The main check on means, of course, is not on means at all, but on ends. The board's concern about effectiveness manifests in the degree to which the staff meets the board's policies about ends. That leaves only one *direct* board interest in staff means: that results are achieved in a prudent and ethical way. This category of board values concerning the "how" of achieving results is composed, then, of policy statements defining prudence and ethics. Chapter Five explores the governance of staff means.

Board-Staff Relationship

The only remaining area is the board's own means. It is with regard to board means that policy is more likely to embody a perspective than, strictly speaking, a value. For mechanical ease rather than conceptual purposes, I divide the board's means into two parts: how the board relates to staff and how the board goes about the job of governing.

Policies about relating to staff include the board's approach to delegation, its view of the CEO role, and its manner of assessing performance. We deal directly with the board-staff relationship or, more accurately, the board-CEO relationship in Chapter Six.

Process of Governance

It is in policies about the process of governance that the board addresses the nature of its trusteeship and its own job process and products. Nonprofit and public boards ordinarily govern on behalf of someone else, an often undefined group tantamount to stockholders of equity corporations. Board effectiveness can be sensibly assessed only if we know *in whose behalf* the board acts. For whom is it in trust?

In carrying out the top job in the organization, the board—like any manager—makes specific contributions beyond just a summation of what subordinates do. What are those contributions or, to put it another way, what is the board's job description? What principles or ground rules does the board use to discipline the process of leadership? What are and what are not legitimate board topics? What is the board's approach to its own discipline? How can the board structurally organize itself?

The issues are numerous, but the question in this category is simple: How do we approach the process and products of governance itself? These subjects form the content of Chapters Seven and Eight.

Summary of the New Policy Categories

Values and perspectives that govern an organization can be divided into four categories, whether or not the board recognizes or uses them. It is my thesis that *explicit* use of these categories will profoundly alter the nature of board dialogue, documents, accountability, and, ultimately, the capacity for strategic leadership. These categories of policy, as further explained in subsequent chapters, can replace *all* other board documents except bylaws, minutes, and pronouncements of the state (articles of incorporation or enabling statutes). They are designed to be the centrally available, exhaustive repository of board wisdom.

Categories of board policies are printed in uppercase and lowercase as shown throughout the remainder of this text. When, for example, "board-executive relationship" appears in lowercase, the reader may assume it denotes exactly what it says, rather than the policy category of the same name. As construed by my governance model, then, all board policies fall into these groups:

1. *Ends:* The organizational "swap" with the world. What human needs are to be met, for whom (outside the operating organization), and at what cost or relative worth.
2. *Executive Limitations:* Those principles of prudence and ethics that limit the choice of staff means (practices, activities, circumstances, methods).
3. *Board-Executive Relationship:* The manner in which power is passed to the executive machinery and in which the use of that power is assessed.
4. *Board Process:* The manner in which the board represents the "ownership" and provides strategic leadership to the organization.

These policy category titles will be used throughout this text, but the exact titles are not important except to maintain continuity of meaning. Indeed, over the years my clients and I have used variants. One client referred to *Ends policies* as *Mission-Related policies*. The category *Executive Limitations* has been referred to as *Administrative Parameters* or *Staff Means Proscription*. The *Board-Executive Relationship* category is often called *Board-Staff Linkage* or *Board-CEO*

Linkage, even in my own publications. The title is not important, but the concepts differentiating these policy types are crucial.

Next Chapter

Having established universal categories in which to conceive and store the board's policies, I will now investigate policymaking in more depth. In Chapter Three, I will look at the traps in policy-making and the characteristics of effective policymaking. I show how the board can gain greater control with shorter documents, and demonstrate how the revered practice of approving budgets, plans, and other administrative material—a process that cripples strategic leadership—becomes unnecessary when boards enact policies that make a difference.

Designing Policies That Make a Difference

Most governing boards conceive of themselves as policy boards. We have a general understanding that board leadership is largely a policy task. A policy approach prevents a flurry of events from obscuring what is really important.

Yet it is rare to find a board that seriously attends to policy more than to the various details of policy implementation. Fewer than 5 percent of the boards I have encountered over the past decade were able to furnish me with board policies! Either they did not have them or what they had was scattered through years of minutes. Documents purported to be policies were almost always executive compendiums in which the board had played a reactive part.

Even searches of minutes failed to turn up much more than single-event decisions disguised as policies. To be sure, there were "personnel policies" and "administrative policies" or general "policies and procedures manuals." But these were basically staff documents upon which the board had stamped its approval. In none of these was it clear what portions or aspects the *board itself* had created or decreed.

The most frequent exceptions to this state of affairs have been school boards. These boards have so many policies that they cannot possibly keep up with them. As would be expected, their policies concern mainly staff practices and are usually prescriptive in detail. Few would qualify as legitimate board policies under the definition developed here.

I divided board policies into four categories in Chapter Two. Before investigating each category separately beginning in Chapter Four, I will explore principles that apply to all categories. This chapter begins by describing what is often wrong with board policy and the general characteristics of effective policy. We next consider how a board can utilize the different "sizes" of policies to govern more efficiently. Then I argue that proactive policymaking can replace approvals as the dominant board style of leadership—and why it should. I conclude by looking at the format of policy and the refinement of policy content over time.

Getting Serious About Policy

Current operational definitions of policy impede governing by policy. Any sort of action by the board is often granted the legitimizing title of policy. The fuzziness of the definition is a loud signal that the whole area of policy has not been taken seriously. Consequently, the claim to be a policymaking board is ordinarily belied by "policy" that is staff material with a large component of implementation specifics, and that the board has only blessed. In practice, I have found that a board's professing to be a "policy board" offers few clues to what the board actually does.

Board policy can be dead but unburied. I once supervised the collection of all existing (but still official) board policies of a large public organization in Indiana. The paperwork was inches thick. Many of the policies were long since forgotten but still on the books. Were these policies really useful in running the organization? They had been painstakingly assembled at considerable cost, for they were sprinkled through a wide range of documents. For all the rhetorical glamour afforded the board's policies, they turned out to be an impotent, self-contradictory collection too unimportant to be kept up to date.

Board policy can be alive but invisible. Although it is hard to find true board policy in written form, it is always possible to find it in unwritten form. Actually, it may not be found so much as suspected. Ironically, unwritten policy is sometimes thought to be so clear that no one feels the need to write it down and, at the same time, so variously interpreted as to border on being capricious. In a sense, there is never a de facto lack of policy; it always exists in the actions taken. *Implicit* policy not only fills in for the missing *explicit* policy, but is even used to excuse the absence of the latter.

Unfortunately, both unwritten and written board policy left un-tended are of questionable utility. We have difficulty in either agreeing on what the unwritten policy actually is (what it would say had it been explicit) or knowing which old written policies are still in effect. Curiously, the criterion used to judge which written state-ments should be taken seriously and which should be ignored is it-self *always* an unwritten policy! Why? Because boards are loath to admit that their policies do not make a difference. Making a major investment in board policymaking means first establishing prin-ciples and formats to guide policy content. Board policymaking, within the categories set out in Chapter Two, is explicit, current, literal, centrally available, brief, and encompassing.

Explicitness. Policies must exist in written form. This is the only way all parties (including the policymakers) can know just what the policy is. It is the best way for members to realize which policies should be questioned or changed. Two forces often make explic-itness more difficult. First, as "everyone" understands this or that precept, it seems silly to dwell on actual language. It seems silly, that is, until the writing begins and we discover our agreement was not as precise as we thought. Second, being explicit carries a dan-ger similar to that of being proactive. It means laying one's values on the table, exposing differences, and confronting them openly.

Currentness. Up-to-date policies are the only ones that work. A board can ensure that it keeps policies current more by compul-sively operating from its policy manual than by vowing to do an-nual reviews. When a board lives from its policies, the policies will either work or be changed. They will not then collect dust. Poli-cies must never end with a whimper but a bang; they must not be allowed to fade away into oblivion. Staff can help by acting as if the board sincerely means *every* policy that the board has not yet rescinded.

Literalness. Policies must mean what they say. If they do not, then they should be amended or deleted. We have come to accept organizational language that is meaningless. Learning a job is time consuming when you must discern bit by bit which words mean what they say and which do not. Governing is a verbal job; if a board's words have little integrity, governance cannot be excellent.

Central availability. When board pronouncements are all kept in one place, the task of determining what the organization represents becomes easier. Policies are virtually the only medium through which the board speaks, and thus should not be scattered about, discoverable only by scouring years of minutes and multiple staff documents. Centrally visible board values go far in preventing board intentions from being idiosyncratically interpreted by individual members, officers, or committees. To make a difference, board policies must be in a single repository that has obvious preeminence over other organizational documents.

Brevity. Brevity may be the unheralded secret of excellence. Peters and Waterman (1982) point out the stultifying effect of reams of procedures. It is certainly possible to tie an organization up in procedures manuals. Similarly, in board policies, "too long" and "too many" are enemies of good leadership. Organizations seem to be impressed with complexity, however, so brevity in policymaking confronts the need to look sophisticated ("It just *can't* be that simple!"). Boards need to seek the compelling elegance of simplicity.

Comprehensiveness. The board policy framework must encompass the entirety of that which is governed. That is, the design must enable all aspects of the organization to fall under the stated values of the board. Then, the board need not address all value issues, only the larger ones. By sticking to the discipline of resolving larger questions before smaller ones, starting with the broadest in each category, the board ensures that its policies will encompass the entire range of corporate possibilities. By examining the nature of policy "sizes," the next section explains how policy can be encompassing.

Policies Come in Sizes

Inasmuch as there are fewer policies than decisions based on those policies, the board's task is already easier than if it had tried to address all the single decisions. Dealing with policies moves the dilemma from the impossible to the merely improbable, for there are also more policies than a board has time to consider. As policies merely represent our values or perspectives, written or unwritten, they can be revealed in every event that occurs in an organization. We value one pen over another. We have values about length of meetings, coach airfare, group insurance, wax for the floor, and the need for a waste treatment plant. How can the board address such an inherently pervasive, large body of policy material, yet have a manageable task and product? This dilemma of too many policies to deal with has, happily, a simple key: policies come in all sizes.

Logical Containment of Policies

Larger values or perspectives logically contain, that is, limit the logical content of, smaller ones. Once a board has chosen an encompassing value, a plethora of narrower value issues still remain to be settled. It is this characteristic that leads many board members to see policy as vague or not specific. A board is just as likely to be too broad as to be too detailed, so board members' anxiety is not without foundation. The phenomenon of logical containment can help boards debate the question of policy breadth in an organized manner.

No matter how broad a policy is, it is always *more specific* than if it had not been said and *less specific* than it might have been. Therefore, it delimits the universe of specificity yet to be encountered, though it does not resolve those specificities. In other words, the *range* of further possible choices is smaller because the large value has been resolved. Say that you personally place more value on owning a new car than on having $15,000. This value statement both introduces and delimits further value issues about colors, models, and stereo systems. Similarly, selecting a mission involves the broadest level of values about organizational results. Making that choice leaves many questions of priority unresolved, but it clearly limits the range of remaining choices.

A community may feel that the goal of establishing a "healthier local economy" is sufficient reason to operate an economic development agency. Bringing about a healthier local economy is an appropriate choice of mission. Whether to establish a broader employment base or to be a regional retail center is a subsequent, and slightly smaller, value choice confronted *within* the mission. Similarly, a public school mission to produce "competent, employable citizens" still leaves large issues to be decided, though at a level of abstraction lower than that of the mission. These issues include the balance among academic, job skill, and life-planning competencies.

An exercise in values clarification challenges boards who would govern by policy. Policies within each category, described in Chapter Two, can be arranged by size. Like mixing bowls, they are "nested," largest to smallest. After addressing the largest of value choices (the biggest bowl), the board can either address the next level (the second largest bowl) or be content with having clarified the first level. The CEO then inherits the right to make choices within the second and subsequently smaller levels.

By attending to the largest issues in each category, the board can responsibly limit its work. As it attends to the specificity in each decreasing level of policy, it reaches a point at which a majority of members are willing to accept *any reasonable interpretation* of the policy language. Until the board feels that the full range of choices permissible under this rule are acceptable to it, it has not reached the stopping point. When it does reach that point, the board can safely stop. It is not relevant whether the remaining range is vague, only whether it is acceptable. How much the board trusts the CEO is not relevant, only whether the range is acceptable, because if the board "trusts" the CEO to make a certain choice, then the board is harboring an unspoken expectation that they should commit to further policy specificity. When Ends and Executive Limitations policies are created with this integrity, management can be safely entrusted to make all further choices.

Phyllis Field of the Rhode Island Board of Regents refers to this phenomenon as "controlling the inside by staying on the outside." As the board writes its policy, there should be no doubt about the size of "mixing bowl" at which the board stopped, nor what the board has explicitly pronounced. Without such a scheme for creating policy, boards tend to make a policy about this, that, and the other. A patchwork of policies can leave dangerous gaps. Boards are reasonably fearful of having overlooked some important policy feature, so the solution is to become supermanagers, reviewing and approving everything. Powerful delegation is impossible in these circumstances, as is the freedom of the board to attend unceasingly and vigorously to the big issues. Making use of logical containment enables a board to have its hands firmly on, though not in, an organization.

Board Policy Versus Staff Policy

Starting with the big questions first is simply a good problem-solving technique, even for individuals. But when delegation is involved, the utility of this approach goes beyond merely good problem solving. It enables the board to define the boundary between itself and its executive. The boundary always lies just below the point that the board last addressed. There is *no set boundary* for all boards or even for the same board at different times. As long as the board approaches all policymaking from the largest to the smallest issue, this method will continually redefine the boundary as circumstances and board values shift.

The board's job differs from staff jobs, then, not by topic but by *levels within topics*. Exceptions to this rule are the unique board job contributions to be discussed in Chapter Seven. This approach recognizes and legitimizes that everybody, not just the board, makes policy. Every clerk and janitor, by her or his actions, is making implicit policy at all times. It is inescapable that everyone does so, though the policies made are of vastly differing sizes. What is important is that all policies that live in the organization be consonant with the broader policies enunciated by the governing leadership. Thus, the board can control without meddling.

In dealing with policy issues of different sizes, the board can create policies that make a difference if it observes the following principles:

- *The board should resolve the broadest or largest policy issue in each category before dealing with smaller issues in any category.* This means having the discipline to stick with the highly subjective, tough choices to be found in the broader policy issues.
- *If the board wishes to address smaller levels, it should never skip levels but should move to the next smaller levels in sequence.* This requires having the discipline not to reach into the organizational decision process for instant fixes, even if specific board members are more expert in a subject than staff.

- *The board should grant the CEO authority to make all further choices as long as they are "within" the board's Ends and Executive Limitations policies.* This requires the discipline to let go, to delegate.

The provisions of Ends and Executive Limitations policies are binding directives, but within those bounds, the executive is free to choose and move without the board's stultifying, over-the-shoulder involvement (some might say meddling). If the board has done its job, such detailed involvement is not only unnecessary, but it also destroys staff creativity and efficiency. Only boards that have failed to be proactive policymakers have any need to meander in or retain approval authority over staff activity and plans. Moreover, unless the CEO has such authority, he or she can never delegate parts of it to subordinates without onerous bureaucratic strings.

Prerogatives that fall within board policies in the Board Process and Board-Executive Relationship categories may be given to the board chairperson. Because these categories deal with the board's own means, they should not be delegated to the CEO. But within the Ends and Executive Limitations categories, the CEO *must* be the person authorized to make further decisions. In any event, it is in delegation to the CEO that board fidelity to good principles is most critical. Even when the staff is small, by far the preponderance of further decisions lie in the executive's arena. Consequently, almost all my further comments on the concept of residual decision latitude relate to the Ends and Executive Limitations categories.

There need be no prescribed limit to how far a board may delve into smaller issues, as long as it starts with the largest and progresses *in sequence.* The likelihood of a board's going "too far" (even in the judgment of staff!) is small, simply because the further it goes, the more complex the task becomes of balancing all the ramifications of any one choice. Lower-level issues branch out much like a table of organization does, so the number of factors to coordinate increases at lower levels. Juggling such permutations is one reason a full-time staff stays busy.

It is instructive to envision the "size of issue" phenomenon as a matrix. The board's level of involvement is across the top of all subjects. Just beneath the board's level is the CEO, and just below that the first echelon of staff, and so forth throughout the organization. Everything below the board is the CEO's domain, though the executive turns over lower-level issues to staff. Columns cutting down through all levels consist of any topic with which the agency might deal.

Each topic includes issues that are very large (at the top) and those that are very small (at the bottom). A budget, for example, embodies a few sweeping values and a great many small ones. The board itself fills in the top cells with policy. The CEO and his or her subordinates fill in all other choices consistent with the board's statement. Board policies are embodied in a board policy manual consisting of all the board's pronouncements, but not cluttered by the more voluminous ones subsequently made by staff.

In other words, instead of an agency "policy and procedures" manual, there should be a board policy manual separate from staff-written, staff-owned documents. Rather than a board-approved budget, there should be a board budget policy. Instead of a board personnel manual, there should be a board policy on the treatment of personnel. Rather than a board-approved wage and salary administration plan with compensation schedules, there should be a board policy on compensation. Each policy might be approximately one page in length. The board's document would be a conceptually *horizontal* collection of these three and other board policies (see also Carver, 1995f).

Contrast this with the conventional approach in which agency documents are arranged *vertically* by topic. Commonly, we would have an agency personnel manual, a budget, and a compensation plan. Each document is a mixture of the trivial and the profound, mostly trivial simply because the greatest number of issues are at the lower levels. Moreover, document content is not explicit about values at all. Board-level choices cannot be distinguished from staff choices. The content overwhelmingly consists of the specifics of implementation, generated largely by staff, from which the controlling, broadest values *can only be inferred*.

Policy Architecture

When a board policy is longer than one sentence, the internal structure of the policy reflects the nested levels of issues it addresses. An outline form serves this need handily. The policy preamble would be the highest level, major headings the next highest level, and so on through the outline format. The board will have debated and resolved higher levels prior to lower levels within what will become a single policy. It will not have dealt with the document as a whole, except perhaps in the final review.

Consequently, the very format of board policies in nested sizes reflects the discipline of the board's values and perspectives. Policies can be rigorous and yet succinct. To be a compact document wherein every word counts, a policy must not repeat what can be found elsewhere.

The Approval Syndrome

This kind of unembellished policymaking may appear stark and suspiciously terse to boards accustomed to adopting policies in monolithic rather than articulated format. It can be quite difficult to find, much less to extract, the broadest, most encompassing policy issues from such conglomerations. It is customary not only to adopt various levels of policy as an undifferentiated mass but also to adopt whole documents. Whole documents, like budgets, personnel "policies," and compensation plans fill multiple levels from the least to the most detailed. Boards are handed entire documents complete with a preponderance of trivia. So it is that boards' approval of whole management documents is the current norm in governance.

Only respect for tradition prevents our noticing how ritualistic, trivializing, bottlenecking, and reactive this "approval syndrome" is. The inherent flaws in this time-honored method are severely detrimental to the quality of both governance and management. I will now examine these flaws.

Reactivity. Document approvals place the board in a reactive position. The board is moving after the fact inasmuch as the document has already been created (using criteria the board did not establish). For practical reasons, the board can often do little but approve the measure. Many times, to avoid feeling like rubber stamps, boards nitpick, particularly in approving budgets. No matter how much intelligence goes into playing this reactive role, it is clearly not leadership.

Sheer volume of material. Board members must read and understand sufficiently to critique. That calls for studious attention to many low-level issues. Boards are burdened with material to study. The resultant tomes are necessarily filled with staff-level material and issues on which board members spend conscientious and prodigious time. It is unlikely that boards can be truly complete in this endeavor, and they may therefore overlook important items in the flurry of small ones.

Mental misdirection. A strategic leader must continually struggle against smallness. The larger, important values are vulnerable and easily displaced by concrete, short-term matters. The "approval syndrome" invites boards to deal with primarily low-level issues and detracts their attention from high-level, more subjective issues. One board I worked with spent time going over every nook and cranny of an almost $200 million budget each year. Looking back over several years of such exhausting work, they were hard-pressed to find even one half of 1 percent of budget improvement thus produced. Yet during the same time, they had failed to wrestle with and clarify just what this large organization was to produce!

Letting staff off the hook. When the board gives formal approval, it becomes the owner of the document. Whatever is inconsistent with what *would have been* a board policy (had there been one) can no longer be held against the CEO. Who is to be held accountable when a board-approved staff plan fails to accomplish the desired results? The board has been co-opted in the process. But staff judgment may have been co-opted as well, inasmuch as staff plans are designed not only to accomplish results but to garner board approval. It is not uncommon for staffs to give disproportionate attention to this political feature. Under these conditions, CEO accountability to the board loses both legitimacy and rigor.

Short-term bias. Low levels of organization generally have a short time horizon. Because the document is created from the bottom up, rather than on the basis of high-level values pronounced by the board, it may have a short-term bias.

Lack of clarity in the board's contribution. When the document is approved, it is impossible to determine just what the board said! The board either said everything because it now owned the document in its entirety, or it said nothing because it merely passed what someone else contributed, or said something between these extremes. But no one can tell. There is no distinct pronouncement expressing the values of the board. Thus, the voice of leadership cannot be heard. Under such obscurant conditions, a board may remain busy reviewing and approving, but *making no substantive contribution at all,* and no one notices.

Subsequent staff agility. Since we cannot tell what the board has said, we cannot tell what others in the hierarchy have said. Consequently, we cannot tell who has the right to restate or change some part of what has been decided. Any request for change must be put to the board, regardless how undeserving it may be of their attention. Thus, the board is involved in trivial matters both in the initial approval and in amendments. The management either floods the board with staff-level issues in order to be agile and flexible with activities and plans, or accepts the bottleneck caused when plans and procedures cannot be amended in a natural flow by the persons most intimate with implementation.

Fragmentation. The board faces a sequence of disconnected and unmanageably voluminous vertical slices of the whole instead of a holistic, manageable fabric of horizontally connected policies. We all profess that boards should view the big picture. Yet what most boards confront in meeting after meeting are pieces that are too specific.

The approval process provides boards with a handily available, easy, tradition-condoned *imitation* of leadership. Instead of separating the board's domain from the staff's domain, the "approval syndrome" confounds both domains into an undifferentiated mass. The stage is set for the board to do unnecessary work at the staff level or for the staff to wield undue influence at the board level. The former result, depending on one's point of view, is perceived as detailed, trivial, burdensome, or involved. The latter is perceived as rubber-stamping, staff dominance, or comfortable passivity. Of course, both situations may exist at the same time, with the board doing staff work and the staff doing board work. However talent is wasted, neither strategic leadership by the board nor effective management by the staff occurs. When the approval process is taken lightly, it reduces board action to a charade. When it is taken seriously, it reduces the CEO concept to a charade.

Curiously, there are times when the board goes through the approval process not intending to withhold authority from the CEO, but to confirm it. A board might declare its support for the CEO by cloaking some controversial executive decision in the prestige of the boardroom. Board motivation is usually expressed as, "We want the staff (or others) to know the board is really behind the CEO on this." As long as the board and CEO understand that the decision is truly the CEO's, this approval not only seems harmless, but appears to be a healthy show of solidarity. The board should, however, consider that such a gesture of board support is called for only if the board has been sending weak signals about the nature of delegation. This kind of support is ordinarily not warranted if the board has made it clear to all that the CEO's decisions within board-stated bounds are *always* supported by the board. Official support of a specific action implies that such support is necessary or, conversely, that the general philosophy of delegation is weak.

Policy Development

Policymaking, then, is proactive concerning the broadest issues, rather than reactive on issues of all sizes. Policies of the board, brief though they may be, become parents to all executive action. Because these policies are central, their currency is critical. Brevity will make it far easier to keep them up to date. Such brief, current policies developed by a state board in Ohio were said to "reduce the Board's Policy Manual to 34 pages from 422 pages and make it a constantly used reference rather than a collector of dust," according to Dr. Robert Bowers (personal communication). Governing by policy means governing *out of* policy in the sense that no board activity takes place without reference to policies. Most resolutions in board meetings will be motions to amend the policy structure in some way. Consequently, policy *development* is not an occasional board chore but its chief occupation.

From time to time, a board discovers that its values and perspectives have changed, that a previous statement was not fully cognizant of the range of options, or that the risks and opportunities in the external world have shifted. Even large shifts in board values can usually be accommodated more by altering existing language than by adding to it, thus changing the volume of policies very little. It is very important that the collection of board policies not grow so large that it fails to remain a truly living document.

Policies or policy changes can be initiated anywhere. It is not important to restrict the sources from which the board receives its impetus to establish or change its policies. But it is important to affix the *responsibility* for continual, informed weighing of policy issues. That responsibility must rest squarely on the board itself, not on the CEO. In practice, the CEO plays a meaningful role in the board's continuing inquiry. But to remove from the board the central responsibility for its own job would be a rash flight from responsibility. The board may charge its officers or committees with parts of its task, but let there be no mistake about *whose* responsibility is being assigned.

In an optimally working board, the nature of its discourse constantly presents it with ways to develop policy. Proper boardroom dialogue spots value inconsistency, seizes upon value issues, and is impelled on an exciting discovery in relative worth. Meaningful policies are an expression of the board's soul. While they may not embody everything a board believes, when done in the Policy Governance manner, they embody everything about which *one can be certain* the board is and stands for (Carver, 1995d). In an environment of value awareness disciplined by principles relating to value size and category, a board can enact policies that make a difference.

Next Chapter

Now that we have better defined the nature of effective policy-making, we will study each policy category in turn. In Chapter Four, we examine those policies that direct the most critical feature of any organization: the Ends. No feature is more central to the policymaking responsibility than the governing of organizational ends.

Chapter Four

Focusing on Results
Clarifying and Sustaining
the Organization's Mission

The most important work of any governing board is to create and re-create the reason for organizational existence. This is not simply the approval of a purpose statement. Nor is this a task done once, then forgotten. It is a perpetual obligation, deserving of the majority of board time and energy. It is far more important than any other board undertaking, including budgets, personnel issues, risk management, and even choice of chief executive.

The only justifiable reason for organizational existence is the production of worthwhile results. Worthwhile results always relate to the satisfaction of human needs. Whose needs, which needs, and what constitutes "satisfaction" are the unending, subjective quandaries confronting a board. Resolving the important, even existential value dilemmas inherent in these questions is the very heart of leadership in governance.

In this chapter I begin by arguing for boards to focus more on the world outside the organization than the one inside. I then relate that external focus to the creation of mission and the results-related (Ends) policies built on mission. Next, I look at two powerful distractions that draw boards away from Ends: the confusion of ends with means and premature anxiety about evaluating Ends. I conclude with the board's largely Ends-related role in long-range planning.

Transcending the Organization

Board leadership of an organization is jeopardized more by the organization itself than by any other threat. I am not referring to the reluctance of staff to be governed, but to a more insidious phenomenon: the captivating allure of organizational events and issues. Typically, a high percentage of board time is spent on internal matters. Even when the subject matter is related to services or programs, the focus tends to be on personnel, fiscal, logistical, or other organizational aspects of programming. In other words, the most compelling subject matter deals with structure and method, not results.

Leadership for results begins outside, not inside the organization. Because of the seductive intrigue of organizational activity, board discipline must be designed to overcome entanglement in internal matters. Our understanding of what constitutes board "involvement" must change. The most effective way to help a board rise above organizational myopia is to let the board taste the grand expanse of the larger context.

The Larger Context

Although organizations are worlds in themselves, each is part of something bigger. We must start from this larger context to grasp the underpinnings of an organization. This outside world existed prior to, is larger than, and likely will go on after the organization. It is this larger context that gives meaning to the organization's mission and makes the organization's very existence possible. Further, board members' primary identity lies not within the organization, but in some part of the external context.

To the extent that a board fails to consider its results from a context external to the organization, it narrows the vision of which it is capable. Sometimes, leadership differs from nonleadership only in that leadership views the world with a slightly wider lens. That wider lens or, if you will, taller perspective, is achieved in governance by viewing not the organization but its environment as the setting for analysis and debate.

Transaction with the Environment

The organization lives in this larger context and, hence, affects it. That the organization exists makes a difference to this larger world, and the difference it makes can be characterized in two ways: (1) the world is richer, happier, and less in pain because of the care, knowledge, cure, or support produced; and (2) the world is poorer, more depleted, and more in pain because of the talent, capital, and space consumed. These two impacts on the world, corresponding to benefit and cost, should be the chief interest, even obsession, of the governing board. The board should ask itself, What good shall we accomplish, for which people or needs, and at what cost? It is important that boards view organizational results in terms of both cost and benefit.

The concept here is exchange, a transaction between the organization and the world. Something of value that is consumed is swapped for something of value that is produced. I use the words *results, ends,* and *outcomes* interchangeably to describe the organization's swap with the world. So these terms, as used here, refer to both product (changes for people) and efficiency (amount of change per dollar).

The usual organizational vocabulary contains *goal* and *objective.* But, alas, both goal and objective can be applied to either means or ends. Legitimately and commonly, objectives are established in the drive to attain a desired amount of activity or a desired outcome. Therefore, it is misleading to equate *goals* or *objectives* with *ends.* Although I use these terms in their common meaning, as some desired achievement, I do not employ them as special management concepts, choosing instead to focus on the ends-means difference.

Similarly, the word *strategy* includes both ends and means components. A planned shifting of outcome priorities over the next five years is an Ends issue. Long-term staff retraining and replacement strategies to make the shifts possible are means issues. As important as strategy is, the concept itself confuses ends and means. So as much as this text is a plea for boards to be strategic leaders, good strategy flows from the board's proper treatment of the ends-means distinction.

Confusing Ends and Means

My point is not that means are unimportant, just that means and ends should not be confused. Means will be best decided by the people who must use them, those who measure their choice of means chiefly by whether they achieve the expected ends.

Kirk (1986, p. 40) charged that boards "become so engrossed in doing an infinite variety of discrete things, pursuing an endless number of routines, that they lose sight of the results, if any, that the activities are supposed to accomplish." The distinction between ends and means seems simple. Ends and means appear often in the common language as a way of usefully classifying events around us. But closer inspection reveals difficulty in this apparent simplicity. For a board to take advantage of the ends-means opportunity for governance, it must recognize the ways in which ends and means are confounded.

Means Mistaken for Ends

In the absence of clear dictates about intended effects on the world, boards come to treat a number of means as if they were ends themselves. In some nonprofit and public endeavors, these counterfeit results have received the blessing of tradition, an unearned legitimacy that is accorded to the familiar more through default than through deliberation.

Commendable Activities

The most insidious counterfeits are activities associated with good intentions or with well-accepted reasoning. For example, because making more handouts available for training sessions shows good intent or sense, the number and quality of handouts can come to be judged as more important than the effect of the training. The bounds to which such confusion can extend are endless. In response to public clamor in the mid-1980s to compensate teachers on the basis of competence, numerous plans were proposed to establish incentives for those teachers who took more graduate courses!

In social service fields, a revered counterfeit is unit cost. Unit cost is the cost in dollars for providing a time unit of service. Pupil-day expenditure is a comparable public school term. Unit cost comes to be the measure of whether a service organization is doing as much per dollar as it should. But unit cost is not related to the effectiveness of the service, so it does not measure productivity (efficiency in producing benefits per dollar) as social programs pretend it does. For example, the unit cost mentality leads to the assumption that $50 per hour is better than $65 per hour when there is absolutely no reason to believe so. Perhaps the $65 per hour service is 150 percent more effective in attaining the results sought! Unit cost would simply be an innocuous measure if institutions had not come to rely upon it.

An organization can become so permeated by the belief that well-intended or reasonable actions (rather than results) are the reason for existence that no one realizes something is awry. A striking example is the allegiance given to services and programs as if they were results. Services and programs are often treated as if they have value in themselves; however, these are only packages of prescribed activities. Under a results orientation, services and programs are seen only as means to some end. It is that end that should be judged. Otherwise righteous busyness becomes not just as meaningful as results, but *more so.*

The *threat of good activity* is so great that it can hardly be overstated. Without constant vigilance and systems to support it, said Odiorne (1974, pp. 1–7), "People tend to become so engrossed in activity that they lose sight of its purpose. . . . They become so enmeshed in activity they lose sight of why they are doing it, and the activity becomes a false goal, an end in itself. . . . Falling into the activity trap is not the result of stupidity. In fact, the most intelligent, highly educated people tend to be those most likely to become entrapped in interesting and complex activities."

It is not that good intentions or sensible actions by staff are unimportant. It is that they in no way constitute the reason for an organization's existence. Commendable activities are only a means to an end.

Commendable Conditions

Similarly, commendable conditions can also masquerade as results. Staff credentials may be the foremost of these conditions. Credentials and training can easily inspire admiration. It surely seems reasonable to think that a person with impressive training will do a better job than one without such training. Such reasoning has been called "paying persons for where they've been, not for what they are contributing." On this basis, for example, a professor with an impressive publications list is assumed to be a better teacher than a professor without such credentials.

High staff morale is another commendable condition. Some boards show more interest in staff morale than in results. They think, if morale is high, then we must be okay; if turnover is high, something is wrong. One does not have to favor low morale or high turnover to see that although these indexes may be symptoms, the organization exists neither for high morale nor for low turnover. The point here is not to ignore the signs of possible problems, only to put them in perspective. Boards that monitor morale but not results have an inverted ends-means perspective.

Conditions within an organization are important, but they are not the reason the organization exists. Commendable conditions are only a means to an end.

Commendable Structure

The arrangement of jobs, reporting lines, and distribution of decision centers through an organization constitute the structure of an organization. A shorthand representation is the table of organization. Structural factors have great influence on how an organization functions.

To illustrate, narrow spans of control may reflect undeveloped management potential and extra hierarchical levels. The existence of a majority of staff officers (as opposed to line officers) in close proximity to the CEO suggests fragmented delegation and underutilized, underdeveloped line managers. A very wide span of CEO control may demonstrate unusually precise delegation, but could also mean that the CEO is too busy and not sufficiently reflective. A deputy CEO to whom everyone else reports when the CEO is unavailable is almost sure to represent wasted managerial power. More than two executives vertically configured, each with supervision over only one person, almost certainly means someone has a position but no job. Structure does make a difference.

Streamlined, efficient structure is to be admired and much sought after. But an organization neither deserves points for it, nor loses points for lack of it. Whether an organization is good or bad is revealed in its results and in its prudence and ethics. If performance is measured against the criteria set forth in board policies and shows no problems, then the concern was misplaced anyway.

Organizational structure is important. Yet even the best structure is not the reason an organization exists. Structure is only a means to an end.

Commendable Technology

High-technology electronics has become increasingly important in nonprofit and public organizations, but the technology of operations has long been an issue for managers. Examples range from the hardware technologies of typewriters, filing systems, and telephones to the conceptual technologies of queue theory, operations research, and decision-making techniques. Management has graduated to word processing, extensive data banks, and the Internet. But techniques and technologies can be undeservedly promoted from supporting to leading actors.

In the late 1970s, the Environmental Protection Agency was set to require use of a certain type of scrubber to rid smokestack discharge of particulates. The EPA intended that particulate emission be no greater than some critical level. Yet its criterion was that certain technology be used to reach the result. By diverting attention from the desired result, the EPA would have sabotaged its own long-term effectiveness. Government bureaucracies often operate in this manner. Although they sacrifice long-term effectiveness, in the short run they maximize control (even over the wrong things). In a supervisory situation, this might be viewed as the difference between managing and bossing. Technology-driven operation, very much like commendable activity–driven operation, is susceptible to what has been called the "tool illusion." To a child with a hammer, objects to be pounded become the most important things in the world. An object's "poundability" becomes its most salient characteristic.

Technology within an organization is important, but even the best technology is not the reason an organization exists. Technology is only a means to an end.

Ends Mistaken for Means

In failing to focus on the ends-means distinction, we can also confuse ends for means. In some instances, there is such a single-minded focus on means that results are not recognized when they come along. I observed a public school board spend its usual long, cluttered meeting moving from one executive means issue to another. Most of the means issues were not very large. In the midst of this unnecessary flurry was an agenda item concerning the outcome of extensive tests of reading ability throughout the system. The busy board spent only enough time to notice the item, say something nice, and move quickly back to the flurry of trivia!

The confusion that surfaces most often is between "sub-Ends" and means. Parts of the overall result can accurately be viewed as means to the final end. The concept of means in such a case differs materially from the concept of means used here. In everyday language we use the word *means* for both.

Assume that the board's overall result (mission) is "normal community living for the developmentally disabled." The board, in dealing with the next lower level of abstraction, determines which "products" make up the mixture that most closely corresponds to its vision of the broad result. Perhaps the board will decide that the desired mixture comprises independent living skills, occupational skills, and receptive employers. The megaresult (the mission) will comprise several subresults, which in turn will comprise subsubresults, regardless of where the board chooses to stop and allow executives to take over. This procession of ever smaller subresults continues to the most specific short-term result concerning an individual consumer. One *could* look at any subresult as a means to the next higher result.

Returning to the example, occupational skills can be viewed as a means to "normal community living." There is nothing wrong with this construction, but it is not the kind of construction that yields a managerially useful differentiation between ends and means. The hybrid *subresult as means* represented by "occupational skills" is quite different from the *pure means* represented by, say, "skills training." Skills training, an activity, is a means now and forever; it cannot be an outcome. On the other hand, it is easy to conceive of occupational skills as an outcome—a reasonable organizational result in itself. Occupational skills can even be pictured as the single product of a smaller or less ambitious agency, that is, the mission itself. Occupational skills can be mistaken for a means *only* if there exist broader results of which it is a part.

In the ends-means differentiation discussed in this book, the sense in which a subresult like occupational skills can be considered a means will never be used. The powerful utility of the ends-means differentiation in enabling better governance rests on using one definition rather than the other. *Activities are always means, no matter how complex or important. External outcomes, results, and impacts are ends, whether or not they are parts of a broader end.*

Mission as Mega-Ends Policy

A written mission can be conceived in different ways. One popular and creditable manner is to summarize in a short statement all the major values to which an organization aspires. For example: "We will be the most respected regional provider of widgets by our customers, our employees, and our suppliers." This type of mission can be extremely useful, even inspiring. I make no case against such a formulation when I call upon boards to produce another kind of statement—one that focuses on the *difference* the organization is to make in consumers' lives. The two (this type and the one I propose) could, in fact, coexist. Because the mission described in this book is a different sort, there is a danger in using so familiar and widely defined a label as a mission. It is very important that nonprofit and public boards develop the type of mission I describe. It is very unimportant that they call it a mission.

Although Ends can be considered at various levels, it is only the broadest expression that should initially concern a board. Mission, defined as the briefest, broadest Ends statement, does not determine everything about an organization's intended results, but it tells us the range within which all further results will occur. A mission defines the arena and answers these simple questions: "What is this organization for? How will the world be different as a result of our being in business?"

Stating a mission can be the most powerful single action a board takes, or it can be a waste of time. Not infrequently, boards engage in meticulous mission-writing sessions. This intense exercise takes much more time than most boards intend, particularly in the light of the physical product. More times than not, the completed work finds a quiet resting place in a grant application, annual report, or brochure. It bothers no one until it is time to find it, dust it off, and go through the grueling project once again. Often, the board is driven by one member who is sold on the importance of writing mission statements.

A powerful mission is a broad Ends statement with six critical characteristics:

1. *Results terminology:* The mission should not be couched in terms of the activities necessary to achieve some change. *The change itself* is the mission.
2. *Succinctness:* A long statement usually means that a board has not come to terms with its mission. Long statements clutter and smother the actual mission with explanation, intended methods, and excess verbiage. The real mission is often buried in the paragraphs, but boards are hard pressed to identify it and CEOs are not able to organize around it. Ideally, the mission should be stated in a few words, no more than a sentence.
3. *Authoritative generation:* The mission is too close to the heart of governance for the board to act passively and simply approve someone else's statement. If the board is not actively involved in determining the mission, why should it be involved in anything else?
4. *Horizontal integration:* The mission is developed from the extraorganizational context by a board accountable to an "ownership." That same ownership may have other boards doing its business. There is disjointedness in public service and weakening of the public fabric when boards do not speak with other boards. There is no more meaningful subject about which community boards can converse than mission.
5. *Ubiquity:* Unless a mission is pervasive, it will lose its compelling power in organizational affairs. It simply cannot be repeated too much (which is another reason for succinctness). The mission should appear on all documents, on the phones, and in the conference rooms. *Live* with the mission.
6. *Vertical integration:* The mission must be the theme and the backbone of the organization. An elegant mission does little good if it is not connected to the goings-on of the organization. The mission connects the board's job with the CEO's job and thence to all others. Every department, every program, every job, and every objective must be tied to the mission. Placing the mission on this pedestal is comparable in a summative sense to a "bottom-line" mentality. Because of their peculiar market status, nonprofit and public organizations have been able to develop disjointed, internal islands of excellence that are not forced to sum to a bottom line.

Examples of statements that fulfill the first two requirements are "a community free from poverty" (a community action agency) and "every child a wanted child" (American Birth Control League, then its successor, the Planned Parenthood Federation of America— though this was never either organization's formal mission). To cover the "swap" aspect of Ends accurately, the actual policy document might add "at state-of-the-art efficiency" or some other expectation pertinent to the acceptable cost of producing the desired effect. This part could be omitted when the mission is used for slogan purposes.

Expanding on the Mission

The first "vertical integration" takes place in the mission's clear connection to further policies that the board creates. The board, not the CEO, is therefore likely to be the first to expand upon mission, and it does this by creating a second level of Ends policies, just one order of abstraction below the mission itself.

I have argued for phrasing mission in a few carefully chosen words, then adding more detailed policy statements that further determine the organization's results. It is common for boards to write paragraph- or page-long missions. Aside from obscuring the focal mission statement, this *conglomerate form* is far harder to debate and to amend. In contrast, mission-related expressions espoused here are in an *articulated form,* that is, characterized by a progression of cautiously segmented parts beginning with the broadest and moving toward the more discrete. The process of deciding on "headings" before "subheadings" (as in an outline) yields greater integrity in establishing intended results than lumping results into an undifferentiated mass. In effect, the articulation of results into separable, descending parts yields a "value map" that both boards and staffs find instructive, with respect not only to what has already been resolved, but also what is to be addressed next.

The brief mission statement at the very highest, broadest layer encompasses all further value choices about results. It might be more instructive to call this the "mega-Ends" statement. Though unlikely, the board may choose to address no further results after it has adopted a mission. If the board were to agree that any reasonable interpretation of the mission language by the CEO would be acceptable, then it need say no more. That is, if all the possible priorities, choices, and costs are acceptable, there is no reason for the board to narrow the expected results by passing more policies. The board would simply refrain from further pronouncements and allow the CEO to resolve all submission choices among Ends. Most boards are understandably reluctant to leave such broad issues to the CEO, so they do not stop at this point.

The Ohio State Board of Education policy (Exhibit 4.1) illustrates a slightly expanded mission statement. The board collected in this statement the megaproduct of the department and, if you will, the three "product lines" or major outputs. Note that the outputs are what the state agency contributes to the whole of education; there is no pretense that it is contributing what local school systems are producing.

Throughout the text, I will illustrate various aspects of policy development by reproducing policies actually drafted by real organizations. In each case, I will cite the organization by name. In Chapter Nine, I will depart from this practice to illustrate policy development through stages; in that process, I will use sample policies I have created myself. For the real policies, however, due to the possibility of amendments and other governance changes, I make no claim that the policies shown are currently in effect.

Exhibit 4.1. Ohio State Board of Education Policy: "Mission."

This mission of the State Board of Education and the Ohio Department of Education is *Literate Ohio Citizens.* Necessary to that mission, consistent with the State Board's unique representation of citizens with respect to education, and statutorily appropriate to the Ohio Department of Education, there are three distinct Department contributions to Ohio.

Statewide Vision: There will be, enriched by diverse viewpoints, a common public vision of what education is to be and to achieve in the future.

Quality Outcomes: There will be statewide definition of quality in education, and the actual achievement of that quality by Ohio school districts.

Informed Decision Makers: There will be ample information about realities and possibilities that enable the governor, general assembly, and individual citizens to make informed judgments about education.

Source: Ohio State Board of Education.

Consumers, Products, and Costs

The board's next step after stating the mission is to discuss which portions of the topic it wishes to define more narrowly, thereby reducing the submission latitude available to the CEO. The board may choose to create further policy about results, recipients, or cost of results.

Products

Mission statements are broad enough to encompass a wide range of potential products. Products are the benefits to be produced, such as cure, knowledge, broader employment base, housing, or job skills.

As a trade association, the Metropolitan Indianapolis Board of Realtors (MIBOR) exists, as is clear in their policy (Exhibit 4.2), so that members can thrive. Like the Ohio State Board of Education, MIBOR stated no priorities among the five outcomes. The executive director would, therefore, have the right to make that decision, as well as to decide, for example, just which skills will be emphasized in Area 2. The board can, of course, create another policy, expanding on any part or parts of this policy. It is

---

**Exhibit 4.2. Metropolitan Indianapolis
Board of Realtors Policy: "Purpose of MIBOR."**

The mission of the Metropolitan Indianapolis Board of Realtors is enhanced demand for Realtor services. In pursuit of this mission, MIBOR will bring about results in five areas:

1. A positive public image of Realtors.

2. A highly skilled Realtor membership.

3. A favorable environment for Realtors' commerce in real estate.

4. Accurate and timely information and business tools for the conduct of Realtors' business.

5. Free housing choice and equal professional services to all persons as prescribed by the Voluntary Affirmative Marketing Agreement and the Code of Ethics of the National Association of Realtors.

Source: Metropolitan Indianapolis Board of Realtors.

obvious how such expansion would reduce the executive director's latitude.

Beneficiaries

Mission statements are broad enough to encompass a wide range
of potential benefits and potential beneficiaries. Beneficiaries
might be differentially "targeted" by age, type of disorder or deficit,
severity of need, party membership, location, income, or other
consumer characteristics. Varieties of benefits, all fitting reasonably within the broadest statement of ends, can be given differing
priorities as well. In fact, they *will* be given varying priorities just in
the nature of operation. The issue for the board members is
whether they themselves will decide these relative worths.

The mission statement of the Algonquin Students' Association
(Exhibit 4.3) apportions results between the subtly different benefits (for example, awareness and comfort) and beneficiaries (college
community and students). This policy is one of several that this
board uses to describe further its more global ends policy (referred

---

Exhibit 4.3. Algonquin Students' Association Policy: "Culture Conducive to the Needs of the College Community."

As a portion of its overall mission, the Algonquin Students' Association shall
bring about a culture conducive to the needs of the college community:

A harmonious and comfortable environment benefiting students.

An informed college community.

Students are fully aware of entitlements, services, policies and activities
established within the college community.

A college community that is fully aware of all Students' Association policies, services, entitlements and activities.

An official and formal system of student representation that reaches into
the classroom.

High quality gathering environment.

A place to gather which promotes unity, friendship and networking.

A presentable environment which is clean, uncluttered, aesthetically
pleasing, well maintained and accessible.

Source: Algonquin Students' Association.

to in their document as the mission) in which the broader focus was on an enhanced quality of student life during college.

Cost

Although putting a dollar value on changes in the human condition is not an easy task, we do so implicitly all the time. The board may decide how much any given benefit is worth or, at least, the cost not to be exceeded in providing units of that benefit. The apportionment of cost also might be addressed, for example, the subsidy of certain consumers by other consumers, by donors, or by the public.

There is interaction among these three areas. Consider, for example, a dental health project in a ghetto. For a given level of expenditures, we can fill the cavities of 500 children *or* we can fill the cavities and straighten the teeth of 150 children. Which is the best choice? We must juggle product and worth to resolve the issue. In a public school system, students with behavior problems cost more to educate. The extra costs mean that other children do not get as much as they otherwise would. To what extent should the benefits to some children be sacrificed so that troubled children can be more fully served? Public library products cost more per user in rural areas than in urban areas. What is the right balance between cost per rural user and cost per urban user?

The "Mission" policy of the Law Society of Manitoba (Exhibit 4.4) addresses the board's concern that various outputs or effects be included in the definition of the overall "public well-served by a competent, honourable and independent legal profession." In this case, the board chose to include the mega-Ends statement along with six further definitions in one document.

Obviously, these are but a few of literally thousands of value choices regularly facing organizations. Usually they are hidden from direct view, buried in the many pages of program descriptions, budgets, and other staff documents. Board leadership, newly aware of this hidden richness, will at first seem to have uncovered an unmanageable number of value dilemmas. These were always present but were previously settled by default; the board had decided about these massive value choices about organizational nature and destiny by not deciding.

These all-important variations on "What are we here for?" should be the board's consuming business. Reducing the clutter

Exhibit 4.4. Law Society of Manitoba Policy: "Mission."

The aim of the Law Society of Manitoba is a public well-served by a competent, honorable and independent legal profession.

1. Lawyers are qualified upon entry to the profession.
2. Lawyers are honorable and ethical in the practice of their profession.
3. The legal profession is independent of government.
4. Legal services are reasonably available to the public at a reasonable cost.
5. The public are protected from financial loss arising from dishonest or negligent lawyers.
6. There is an absence of systematic barriers to entry to and practice within the profession to persons who are members of groups against whom discrimination is prohibited by law.

Source: Law Society of Manitoba.

of conventional governance enables boards to approach these choices systematically. The first step is determining mission. The second step is establishing those aspects of products, consumers, and costs about which the board feels strongly enough to make further pronouncements. The third step is subjecting those issues to analysis, debate, and vote.

With these policies in place, the board has the opportunity to venture still further. The policymaking process is fluid. Policymaking stops at whatever point the majority of the board is willing to allow the CEO to make further decisions. The idea is not to extend policymaking to the smallest possible value choice. It is necessary for the board to go only as far as its values compel it to go.

Staffs sometimes worry that a board will address the lesser values so extensively that no latitude is left for staff decisions. Such overextension by the board is improbable. As a board addresses increasingly lower-level issues, relatedness among issues grows geometrically. It becomes exceedingly difficult to coordinate all the many value choices, much as traditional personnel and finance committees must take extra time to deal with the interface of their respective work on staff salary increments. The board finds that time requirements get out of hand. Coordination of these many interdependent variables is part of the reason a staff is needed. As long as the policymaking principles presented here (particularly, going one level at a time) are followed, a board's incursion into lower and lower levels of involvement will be self-limiting.

Policy Product

The concrete product of this series of value considerations by the board is a set of Ends policies. Most boards are able to govern well with only a handful of Ends policies, including the mission. Because the number of policy issues and the depth of value levels addressed vary from board to board, the exact number of such policies a board should have cannot be stated. The Ends policies illustrated here are targeted to a single level of achievement in the sense that organizational performance either reaches a reasonable interpretation of their provisions or it does not. It is certainly conceivable for a board to create Ends policies in terms of that which minimally passes and, say, that which meritoriously passes. Indeed, a carefully reasoned argument can be made for this two-or-more-tier approach (Argenti, 1993).

I have chosen not to present Ends policies in this manner for two reasons. First, the format is a more complicated one for illustration. Second, any board can convert to a two-tier method once its Ends policymaking is in good order. My experience is that the self-discipline required to craft a full set of the pass-fail Ends policies shown here is a momentous achievement in itself. In any event, under usual conditions, it would be surprising for an ordinary community social service agency board to have much more than a half-dozen Ends policies averaging a page in length. Reams of staff program descriptions, of course, will be developed on the basis of these brief board directives.

Long-Range Planning

It is important that the board prescribe results from an appropriately long-term perspective. *Creating Ends policies with a long-range perspective is the greatest board contribution to long-range planning.*

It is mandatory that boards be forward thinking. It is important that organizations have long-range plans. By extension of these two ideas, boards should be involved in long-range planning. Boards should, indeed, do their work with excellence and never be involved in actually constructing the myriad parts of a planning document.

Good governance calls for the board role in long-range planning to consist chiefly in establishing the *reason* for planning. Planning is done to increase the probability of getting somewhere from here. Enunciation of that "somewhere" is the board's highest contribution. In a manner of speaking, boards participate most effectively in the planning process by standing just outside it. Boards can make an invaluable contribution to planning; however, except for planning the improvement of governance itself, *boards should not do the actual long-range planning.*

By casting its Ends policies out toward the planning horizon, a board lays out those values on which the staff makes plans. Of course, planning can become mere "blue-skying" if the board has spoken to its Ends policies too cavalierly. To deliberate responsibly, a board must interact greatly with staff and outside parties. This interaction does not relate to the staff's present concerns and job undertakings. Staff-board interaction here is designed to ensure inclusion of staff insights, passions, and environmental scanning in board deliberation. It should not be, as is common in conventional board-staff communication, that the board moves to staff-level issues. To the contrary, this process richly stretches staff upward to the board's long-term, deeply value-laden world so that all participants grow a little.

The board's creation of Ends policies requires penetrating deliberation about big questions. There is simply no time to drift into current staff issues. Difficult as this challenge might be, it is easily the most exciting, creative, responsible task in which a board can engage. Board data, dialogue, and decisions include the probable environmental circumstances of the future, shifting public needs, big-picture strategic swaps, and the intentions of other boards working on their own visions—in other words, highly informed dreaming.

Planning is more effective when kept simple, yet the greatest resistance to board leadership as defined here is that, although it is not easy, it seems so simple. The principle is not "so complicated that it's hard to grasp," as R. James LeFevre of Planned Parenthood of Northern New England in Burlington, Vermont, puts it, "but rather, because it is so maddeningly simple it's easy to have it slip away" (personal communication). There is a fair amount of rigor involved in determining even at a broad level what an organization's contribution to the world should be. But when that has been done, the nuts and bolts of planning become merely the executive tool with which to bring it about. Waterman counsels to "think and rethink basic direction, but keep the statement of it simple and general [even though] you will frustrate the people who are looking for 'the strategy.' Our idealized image of strategy as a complete game plan is so strong that general statements . . . seem unsatisfying" (1988, p. 71).

In short, the board's job in long-range planning is not long-range *planning* itself, but exploration of vision. The board's job is to maintain and behaviorally demonstrate a long-range *mentality*. And they demonstrate that critical mentality by obsessively deciding what good is to be accomplished for which people at what cost. These value issues about ends lie at the core of organizational existence. They are reduced to a few, succinct Ends policies. So it is that with the same stroke, boards can do their part in long-range planning *and* govern organizational results.

Evaluating Ends

Evaluation of Ends is an integral part of the management process. And it must be integral to governance as well. Evaluation (as discussed in Chapter Six under the larger rubric of monitoring) should ideally be a precise, systematic, nonintrusive, criteria-focused method that constantly answers the question: "How are we doing?"

The word *evaluation* has come to be associated with service or program success more than with other areas of performance, such as financial status or compliance with purchasing guidelines. The model presented here does not differentiate, however, among these various instances of performance monitoring. The board is obligated to check performance against those matters that it found important enough either to prescribe (in the case of results) or to proscribe (in the case of staff means). As with other policy types, then, evaluation of Ends is important to leadership for three reasons: it discloses unacceptable deviation from the desired values; enables the board to relax about the present so it can keep its mind on the future; and keeps board policies constantly in the spotlight and, therefore, more likely to be amended as they grow out of date.

Well-Placed Concern for Evaluation

Nonprofit and public organizations—generally free of the harsh, inescapable Ends evaluation of the market—often find their results difficult to evaluate. If, through the mechanism of the market, consumers could tell nonprofit and public organizations what their products are worth, the topic of evaluation would never have attained its lofty status. Business organizations do market research and product research, but never have to do the type of program evaluation popular in nonprofit and public agencies, at least not for the same reasons.

Public and nonprofit organizations need to evaluate their services precisely because they have no natural, consumer-based, behavioral measure of whether a service is effective enough to be worth the cost of producing it. They claim that evaluation is difficult because they are producing services, not widgets. The argument is specious. Consumers are as able to evaluate services as they are concrete items. There is nothing inherently more difficult in evaluating a service *when consumers do the evaluating*.

Evaluation assesses not simply whether organizational activity is effective, but whether it is sufficiently effective to be worth the cost. If a board is to overcome the muted market voice (that is, if evaluation is even possible), the relative worth issue cannot be neglected. The separation of effectiveness from worth is a rampant disease among nonprofit and public organizations. It is a fundamental flaw of public administration. This is why the model presented here assiduously focuses on the simple idea of the organization's swap with the world: what is consumed compared with what is produced.

In the face of this difficulty, it is understandable that professional evaluators and laypeople alike bemoan our inadequacies in evaluating nonprofit and public services. The field of "process

evaluation" attempts to circumvent the problems by intentionally evaluating the means rather than the ends. Texts on the problems of measurement validity and reliability often suggest
well-considered strategies around the dilemmas. Evaluation of
effectiveness is primitive even without the conceptually burdensome question of whether what is achieved is worth the cost. We
truly are not very good at it.

This technical inadequacy in *how* to evaluate is not the largest
evaluation problem facing nonprofit and public boards. The
biggest problem, far and away, is that we do not know *what* to evaluate! Misplacing our concern for evaluation is part of the cause for
this dilemma.

Misplaced Concern for Evaluation

Ironically, premature concern about evaluation of Ends can be a
formidable deterrent to leadership. This problem exists in evaluation of the prudence and ethics of staff means and, particularly, in
the evaluation of results.

Driven by anxiety about evaluative shortcomings, board members often stop short their discussions of program outcomes, saying: "But we can't evaluate it." "But how would we evaluate that?"
People are loath to answer such an obvious stopper. An enthusiastic "Oh, yes we can!" surely brands the speaker as naive, which may
well be true. It seems that well-read people are armed with impressive proofs that evaluation schemes just do not work well
enough even to discuss. Given the obvious inadequacies, these people make a fine case.

Fearing they might decree something that cannot be evaluated
cleanly, boards retreat from decreeing at all. They let a reasonable
worry about evaluating prevent them from saying what the outcomes should be. This process can deteriorate into their deciding
where to go based on whether evaluators can determine when they
have arrived there. "What do you want to accomplish?" is met for
practical purposes with: "It depends. Tell us what you can measure."

Imagine that board members are in a taxi surrounded by fog.
Though their view of the surroundings, their progress, and even
their arrival might be clouded, they would not refrain from telling
the driver where they want to go. Yet that is exactly what many

boards do in the face of countless, admittedly tough questions about evaluating program results. The stage is set for them to slip into the trap of evaluating means, because they can see means better and count them more easily than results. Professional evaluators and boards miss the most relevant point: stating the desired results is too important for them to wait for defensible evaluation.

An authoritative, clear statement of what is to be accomplished has a powerful effect on organizational behavior, even if the results are never evaluated. This is not an excuse for omitting evaluation. But there is merit in letting people know what you want, even if you cannot be certain that you got it. The single most intimidating aspect of program evaluation is not the technical difficulty but the blockage resulting from premature consideration. We simply place the concern for evaluation too early in the process.

Where to Place the Concern for Evaluation

No place. One option is not to be concerned about evaluation at all. Start at the beginning by stating what the organization is to contribute to the world, what condition is worth achieving, and what you would evaluate if you could. That process is best done in the ends-oriented, stepwise fashion I have described, and must be done without regard for evaluative difficulties.

Wrong place. Another strategy is to avoid evaluating the wrong things. Measuring the wrong things is damaging in two ways: (1) "You get what you inspect, not what you expect" is a valid principle of behavior. Measuring the wrong things sends a strong message through the organization about what matters. If, in understandable frustration, you throw up your hands and yield to measuring busyness, you are sure to get more busyness. (2) The pressure, even the embarrassment, of having no stated outcomes to evaluate is a powerful motivator toward developing at least a first, faltering approximation of the results to be achieved. Evaluating the wrong things removes much of the healthy pressure, even more so if you do it well. When we are able to take pride in how well we do the wrong things, there is little incentive to begin a wobbly start toward the right things.

Right place. Only when the board has created Ends policies should it stop to consider evaluation, because only when the board knows what it wants the organization to accomplish can it intelligently discuss evaluation. Evaluation without these targets is ludicrous; fretting over evaluation prior to these targets is dysfunctional. The issue of evaluation is merely this: What is the most convincing evidence board members can find (and choose to afford) that will show them they are getting what they sought? Evaluative purity is wonderful, but purity is not mandatory. What is called for in evaluation is *reasonable assurance for the cost,* not academic accuracy.

We forget that evaluation in the form of performance monitoring is an issue not of research but of management. The topic of evaluation is dominated, one might say handicapped, by the academic mentality. We unwittingly apply standards of pristine, laboratorylike evaluation to the real-world necessity to determine whether what we do is worthwhile. Managerial mentality, unlike academic mentality, would counsel us thus: with respect to influencing organizational behavior, *a crude measure of the right thing beats a precise measure of the wrong thing.*

The best approach a board can take in program evaluation, then, is to stick rigorously to the results, not to cop out by prescribing means. If the evaluation is crude, so be it. If it is worth doing, it is worth doing poorly if that is the best that can be done. But never, never forsake specifying the desired results in favor of a less crude evaluation.

The most important real-world evaluation in almost all nonprofit and public organizations is extremely crude. The public judges an organization's worth constantly. These evaluations may be too global to be managerially useful. They are usually too hard or too soft on management, because authoritatively pronounced criteria on which to base fair judgment are rarely available. In other words, implicit crude evaluation of results occurs anyway. The board's task is to make that judgment explicit, to direct it at preestablished criteria and away from capricious or confounding expectations, and only then to fret, deliberate, and attempt to make the evaluation less crude.

Board leadership in the matter of results evaluation lies not in being seduced by sophistication but in persevering in a compelling, disarmingly simple quest: "What did we want to accomplish? Are we achieving it?"

My contention, of course, is that what really matters in the long run is the effect an organization has on its world. Boards betray their trusteeship when the attractions of staff practices prevent boards from having an undeviating obsession with attaining desired ends. To return to the cab ride example, as long as board members know they are not being cheated, it is usually best to let the taxi driver choose the route and the lanes in which to drive.

Next Chapter

Strategic leadership lies in the board's Ends policies more than anywhere else. But the board is also accountable for how its staff members achieve these results. In Chapter Five, I invite you to consider how the board can safely keep out of staff business yet still be accountable for the conduct of business. We will see how a relatively few Executive Limitations policies can give both the board and its CEO the freedom to be innovative, bold, and attentive to their respective jobs.

Chapter Five

Setting Limits
Standards of Ethics and Prudence

The board must have *control over* the complexity and details of staff operations. It is also important for a board to be *free from* the complexity and details of staff operations. The board needs control because it is accountable for all organizational activity, however obscure or far removed. Yet the board needs to be free from operational matters because it is a part-time body with little time to get its own job done.

It is common to sacrifice one need for the other. Some boards relinquish control to be free from details or to grant the CEO freedom from board intrusion; such boards may be guilty of rubber-stamping. Others forgo freedom in order to control many details; such boards may be guilty of meddling.

The responsible board cannot escape its obligation to prescribe at least the broad sweep of Ends and perhaps a few levels below. In other words, with a broad brush the board determines where the organization is going. In this chapter, however, I am concerned not with where the organization is going, but with what staff members do to get it there. I deal with the myriad of "how to" questions facing the CEO and his or her staff. Or, more accurately, I deal with how the board might best relate to the staff's "how to" issues. The board's challenge is to be reasonably certain nothing goes awry and at the same time to grant as much unimpeded latitude as possible to those with the skill and talent to get the work done.

To make the case for freedom through limits, I start with the often dizzying array of organizational means, their seductive appeal, and the board's legitimate interest in them. I then look at how a board can maintain control of internal operations by setting limits instead of becoming directly involved. Next, I deal with developing the documents capable of exercising proactive control (Executive Limitations policies) and I follow this with a discussion of typical policy topics in this category.

The Enticing Complexity of Operations

For most boards, the greatest source of complexity is not the Ends but staff operations. Boards struggle with budgets, personnel procedures and issues, purchasing, staffing patterns, compensation, and staff plans. Self-perpetuating cycles are in effect wherein staff members bring their issues to the board because they think the board wants to hear them. Board members request information and attend to staff-level issues because they believe that the staff will feel abandoned if they do otherwise. Sometimes, staff members bring matters to the board to avoid making choices: "This item is a hot one; we'd better get the board to decide." Often, no prior board guidance has been given; consequently, there are no parameters within which the board protects the staff's right to make such choices.

On the other hand, boards delve into staff matters because a particular board member has either the relevant expertise or mere curiosity about some aspect of operations. It is not uncommon for an entire board to be drawn into an issue only because of the minority concern. The board's job is thus defined, not by a carefully constructed design of the task, but by the laundry list of individual interests.

Boards study, invest meeting and committee time in, and worry and argue about that complex, never-ending, intriguing body of staff activities. To the detriment both of carefully deliberated results and of effective board process, boards are entangled in and seduced by the means of their subordinates. The following staff issues draw in board members.

Personnel: Job design, hiring, firing, promotion, discipline, training, grievances up through the CEO, deployment, evaluation

Compensation (except that of the CEO): Salary ranges, grades, adjustments, incentives, benefits, pensions

Supply: Purchasing, bidding, authorization, storage, inventories, distribution, salvage

Accounting: Forecasting, budgeting, depositories, controls, investments, retrenchment, growth, cost center designation

Facilities: Space allocation and requirements, rentals, purchases, sales, upkeep, refurbishing

Risk management: Insurance, exposures, protective maintenance, disclaimers

Consumer record keeping: Forms, waivers, consents, service tracking, actions taken or services rendered

Reporting: Grant reports, tax reporting, law and regulation compliance

Communications: Memoranda, telephone systems, meetings, postings, mail distribution

Management methods: Objective setting, staffing patterns, team definitions, feedback loops, planning techniques, control methods, participation levels

The foregoing list is not exhaustive. Means issues with which staff members contend are endless. There are always far more issues than any board can keep up with, even if the board totally neglects its own job in order to do so. Keeping up with all these issues—much less providing leadership for them—is utterly impossible. The ideal of reviewing and approving everything is illusory. Yet the board must attend to its legitimate interest in these matters, an interest that can be overlooked only with severe damage to the organization's concept of board accountability.

The board's challenge is to exercise oversight with respect to staff operations without obscuring role differences and without taking the staff off the hook for making decisions. The appropriate expression of the board's legitimate interest is not to make a staff issue into a board issue, but to curtail or confine the available staff choices to an acceptable range.

The Board's Stake in Staff Practices

The preceding partial list of executive means includes important aspects of corporate life. Such material in board mailings and meetings may be so impressive that it seems to capture the essence of the enterprise. No matter how important, how technically sophisticated, how impressively carried out, or how great the professional training of experts in the various areas, these items are *means*, not ends. They are not what organization is all about; they *serve* what organization is all about. And, for the most part, the degree to which they serve Ends well is the source of their value.

For the most part, but not totally. Boards have more than one interest in staff practices.

Effectiveness

By far, executive means are of importance to a board because of their effectiveness. Do they work? That is the primary test and the only justification for having means. The major measure of means is to look not at the means but at what they were intended to produce. Means are assessed best by focusing on Ends. In fact, the greatest impediment to measuring the effectiveness of means is to look at the means themselves.

In this area, nonprofit and public administrative practice is prone to a monumental flaw. People inspect means through site visits, certifications, and agency evaluations, but there is very little inspection of results. Rewards are handed out on the basis of the means' purported excellence rather than attainment of results. Organizational means come to have a life and momentum of their own, driven by the overpowering tendency to assess them apart from their ability to produce results. Perhaps this source of managerial perversity should not surprise us. Individuals and particularly disciplines or professions are heavily invested in—and, in large part, formed around—distinctive methods or practices.

So if a board is willing to make judgments about means based primarily on attainment of ends ("effectiveness"), then this largest single concern about executive means can be laid aside. I dealt with it in Chapter Four, and the board deals with it by measuring how well the organization performs with respect to the board's Ends policies.

Approvability

Granting that the board discharges its central legitimate interest in executive means by assessing Ends, we must now deal with the fuzzy concept of approvability. Most boards would be unwilling to rest with mere effectiveness as the only test, but would require that, apart from effectiveness, executive means be carried out in an *approvable manner.*

What is meant by an approvable staff activity or plan? By observing boards proceeding through a traditional approval process, we note three phenomena. First, as a body the board is not quite sure what "approvability" means. Consequently, boards tend to go through the motions. Different board members question different items, usually against idiosyncratic criteria. Sometimes, they question effectiveness, but are likely to fall back into the trap of trying to judge effectiveness by closely inspecting the means. A telling test is for a board to ask itself what it would *disapprove.* If a board does not know what it would disapprove, its approval is a process without direction and, at worst, a sham.

Second, board members may equate "approvability" with the question "Would I do it this way?" When an approval is rendered from this point of view, the real chief executive finds that there are a number of would-be executives to contend with. Board members sometimes see it as their prerogative to play part-time CEO. This phenomenon leads a politically inclined CEO to manipulate documents so as to satisfy the various board member interests. Such maneuvering is not without cost. Ends suffer a loss of primacy, and the staff's selection of means is less true to its own best judgment.

Third, board members want to ensure that staff means—however effective in reaching prescribed ends—are prudent and ethical. And to the extent that inspection and approval of executive means fulfill this board interest, they are justifiable.

Legitimate Control of Means

To summarize the foregoing points: (1) effectiveness requires no inspection of means and, in fact, is best measured by intentionally not looking at means; (2) a simple preference that means be arranged or selected in a certain way is an indulgence the board may want to allow itself, but one that reduces the integrity of management; and (3) boards cannot ensure prudence and ethics by measuring the attainment of Ends—but unlike mere preference, the board has a moral obligation to ensure the prudence and ethics of operations.

Consequently, the only legitimate, direct interest a governing board need have in how the staff conducts its business is that all is prudent and ethical. Stated more pointedly, *apart from being prudent and ethical, the activities that go on at and below the level of chief executive are completely immaterial.* The board need only involve itself in executive means to determine that acceptable standards of prudence and ethics are being met. This can save much board time, as well as a great deal of executive frustration. And it becomes clear *what* the board, in its best moments, was approving or disapproving.

Control Through Proactive Constraint

Most means are justified by the ends because producing results is what justifies means. Some means, however, are not justifiable regardless of how effective they are. If this were not so, a board would not need to test anything about executive means except their effectiveness. Focusing on which means are *not* approvable, rather than on those that are, simplifies the task and makes it less onerous on management as well.

A board that wishes to ensure that the organization's actions are prudent and ethical must delineate *ahead of time* exactly what is imprudent and unethical. Any staff action that does not violate the board's standards, then, is automatically approvable. Note that the board's standards are negative or limiting rather than positive or prescriptive. The board has neither the time nor the expertise to state everything that should be done. It does have the sense of values necessary to recognize what should not be done. The principle is simple and, perhaps more than any other principle, enables excellence in governing.

Although the board speaks to Ends prescriptively, *with regard to executive means the board should remain silent except to state clearly what it will not put up with.*

A small number of policies can enunciate the board's values with respect to minimum levels of prudence and ethics. The board can govern the vast array of executive means through policy, not through direct involvement in staff activities. The category of policies that limits or constrains executive authority is called Executive Limitations.

The total message the board sends to staff, then, consists of what outputs are to be achieved (Ends) and what may not be done in the process of achievement (Executive Limitations). Board thought is proactive and general rather than reactive and specific. Such a policy saves the board from making countless separate decisions in the future.

Despite the breakthrough in board effectiveness that this approach makes possible, some board members find it difficult to place limits on staff means. As persons and as governors, they desire to be positive rather than negative. Such a motivation is commendable, but it overlooks an irony of downward communication in an organization.

The most positive approach a board can take toward its subordinates' means is verbally negative. Conversely, the most negative approach is prescriptive and positive. Telling a subordinate how to do a task automatically eliminates all other methods. Telling a subordinate how not to do it leaves open all other possible methods. Better supervision leaves as much freedom as possible.

No one can presume to know ahead of time all the innovative combinations of means. No one can divine all the possible ways to improve tasks, systems, structures, and relationships. Even people carrying out a task stumble across innovation as often as they bring innovative ideas to the task at the outset. Moreover, running an organization involves not only innovation within single tasks but also continual re-creation of interrelationships among tasks and persons. The ability to make and change decisions and to move quickly, particularly on the part of those closest to the action, is paramount. In the best of enterprises, leaders "define the boundaries, and their people figure out the best way to do the job within those boundaries" (Waterman, 1988, p. 7).

Board prescription of means is a stultifying and anti-innovative process of control. This would be true even if a board were available full-time and were fully versed in all organizational areas of expertise. But boards are available to render decisions only a few hours per year and do not have knowledge of every part of organizational life. The common, albeit incomplete, prescription of means not only produces an untenable amount of work for the board but unduly hampers staff effectiveness. Such board positiveness is a serious cause of lost staff potential. Given the availability of a more effective alternative, it is completely unnecessary as well. In Fram's fictional exploration of the "Corporate Model," a character boasts, "We have a REAL BOARD. . . . A real board tells its executive director exactly what to do." Fram's protagonist politely withholds his thought: "You don't have a real board. What you have is a parent-child relationship" (Fram, 1988, p. 74).

There is a subtler way in which a board does the same damage without directly prescribing executive means: it retains approval authority over staff plans. When staff must bring specific decisions to the board for approval (for example, of annual budgets and compensation changes), the board implies that only the staff actions it approves are legitimate. Although staff members generate the board-approved actions, the board empowers them. For staff, means that have board approval, regardless of their origin, are frozen in place until the board has time and sees fit to approve changes. The effect on management is only a little better than if the board had generated the means prescription itself. Consequently, board approvals, even of staff-submitted documents, constitute unnecessary interference with the CEO's staff delegation system and decision flow.

Consider the alternative of being minimal but "negative" in dealing with staff means. *Ignoring* staff means, except to prohibit them with explicit policies, frees both board and staff. The board is free of the endless details of staff work and can do its own job. The Rev. G. Taft Lyon, Jr., chairperson of Life Management Center, El Paso, Texas, was happy that he "didn't have to get involved in [the CEO's] business and tell him what he needed to do." Anne Saunier, chairperson of Planned Parenthood Federation of America, speaks of the ability to "safely withdraw, as a national board, from administrative details, with the emphasis on being 'safe.'" The staff is left free to choose, change, and create within clearly stated boundaries. Norman Barth, CEO of Lutheran World Relief, New York, is happy to be "freed . . . not that I can do anything I want to, but rather I know the bounds of my authority. . . . The board does not second-guess me." Without this explicitly bounded freedom, the CEO of a large zoo wrote that she "continues to feel as though I am walking through traps and land mines. Fortunately, I am guessing where most of them are; I am guessing a lot." J. Gregory Shea, CEO of Tri-County Mental Health Services of Lewiston, Maine, says his board "clearly feels . . . that it knows . . . how far the CEO can and will go . . . that both my day-to-day functioning and the board's policy setting and oversight are done with much greater freedom . . . and [with] flexibility . . . to sometimes very rapidly changing circumstances. Without those policies, there would be a lot of 'Monday-morning quarterbacking'" (all personal communications). As long as the board-stated Ends are accomplished and the board-stated Executive Limitations are not violated, staff action is by definition supported by the board.

Using this approach, the board is proactive. Approval of staff documents, discussed more fully in Chapter Three, is reactive. Further, approval is a practice in which the board is always "one down"; it can never know quite as much about the details of staff action and planning as the staff itself. Moreover, by being proactive, the board can be more confident that it has dealt with the issues of prudence and ethics. As painstaking as many approval processes might be, they ordinarily focus on the acceptability of *specific* actions or documents rather than on the underlying values that form the basis for board decisions on those actions and documents. Consequently, after the board approves specific actions or documents, its *policy* remains unstated. Another payoff, more important than it seems, is reducing the board's burden of paperwork. The board can then invest the bulk of its leadership in determining expected results rather than in helping staff be staff.

Policies to Limit Staff Action

The task, then, with respect to board oversight of staff means is to create a workable set of policies that constrain or limit executive latitude. In this section, I first review the necessity of saying what seems unnecessary to say, even at the broadest and most obvious level, in a negative or limiting fashion. Second, I argue that broad policies should grow out of the *board's,* not the staff's, values and perspectives. Last, I consider the board's worry areas as a natural origin of these Executive Limitations policies.

As with all policy control, proper governance lies an uncomfortable arm's length from the action for some board members. "Being relegated to a position of *simply* setting policies," comments the Rev. Lyon, "seems like a less important job to them." There may be discomfort, but not difficulty, because it is not hard to write policies that safely allow board withdrawal from the prescriptive details of staff means. Doing so does require close attention to the few simple rules proposed here for policy development. For example, as discussed in Chapter Three, we must start with the largest, most inclusive level before moving on to lesser levels.

Remember that the intent of the Executive Limitations category of policies is to prohibit staff practices that the board regards as imprudent or unethical. Though this will be further defined, note that preventing imprudent and unethical behavior is the board's *sole* aim in setting these policies. Note further that the wording here is negative. We could as easily say positively that the board is trying to ensure that behavior is prudent and ethical. The meaning is the same; however, because boards face the almost irresistible temptation to slip back into prescribing staff means, they are wise to maintain a proscriptive demeanor throughout, even when it seems pedantic to do so. Establishing the limiting approach at this basic level ensures a board's ability to maintain that discipline in more complex issues.

The board's first and broadest staff means policy position is a simple constraint on executive authority: "The chief executive may neither cause nor allow any organizational practice that is imprudent or unethical." This sentiment is so obvious. Why should the board have to dignify it as policy? There are two reasons for beginning at such a simple level. First, this position is the source from which all further constraints spring. It is the beginning. As further policies are built on this foundation, it becomes increasingly important to maintain simplicity or, at least, clear connections with simplicity. In addition, as we must learn again and again, organizations attain excellence by doing the simple things well.

Second, approaching constraints from the broadest perspective, regardless of how simplistic this appears, ensures that the board can never, through oversight, leave a policy vacuum. Although the "backup" policy may be broader than the board would like (allowing more room for interpretation), it is impossible for an issue not to be covered by board policy at some level. If the extent of reasonable latitude under a constraint of "imprudence" is greater than the board desires, then it needs to create further policy. But at no time will there be a lack of policy. In organizations where this principle of logical containment is not followed, executives or boards continually find issues not covered by board policy. Consequently, forceful staff action can be bottlenecked or staff members may take an unnecessary risk or miss an opportunity while the policy hole is being plugged.

Conventional, prescriptive policy development on staff means requires that the board foresee all possible actions and create policies targeted at these actions. Perfect foresight is, of course, impossible, and such an approach leads to patchwork policymaking. This approach also ensures that the board forever remains a step or two behind staff, as staff members are continually generating new specifics.

Optimal policymaking produces neither a long list of disjointed pieces nor a mere restatement of approved staff documents. It produces a *fabric of values* that, no matter how thin, effectively blankets all possibilities. Creating this fabric with respect to executive means must begin with the broadest proscription. Without this broad statement there is no all-inclusive point of departure for further, more detailed explicit board constraints.

All CEOs know better than to assume that there is no limit on staff behavior. But he or she would have to assume what that limit is . . . and might not come up with what the board would have stated. The CEO would have two choices: first, to ask whether the board is displeased (this takes us back to approvals) with each concrete plan or activity and all changes thereto; second, to be safe and assume more limitations than the board is likely to intend. Unnecessary constraint often reduces performance, a consequence the board may not have wanted. A constraint does so by raising cost or lowering product quantity; nothing is free, including constraints.

The most effective move a CEO can make is to inform the board of the unspoken constraint he or she is assuming and to ask for confirmation. If the CEO asks about the broadest level instead of a specific application, the board creates policy by answering the question. It is simpler to begin from that point, rather than to have the process depend on the CEO's motivation and integrity, not to mention luck.

Making Board Policies the *Board's* Policies

For integrity of governance, the board must generate policies from board values, not parrot them from staff wishes. A side effect of traditional patchwork policymaking is that the staff members repeatedly ask the board for approvals. As the staff members obviously know what they need, boards ordinarily issue approvals after a cursory review. Even a detailed review would not change the fact that the board is passing policy without *the board's* needing it. In the governance design presented here, the board adopts only policies for which its values dictate a need. Board policies are not passed to please staff, even the CEO. The CEO is already empowered to adopt policies, as long as they are consistent with the board's policies. The CEO is unlikely to request that the board restrict executive latitude further. As he or she is already empowered to make such choices, it would be clear that the CEO is merely using the board to avoid making a decision.

Despite the churning commotion of implementation, a board's ethics and prudence standards remain constant. The board's standards written into policy serve as an anchor for all staff action. There is room for staff to move around when tossed about in stormy weather, but there is not so much room that staff loses its bearings or strays from what the organization holds itself to be. Like an anchor, good policymaking is not complicated; its simplicity is why it works. Staff must be given a free hand to do what they know how to do, but should not be stranded by the board's failure to define boundaries.

Boards can provide this leadership only if they are not subjected to the same short-term pressures. If the board is tossed in the same stormy seas as the staff, it will have difficulty seeing past the next wave, much less to the horizon. The stability of a relaxed governance arena allows the board to ride above the fray fairly unperturbed. The board saves its energy for the more contemplative struggle about underlying values. A board that is more hurried than contemplative has probably fallen into staff-level issues and ceased to govern.

Having prohibited only "unethical and imprudent" behavior, the board may worry that its brush has been a little too broad. Any staff practice that fits within a reasonable interpretation of this range must be considered acceptable. A "reasonable" range is that determined by the board to be a prudent person's reading of the policy. If the majority of board members feel that practices that pass the "reasonable person" test are not acceptable, then the constraint on staff activity must be further defined and narrowed. As might be surmised, I have never found a board that did not wish to constrict the acceptable latitude further.

Transforming Worries into Policies

The broadest constraint (no imprudent and unethical behavior) applies without differentiation to all areas of organizational activity. When building policy beyond this general proscription, the board will doubtless apply its caution more to some subjects than to others. That is why moving to the next lower level takes the form of addressing specific aspects of the organization. Thus, policy not only drops to a lower level, but begins to differentiate among organizational topics.

Subjects differentiated for further constraint could be seen as specific "worry areas." The most common worry areas in which policy is then written, to define unethical and imprudent behavior further, involve financial condition, personnel, compensation, asset protection, and budgeting. Addressing each of these subjects (1) affords board members the opportunity to agree on what is unacceptable; (2) sends the executive a clear message about what must be avoided, an explicitness that most executives find refreshing albeit less manipulable; (3) enables the board to streamline future monitoring because it has established criteria against which to measure performance; and (4) enables the board to codify its anxieties and, consequently, to relax.

In conceiving these policies, the board should not constrain its thinking with *current* worries. A board should create Executive Limitations policies that cover the entire range of unpalatable circumstances. What a board would find unpalatable is not a function of recent agency problems, even though heightened sensitivity to one or another condition might be. Reactive policymaking will seem to be the responsive action at the time, but this would mean the board's leadership is driven by circumstances rather than by ideals. When it is free from immediate concerns, the board uncovers values that have not theretofore surfaced, values that will be relevant to events as yet unforeseen. Still, the safety net effect of the logical containment principle saves the board from having to be perfect in its comprehensiveness.

Listening to worries voiced by board members helps the board establish Executive Limitations policies specific to the organization. One member of an Arizona board wondered aloud how disruptive it would be if the CEO were to be unexpectedly lost. The others were persuaded that this was a legitimate board worry. Converting that worry into an Executive Limitations policy resulted in immediate relaxation about the problem. The board adopted a policy requiring that the CEO never have fewer than two senior staff substantially familiar with board and executive officer activities. The majority of the board members felt that this policy provided all the emergency preparedness needed. The policy fit their values, precluded further worry, and was stated in two sentences.

It is important that policies represent the values of the board that establishes them. Policies are not chosen from a catalogue, issued by an agency of government, enunciated by staff, derived by consultants, or taken from books. Policies are personal for the board.

Typical Executive Limitations Topics

Because Executive Limitations policies spring from a board's sense of prudence and ethics, they are more likely than other categories of policy to resemble the policies of other boards using this model. Prudence and ethics are relatively common across boards, more so than Ends. Note these few, common Executive Limitations policy titles.

Vendor relations	A "floor" for their fair treatment
Treatment of parents	Minimum standards for interactions with parents of students
Asset protection	Unacceptable risk and treatment of fixed and liquid assets
Indebtedness	Limits on circumstances in which the executive could allow the organization to incur debt
Financial condition	Conditions of fiscal jeopardy to be avoided
Budgeting	Characteristics unacceptable in any budget
Funded depreciation	Limits on amounts and conditions under which the executive can spend money from the funded depreciation reserve

| Growth | Limit on the amount of growth that can occur from one fiscal year to the next, regardless of the availability of funds |
| Compensation and benefits | Characteristics not tolerated in any wage and salary plan |

All Executive Limitations policies are messages from the board to its CEO. They are *not* messages from the board to staff, for the CEO is the only staff member to whom the board gives directions. Further, the policies do not give the CEO power to do this or that. They take power or latitude away ("You may not . . ."). The CEO has whatever power the board does not withhold: "Go till we say stop" rather than "Stop till we say go."

To illustrate three Executive Limitations areas, let us look at board concerns with respect to financial management and personnel administration. The financial concern is traditionally expressed in two ways: monthly reports on the actual financial condition and annual inspection of budget. The personnel concern traditionally manifests as approval of personnel "policies."

Financial Condition Policy

Boards put great stock in monthly or quarterly financial reports. Yet a substantial number of board members do not understand these reports. Even in boards comprising persons competent at analyzing financial statements, it is uncommon for the board to know *as a body* what it finds unacceptable (Carver, 1991c, 1993b, 1996i). This gives the approval process questionable importance and repeatedly invites discussion about financial details. Actually, even if the standards were clear to everyone, "approval" of a financial report is simply an acknowledgment that the data exist, that the preceding month or quarter actually took place.

In converting to control by Executive Limitations policies, boards are usually unwilling to let the standard rest simply on avoiding imprudence. Some practices or conditions might not be imprudent in the general sense, but are outside what a given board is willing to countenance. To adopt a policy that further defines the acceptable boundaries of ongoing financial conditions, the board must discuss and debate those circumstances it finds unacceptable. Financial condition is a wavering phenomenon; most of its squiggles are of no consequence. Some aspects, however, are worrisome or even frightening.

Ordinarily, the top level within this policy is that the financial condition never result in fiscal jeopardy or disruption of programmatic integrity. Beneath this broad proscription, foremost among the several considerations is usually that spending never exceed revenues. If the agency has the ability to borrow funds or has reserves, the prohibition might be to limit the amount of indebtedness or withdrawals from reserves. Or it might be to prohibit indebtedness or withdrawal except under specified conditions. Moreover, that an executive has not yet spent more than has been received might be a rather hollow datum if expenses have been put off and revenues rushed into the reporting period. Further, shifts of wealth hidden within the overall numbers may obscure important fiscal jeopardies such as a decreasing ratio of current assets to current liabilities. Fine-tuning the policy language can address these points and, at the same time, enhance the board's appreciation of the issues of fiscal jeopardy.

The board must discuss and understand these and related issues to create a financial condition policy. In the short run, as much value is derived from the new level of understanding as from the policy itself. A board can use expert counsel in producing such a policy, as long as the expert does not create the policy. The expert should help board members attain a more complete understanding. The understanding supplies data on which board members' values about risk, safety, conservatism, brinkmanship, and so forth can operate. The aggregated and debated board values create the policy. For most boards, the list of unacceptable conditions thus derived is more complete and more systematic than the items it would have routinely inspected using the standard approval method. Though more complete, the subsequent monitoring of financial statements (Carver, 1994b) requires far less time than many boards and finance committees traditionally spend.

Voyageur Outward Bound's policy limited its executive director (Exhibit 5.1) on criteria that the board felt to be conditions of jeopardy. The board felt it could accept any reasonable definition of "timely manner" in Criterion 7, though another board might

Exhibit 5.1. Voyageur Outward Bound School Policy: "Financial Condition."

With respect to operating the School in a sound and prudent fiscal manner, the Executive Director may not jeopardize the long-term financial strength of the School. Accordingly, he or she may not:

1. Cause the School to incur indebtedness other than trade payables incurred in the ordinary course of doing business.
2. Use advances from the Cash Reserve Fund or the Building Fund other than for ordinary operating expenses.
3. Allow advances from the Building Fund to remain outstanding for more than 90 days.
4. Allow advances from the Cash Reserve Fund or the Building Fund to remain outstanding on the August 1 next following the advance.
5. Use earnings on the Scholarship Endowment Fund for any purpose other than scholarships.
6. Use restricted contributions for any purpose other than that required by the contribution.
7. Settle payroll and debts in other than a timely manner.
8. Allow expenditures to deviate materially from Board-stated priorities.
9. Allow the Cash Reserve Fund to fall below $90,000 in 1988, 6 percent of operating expenses in 1989, 7 percent in 1990, 8 percent in 1991, and 10 percent in 1992 and beyond.

Source: Voyageur Outward Bound School.

need to restrict the range by using words such as "within the discount period or thirty days, whichever is earliest." Figures in Criterion 9 would be periodically amended.

Of course, an additional Executive Limitations policy specifically focused on investments per se would be needed by organizations dealing with a sizable endowment. A simple form useful even for boards with more modest reserves might merely instruct that the CEO shall not "invest or hold operating capital in insecure investments, including uninsured checking accounts and bonds of less than AA rating, or in non-interest-bearing accounts except where necessary to facilitate ease in operational transactions." Having policy control over investments is normally better than having board members on an investment committee make investment decisions (Guy, 1992, 1995).

Budget Policy

A financial condition policy establishes the boundaries of an acceptable monthly or quarterly financial status. Boards can go further and establish those characteristics of financial *intentions* that would not be acceptable. Financial intentions or financial planning takes the form of a budget and often numerous budget adjustments during a year.

Most nonprofit and public boards consider the budget approval process sacrosanct. To suggest that board budget approval might not be a necessary element of fiscal stewardship runs against a firmly held belief, one so firm that some board members contend that no regularly occurring board activity is as important as budget approval. The reason given is that the board must have control over the budget because of the board's fiduciary responsibility. In addition, some say that the budget is the most important "policy document" the board passes.

Both contentions are correct. The board must have control over that for which it is accountable. And the budget does, usually implicitly, represent much of what is important to an organization—its aims, its risks, its conservatism. Neither argument, however, dictates *how* a board should control a budget and the budget's policy implications. The starting questions for any board are: "What is it about the budget that we wish to control?" and "If we were never to see a budget, what specific conditions would we worry about?"

A budget concerns events that have not yet occurred. It is a plan. Like all plans, it makes suppositions, conveys intentions, and designs process or flow. It is a rather special plan inasmuch as it is denominated in money. Most budgets, moreover, are line-item budgets rather than program budgets or result-package budgets, so they illustrate some of the less salient aspects of creating the future. For example, the expected cost for a certain outcome is of central interest when a board debates its Ends policies. How much the group insurance component of support staff compensation is expected to be has less intrinsic value. What is it that the board wishes to control?

If the board had to list every possible dollar figure and ratio in the budget, it would give up and go home! Only the most compulsive board members want to know the budget for stationery, much less to control it. In fact, there are very few aspects of a budget that even very responsible boards need to control. Boards want and need control over *certain* budgetary characteristics to fulfill their legal and ownership responsibilities. Few boards have any idea what characteristics these are.

To fine-tune its fiduciary responsibility, a board must decide which aspects of the budget to control. If the board has been checking these budgetary characteristics all along, jotting them down will take but a few moments. If the board finds it cannot do this readily, there is reason to question what the detailed budget approvals have been seeking. What, in fact, was approved? Is it possible that the admittedly high principle of fiduciary responsibility has been used to justify a process less effective than board members thought? In my years of watching budget approvals, I have concluded that this is exactly what goes on.

Enlightenment is nearly inescapable when a board sets out to codify its worries about financial planning. What would worry board members about a budget? What would cause them not to approve a budget? The important features begin to stand out and the less important ones recede. The vast array of figures becomes less intimidating for nonfinancial people. Financial people are afforded the opportunity to connect their technical expertise with their wisdom. It is on the wisdom level that they meet the other board members; they are no longer strangers divided by a language barrier.

On this journey, the board gets serious about the meaning of fiduciary responsibility. This responsibility does not mean controlling the number of phone lines, but it does mean controlling the ability to pay the bills. It does not mean controlling out-of-state travel, but it does mean controlling the conservatism with which revenues are projected. Or are those issues the wrong ones? Debate ensues. Values about risk, brinkmanship, judiciousness, proportions of effort, and so forth begin to receive more attention than the mundane factors. And throughout, the process is disciplined by a progression from big questions to small ones, as it should be in all policy creation.

As in all other Executive Limitations policies, the message is directed to the CEO and is one of limitation, not empowerment. The CEO is already empowered by the "Go till we say stop" system of delegation. What he or she needs to know are the limits to power, the acceptable latitude in exercising it. The CEO must ponder these questions: "How liberal may I be in counting chickens prior to their hatching (projecting revenues)? How low may I let the current ratio slip to save programs? How much may I dip into reserves when pinched for cash? To what extent may I meet cash flow necessities by shifting money temporarily among special-purpose funds?" These and other value questions arise during financial planning, whether for next month or next year. Agile, empowered management can address these choices within board values far more effectively than a board can.

An additional bonus to the Executive Limitations approach is the policy's applicability to *all* financial planning, that is, the plans for next month and next year and all the replanning that occurs in the real world of constant change. An organization rarely has one budget for a year. As conditions shift and assumptions fail to pan out, it may have many. Every budget alteration made by the CEO, no matter how many, must meet the test of the board's budget policy. CEOs can respect the stability of this type of board leadership. The only fixed aspects of budgets, then, are the policies on which they are based and the certainty that specifics will be endlessly amended.

Most boards that I have helped through this process have had a hard time coming up with more than half a page of budgeting constraints. What message does this send? All those years of painstaking board budget approvals, not to mention finance committee time, resulted in half a page of unacceptable conditions. The approval process had always gone far beyond checking for unacceptable conditions. Having no policy that delineated the unacceptable conditions, the board foraged about wherever individual interests and fears directed them. Moreover, this painstaking scrutiny seldom resulted in material change to the submitted budgets and not infrequently overlooked dangerous conditions until it was almost too late.

Boards are accountable for budgets, but not more accountable than they are for what the organization accomplishes in actual results for people per dollar. Budgets are simply *not* the board's most important job. Determining what good is done for which people and at what cost is its most important job. Missing the mark with respect to Ends even by a small percentage costs the world far more than most budgetary errors. Gwendolyn Calvert Baker, executive director for the National Board of the YWCA, found that when you deal with financial planning this way, "The program drives your budget, your budget doesn't drive your program" (personal communication).

In Bryan, Texas, the city council created a policy (Exhibit 5.2) to control the budgeting that its city manager does. As complicated as budgeting is for a complex organization, the *governance* of budgeting need not be.

Exhibit 5.2. City Council of Bryan, Texas, Policy: "Financial Planning."

Budgeting any fiscal period or the remaining part of any fiscal period shall not deviate materially from Council Ends priorities, risk fiscal jeopardy nor fail to show a generally acceptable level of foresight. Accordingly, the City Manager may not cause or allow budgeting that:

Contains too little information to enable accurate projection of revenues and expenses, separation of capital and operational items, cash flow and subsequent audit trails, and disclosure of planning assumptions.

Plans the expenditure in any fiscal year of more funds than are conservatively projected to be received in that period or which are otherwise available.

Allows the reserves in the general fund to fall below two months of operating expense requirements.

Allows the reserves of the utility fund to fall below forty-five days of operating expense requirements.

Provides less than $100,000 for council prerogatives during the year.

Fails to provide for an audit or council development.

Is not derived from the multiyear financial forecast.

Source: City Council of Bryan, Texas.

Personnel Policy

When boards are asked to show their policies, they invariably produce their personnel "policies." It is ironic that the one document in which the word *policy* is almost always misused is the most frequent example of board policy that comes to mind. The question for boards, beyond the broader ethics-prudence proscription, is: "What is it about dealings with personnel that we need to control?" The answer is anything that a reasonable person might consider ethical or prudent but that the board does not want to have happen.

The board of the Orchard Country Day School decided that secretive decision processes, which it found unacceptable, constituted mistreatment that might slip by as acceptable under the "Don't be unethical" rule. Another board decided the same about any prejudice toward an employee who had filed a grievance. Most boards have decided to omit references to sex, race, and age discrimination insofar as the law now covers these items. Violation of the law is so patently a case of imprudent behavior that no additional words need be wasted. But a board that believes that the law does not go far enough could increase the constraint beyond the law's protection.

The board does have a personnel policy under this model, but it is unlikely to be more than a page long. The previous board personnel manual becomes the property of the CEO, to change within the board constraints as he or she sees fit.

"Staff Treatment" is the title that the board of the Tennessee Managed Care Network chose to address the personnel issue (Exhibit 5.3). Because they were just dealing with the "don't" list, their only concern about personnel was that they not be subjected to "inhumane, unfair or undignified" situations, as further defined by Points 1 through 4.

Range of Executive Limitation Policies

In Executive Limitation policies, different boards have varying things to say, both in volume and in restrictiveness. One board may find another's policies too restrictive or irresponsibly loose. It is critical only that the CEO and board always know precisely what the marching orders are at any point in time.

**Exhibit 5.3. Tennessee Managed Care Network Policy:
"Staff Treatment."**

With respect to treatment of paid and volunteer staff, the chief executive may not cause or allow conditions which are inhumane, unfair or undignified. Accordingly, he or she may not:

1. Discriminate among employees on other than clearly job-related, individual performance or qualifications.

2. Fail to take reasonable steps to protect staff from unsafe or unhealthy conditions.

3. Withhold from staff a due-process grievance procedure, able to be used without bias.

4. Fail to acquaint staff with their rights under this policy.

Source: Tennessee Managed Care Network.

Although most boards will face a number of policy topics, such as the three just discussed, the full list of policies will differ from board to board within the same type of organization and will certainly differ from one type of organization to another. An international development agency will have policies different from those of a family planning agency. Boards of county commissioners, library boards, chambers of commerce, and trade or professional associations will all differ, though they are subject to the same principles.

The Executive Limitations policies of People Services to the Developmentally Disabled (Exhibit 5.4) and the College of Medical Laboratory Technologists of Ontario (Exhibit 5.5) illustrate two very different types of constraints a board might impose. The first ensures that the board is sufficiently informed and supported to do its job. The second limits the asset risk that the board finds palatable. An Executive Limitations policy may be as simple as the one issued by the board of the Diving Equipment and Marketing Association (Exhibit 5.6).

In practice, most boards get by with fewer than ten Executive Limitations policies. These tend to average less than a page in length. But the vessel is adjustable to have as much restriction or

Exhibit 5.4. People Services to the Developmentally Disabled Policy: "Communication and Support to the Board."

With respect to providing information and counsel to the board, the CEO may not permit the board to be uninformed. Accordingly, he or she may not:

1. Neglect to submit monitoring data required by the board (see policy on Monitoring Executive Performance) in a timely, accurate and understandable fashion, directly addressing provisions of the board policies being monitored.

2. Let the board be unaware of relevant trends, anticipated negative media coverage, and material external and internal changes, particularly changes in assumptions upon which any board policy has previously been established.

3. Fail to advise the board if, in the CEO's opinion, the board is not in compliance with its own policies on Governance Process and Board-Staff Relationship, particularly in the case of board behavior which is detrimental to the work relationship between the board and the CEO.

4. Fail to marshal for the board as many staff and external points of view, issues and options as needed for fully informed board choices.

5. Present information in unnecessarily complex or lengthy form.

6. Fail to provide a mechanism for official board, officer, or committee communications.

7. Fail to deal with the board as a whole except when (a) fulfilling individual requests for information or (b) responding to officers or committees duly charged by the board.

8. Fail to report in a timely manner an actual or anticipated noncompliance with any policy of the board.

Source: People Services to the Developmentally Disabled.

Exhibit 5.5. College of Medical Laboratory Technologists of Ontario Policy: "Asset Protection."

The Registrar shall not allow assets to be unprotected, inadequately maintained or unnecessarily risked. Accordingly, the Registrar shall not:

1. Fail to insure against theft and casualty losses to at least 80 percent replacement value and against liability losses to Council members, staff, or the organization itself in an amount greater than the average for comparable organizations.

2. Allow uninsured personnel to handle funds or College property or pledge credit of the College.

3. Subject plant and equipment to improper wear and tear or insufficient maintenance.

4. Unnecessarily expose the organization, its Council or staff to claims of liability.

5. Make any purchase or commit the organization to any expenditure of greater than $10,000. Make any purchase: (a) wherein normally prudent protection has not been given against conflict of interest; (b) of over $1,500 without having obtained comparative prices and quality; (c) of over $10,000 without an adequate review of ongoing costs, value and durability.

6. Fail to protect intellectual property, information and files from loss or significant damage or unauthorized duplication.

7. Receive, process or disburse funds under controls which are insufficient to meet the Council-appointed auditor's standards.

8. Invest or hold operating capital in insecure instruments, including uninsured checking accounts and bonds of less than AA rating, or in non-interest bearing accounts except where necessary to facilitate ease in operational transactions.

9. Acquire, encumber or dispose of real property. Endanger the organization's public image or credibility, particularly in ways that would hinder its accomplishment of mission.

Source: College of Medical Laboratory Technologists of Ontario.

Exhibit 5.6. Diving Equipment and Marketing Association: "Diving Industry Image."

The Executive Director may not endanger the organization's image or credibility in the diving industry, particularly in ways that would hinder its accomplishment of mission.

Accordingly, he or she may not:

Create the perception of nepotism or conflict of interest.

Distribute documents of poor appearance or with inaccurate, misleading or politically insensitive content.

Source: Diving Equipment and Marketing Association.

freedom that a board feels is right. In the final analysis, however, boards must realize that no matter how narrow a policy is intended to be, there is still room for interpretation. The CEO's job is largely one of making those interpretations as he or she delegates to others. Unless the board itself wishes to do the organization's work, this will *always* be the case. Interpretation is so integral to the nature of management that one could describe managers' jobs as translation from one level of abstraction to another.

Consequently, it is *never* legitimate to complain that board policy with respect to the CEO and staff is fuzzy, open to interpretation, or too general. It is on that *degree of fuzziness,* interpretive range, and generality that board debate must turn. A board member who feels that certain policy language allows too great a range of interpretation is obligated to argue for language that narrows the range. The member only detracts from his or her good argument to complain, in effect, that policy should not allow any range. It is in studious management of the generalities that a board enhances both its contributions and those of staff.

Board and staff need as much freedom as possible to perform. The board is responsible for creating the future, not minding the shop. Chait and Taylor (1989) bemoaned boards' time being "frittered away on operations" (p. 45), mired in minutiae, and thus unavailable for policy and strategy. "Rather than do more, boards would be better advised to demand more" (p. 52). The staff needs freedom from the board's friendly intrusions to do its work. The board cheats the mission by constraining too much; it risks cheating standards of acceptable conduct by constraining too little. Proactively setting relatively few limits for the CEO increases the freedom of both the board and the CEO (Barth, 1992).

Next Chapter

We have now looked into the minimal verbiage and high leverage power of Executive Limitations policies, which are established to ensure that staff action is prudent and ethical. Simultaneously achieving delegation that is simple and powerful, however, requires a certain kind of relationship between governance and management. In Chapter Six, I turn my attention to the relationship between the board and its CEO.

Chapter Six

Strong Boards Need Strong Executives
The Board-Executive Relationship

No single relationship in the organization is as important as that between the board and its CEO. Probably no single relationship is as easily misconstrued or has such dire potential consequences. That relationship, well conceived, can set the stage for effective governance and management.

It is often said that the most important task of a board is the choice of CEO. Although choice is surely important, establishing an effective relationship is even more important. Good CEOs have been rendered ineffective as a result of poor relationships with their boards. Poor CEOs have been allowed to remain because of inadequately structured relationships with their boards.

To describe an effective relationship, we must attend to the board's job, the CEO's job, and the link between them. In this chapter, the focus is on the CEO's job and the link between board and CEO. Board policies on empowerment of staff and the nature of staff accountability constitute a category called Board-Executive Relationship. In this chapter, I begin with a definition of the CEO and the nature of accountability and empowerment it implies. Then, I deal with the kind of information the board needs for responsible oversight of the CEO and what this has to do with the CEO's performance evaluation. I end by discussing how to keep the roles of board and CEO separate and complementary.

Defining a CEO

Except for a few unique functions of the board, almost all organizational activities are performed by staff. Even in relatively small organizations, the sheer volume of staff activity would overwhelm a part-time board. Furthermore, the myriad interrelationships among separate functions in an organization frequently awe even a full-time staff.

Boards ordinarily choose to coordinate these intricate parts by employing a CEO to put all the pieces in place. More than a mere coordinator, a CEO is accountable for making all the parts come together in an acceptable whole. The board is able to govern by dealing conceptually only with the whole and personally only with the CEO. As the board's bridge to the staff, the CEO has a role more distinct than merely lead staff member. A powerfully designed CEO position is a key to board excellence. It enables a board to avoid the intricacies and short-term focus of staff management and to work exclusively on the holistic, long-term focus of governance.

Nonprofit and public organizations have chronic problems with the CEO function, because it is either overpowered or underpowered. In either event, its promise can be lost, and with it much of the board's opportunity for excellence. If a strong CEO causes a board to be weak or if a strong board causes an CEO to be weak, the role has been ill designed. Many boards unwittingly invite their CEOs to be either Milquetoasts or manipulators.

The "Delegation to the President" policy of the Garden City Community College board (Exhibit 6.1) expresses the method in which power is passed. Pay particular attention to Point 4, wherein the board as a body has limited its own rights as individuals to commandeer resources through seemingly benign requests for information. This provision is clearly consistent with a strict interpretation of the "one voice" philosophy—that is, that boards must speak as one, not as individual members.

Placing the CEO Role

Understanding an effective CEO function requires us first to look beyond the distraction of titles and, second, to grasp the peculiar organizational phenomenon of cumulative responsibility.

Exhibit 6.1. Garden City Community College Policy: "Delegation to the President."

All board authority delegated to staff is delegated through the president, so that all authority and accountability of staff—as far as the board is concerned—is considered to be the authority and accountability of the president.

1. The board will direct the president to achieve certain results, for certain recipients, at a certain cost through the establishment of Ends policies. The board will limit the latitude the president may exercise in practices, methods, conduct, and other "means" through the establishment of Executive Limitations policies.

2. As long as the president uses any reasonable interpretation of the board's Ends and Executive Limitations policies, the president is authorized to establish all further policies, make all decisions, take all actions, establish all practices, and develop all activities.

3. The board may change its Ends and Executive Limitations policies, thereby shifting the boundary between board and president domains. By doing so, the board changes the latitude given to the president. So long as any particular delegation is in place, the board members will respect and support the president's choices.

4. Only decisions of the board acting as a body are binding upon the president.

5. Decisions or instructions of individual board members, officers, or committees are not binding on the president except in rare circumstances when the board has specifically authorized such exercise of authority.

6. In the case of board members or committees requesting information or assistance without board authorization, the president can refuse such requests that require—in the president's judgment—a material amount of staff time or funds or are disruptive.

Source: Garden City Community College.

The traditions of various pursuits bring with them preferred CEO titles: superintendent, executive vice president, city manager, administrator, headmaster, county executive, president, and executive director. In recent years there has been a trend among some nonprofit agencies to switch from *executive director* to *president.* The reasons given are "to be more businesslike" or "to adopt the 'corporate' model." When this name change occurs without a change in *functions,* only the cosmetics have been affected. The exact title itself has no managerial relevance. The function is what is important. *Chief executive officer,* sometimes used as a title, is used here to refer to the CEO *function,* regardless of job title.

The CEO function can be vested either in the top staff person or in the board chair, although the latter is "rife with ambiguity and complexity" (Lorsch, 1989, p. 94). There is a long business tradition of one person's both chairing the board and being CEO. Historically, in business corporations, however, entrepreneurs gathered boards around them as their enterprises grew. Even large, publicly held corporations often operate with a "good old boy" circle centering upon the chair-CEO combination. Standard practice or not, some have recognized the conflict of interest this method presents (Geneen, 1984).

Almost all nonprofit and public organizations are best served when they vest the chairing function and the CEO function in separate persons. The CEO holds final authority "outside of the broad powers held by the board. To invest this final authority in the hands of a part-time board member would seem inappropriate" (Fram, 1986). Regardless of the board's choice in placing the CEO function, it is necessary for managerial integrity that a board clearly use one method or the other and not wander back and forth.

Some boards state in their bylaws that the board chairperson is CEO, yet operate as if the paid executive performs that role. On the other hand, some boards clearly state that their paid executive is CEO, but allow the board chairperson to play that role as he or she sees fit. Such caprice in a critical relationship is damaging to an effective board-staff linkage. Still other boards hold the executive multiply responsible to the board treasurer, the chairperson, and several committees (most notably, the executive committee). Such a situation gravely confounds the relationship. A board-CEO relationship is weakened when it is allowed to become an officers/committees/board-CEO relationship.

For board and CEO peace of mind, it is very important to define the board and CEO functions as simply as possible. The CEO's *only* accountability should be to *the board*, not to officers of the board nor to board committees. This seemingly harsh prescription does not prevent a great deal of interaction between the CEO and committees or individuals as long as the CEO is instructed only by the board as a whole. Board process and structure must be in harmony with that wholeness.

The CEO, by definition, is the topmost single person through whom all upwardly accumulating accountability flows. A chief operating officer, one step below the CEO, might be a single funnel, but not the topmost. If the top paid executive must get the approval of the board chair or is seen as being supervised by the board chair, then the board chair is really the CEO.

Being held accountable to the full board for agency performance is a distinct characteristic of the CEO function. That accountability derives from the accumulation of responsibilities in the staff. Upward accumulation of responsibility is a key phenomenon in describing the executive's job, the board's job, and the relationship between board and non-CEO staff.

Accountability as Cumulative Responsibility

Each individual is responsible for his or her own behavior. When individuals come together in organizations, they are still fully responsible for their own behavior. Supervisors, too, are responsible for their own personal contributions and compliance, but they are also responsible for the behavior of their subordinates. Supervisors have, then, two kinds of responsibility: direct or personal responsibility, similar to any other individual, and "cumulative" responsibility, which accrues from the bottom upward.

In designing hierarchical relationships, job design, and performance evaluation, boards must treat these two types of responsibility in different ways. I assign the word *accountability* to the responsibility that accumulates. Therefore, each manager is *responsible* for his or her own job contributions and compliance and is also *accountable* for the total contributions and compliance of his or her team, however extensive that team might be. The accountability burden increases as one goes up the organizational ladder, though responsibility may not. In other words, the personal job responsibility of the CEO may not be more difficult than that of the manager of word processing, but the CEO is encumbered with far more accountability.

From the board's point of view, the important lesson is that the *board's relationship with the CEO be formed around the accountability of the position, not its responsibility.* In other words, the board need not be concerned with what job responsibilities fall to the CEO. The board's concern is confined to what it holds the CEO accountable for.

The City of Burnsville, Minnesota, has a council-manager form of municipal government. The council delegates to a city manager, whom it treats as a true CEO. The "City Manager Job Description" policy (Exhibit 6.2) reflects the simplicity of the CEO's task (in the describing, not in the doing!). Commendably, the Burnsville description is worded as a recounting of outcomes or values added rather than of activities. That is, it focuses on what the city manager position is for, rather than what it does.

Exhibit 6.2. Burnsville, Minnesota, City Council Policy: "City Manager Job Description."

As the Council's single official link to the operating City government, the City Manager's performance will be considered to be synonymous with organizational performance as a total. Consequently, the City Manager's job contributions can be stated as performance in only two areas:

1. City government accomplishment of the provisions of Council policies on Ends. Ends statements are to be developed during the remainder of the 1996 year and shall be in place in 1997. Until that time, the City Manager will be held accountable for the 1996 Goals as established in the 1996 City Manager's contract and 1996 Priority Goals.

2. City government operation within the boundaries of prudence and ethics established in Council policies on Executive Limitations.

Source: Burnsville, Minnesota, City Council.

By the definitions just given, the CEO is accountable for no less than the entire product and behavior of the organization. That means everything except the board and its functions. And the CEO is accountable to the board as a body. This seems straightforward enough, but consider the implications.

The board has only one employee. For most official purposes the board has only one employee, the CEO. The CEO has all the rest. If something goes wrong in the organization (for example, a failure in producing Ends or a violation of the board's Executive Limitations), there is only one person at whom the board can point its finger. The CEO is no less accountable to the board for the actions of the most distantly removed staff member than for his or her own direct actions. Everything is part of the CEO's accountability package. The board has no *official* connection with staff members except at the CEO's behest.

The CEO's work is immaterial. The CEO is accountable for the entire enterprise's meeting expectations. His or her personal work is only a means to that end. The working job description of a CEO (what he or she actually contributes personally) is not for the board to decide and certainly not for the board to use in evaluating CEO performance (Carver, 1996a). The skills sought in a CEO are not those associated with responsibility, but with accountability. For example, grant writing, plant maintenance, and accounting are not the point. Executive job design, leadership, strategic organization, and setting a climate of creative achievement are.

Board members and CEO are colleagues. The relationship between the CEO and any *individual* board member is collegial, not hierarchical (Carver, 1991a). As the CEO is accountable only to the full board and as no board member has individual authority, the CEO and board members are equals. This relationship of supportive peers is true for the CEO and board chairperson as well. They are *not* hierarchically related, because to be so would shift the CEO function to the chairperson.

The job of the CEO is to work whatever magic it takes to ensure an acceptable amount, type, and targeting of benefits in prudent and ethical ways. Although allowing no escape from performance, the board needs a strong CEO. Some boards are reluctant to empower the CEO to this extent. Their reasons vary from being unwilling to let go of the strings on decision making to being unwilling to burden CEO and staff with such momentous decisions. But by delegating less authority, the board must constantly forsake strategic leadership to make tactical decisions.

Leadership is being cheated in either case. As to burdening staff, in most cases staff members work no more in making decisions than they already do in *almost* making decisions, such as writing recommendations or providing support to board committees. Staff members will not perceive the right to make choices as a weight, but as an energizing boost.

Boards would do well to discard the traditional distinction of "day-to-day" management in describing the CEO's purview. Does this imply that the board's job is "month-to-month"? If so, both the board and CEO are working dangerously close to their noses. The board should be looking years ahead, and the CEO should usually look ahead almost as far, except perhaps in quite small organizations. "Day-to-day" management is *not* the CEO's task and, even when said symbolically, misleads more than helps.

The CEO role is sufficiently different from that of both board and staff that the common two-part board-staff relationship would be better conceived as a three-part phenomenon: board-CEO-staff. In a formal sense, the CEO role insulates the staff from the board and the board from the staff. The "insulation" is not one that rigidly prohibits contact between board and staff members. On the contrary, those very human connections are never problematic *if the formal roles are clear.* The rule is merely that the board can never direct or judge staff performance, though it may impose as many requirements on its CEO as it deems fitting.

Because of its summative nature, a list of CEO job contributions (not of job activities) is the simplest in an organization: the CEO is accountable to the board of directors for (1) achieving Ends policies and (2) not violating Executive Limitations policies.

This is the long and the short of the job. The CEO neither takes over board prerogatives nor stands meekly aside while the board does staff work. The CEO position is as invested in having a strong board as in having a free hand. It is a function that, being strong, can afford to bid both board and staff to grow.

This highly focused CEO job description is true only *when the board does its job*. The board's desires must be clear to both board members and the CEO. As many CEOs have discovered, if you do not know what the board wants, it may be impossible to please it. The reverse is also true. Boards that lack standards and systematic monitoring are not displeased when they should be.

Monitoring Executive Performance

With the board operating at policy arm's length from operations and delegating so much authority to the CEO, how can it know that its directives are being followed? Boards receive much information, only some of which is for monitoring purposes. We commonly fail to distinguish among classes of information and, thus, cloud the question of monitoring. It is helpful first to separate information into three types.

Types of Information

Decision information. Decision information is information the board receives to make decisions, for example, to create a budget policy from among alternative positions, to decide on an approach to use for the governing process itself, or to establish the qualities it desires in a new CEO. This type of information is used solely to make board decisions. It is not judgmental; any measure of performance implied is only incidental to the purpose. This sort of information is prospective in that it looks to the future and is used to value some aspect of the future.

Monitoring information. Monitoring information is used to gauge whether previous board directions have been satisfied. It is judgmental in that it intentionally measures performance. It is retrospective in that it always looks to the past. Good monitoring information is a systematic survey of performance against criteria. In being aimed at specific criteria, it is more like a rifle shot than a shotgun blast. It does not demand "Tell us everything," but "Tell us this, this, and that."

Incidental information. Information that is used neither to make decisions nor to monitor falls into the incidental information category. It often masquerades as monitoring information. Thus, boards hear staff reports, read lengthy documents on activities, or even scrutinize performance, but *lack criteria against which to judge the information received.* Such conscientious activity creates the illusion that the board is effectively monitoring agency performance. Even the revered monthly or quarterly financial report stands indicted here. To the extent that the criteria against which the financial report is judged are not obvious, it yields incidental rather than monitoring information. Boards do, indeed, get smarter in a scattered kind of way, but they wallow in information more than monitor with it. I have found that the majority of information received by boards is of this type.

A common board folly is to want to "know everything that is going on." Although this thirst can never be sated, such boards do review and often dabble in much staff activity. Because they spend their time in this impossible attempt to learn all that is going on, they never really know how their organizations are doing. First, boards that are awash in staff material have little time to create the policies that will serve as criteria. Second, even if boards had such policies, the endless stream of data is largely immaterial to a focused, rigorous comparison of performance against criteria. Flailing in irrelevant information can be raised to an art form by committee reports and show-and-tell agendas.

There is nothing wrong, however, with incidental information. Global impressions of it may lead to better policymaking. If a board studiously extracts from such information helpful insights at a true board decision level, then it has been a diversion well spent. Unhappily, it is more common to find a board that is dragged through such information because its members think it is their duty or because a few members subject the entire board to their specific list of operational interests. The gravest trap in incidental information is that the board may delude itself that the need for rigorous monitoring has thus been satisfied.

Criteria for Monitoring

Good monitoring is necessary if a board is to relax about the present and get on with the future. Preestablished criteria are required for good monitoring. Setting criteria ahead of time is so critical to good governance that I will dwell for a moment on why criteria are necessary and then on how setting criteria in a two-step process prior to monitoring taps board wisdom more effectively than simply letting criteria emerge while reviewing a document.

Preestablished criteria save board time. Each act of judging will take more people and more time if the criteria are unclear. Boards can rush through the process with little real inspection, of course, but if rubber-stamping is to be avoided, each judging action will consume material board time repeatedly. Very little more time is needed to establish the range of acceptability, after which assessing performance or plans is an easy task of comparison with these preestablished criteria. The real work is at the front end; savings accrue thereafter. The board avoids the continuing start-from-scratch approval struggle that exists when criteria are unstated.

Criteria are also necessary because they save staff time. Time is lost when staff proposals are based on considerations later found to be unacceptable. In many cases boards so routinely approve staff plans and reports that rejection is not a realistic worry. Even under such rubber-stamp conditions, staff time is often spent "dressing up" the report or proposal to ensure that the ritual is smooth. A great deal of ingratiating manipulation of boards has been known to occur during this process.

A third reason criteria are necessary is that judgment is simply not fair without criteria. Many CEOs have received unearned harsh judgment from boards whose values became clear only *after* executive initiative had been taken. Such boards find it easier and safer to shoot down staff action than to struggle with and declare their own values at the outset.

A fourth reason criteria are necessary is that a board does a far more creditable job of judging staff performance if it does so in two distinct steps rather than one. A single step is the common approach. When a board judges without preestablished criteria, individual board members use idiosyncratic criteria and share their yes/no responses; totaling all the yes/no responses yields an official board action. The vote records the summary of individual judgments against individual criteria. It is tricky to infer from such a process the board's aggregate values. Group judgment on the exact criteria cannot be gleaned from mere recounting of comments and arguments, because the criteria so inferred merely constitute a laundry list of individual expectations.

A two-step process leads to a far better product. Board members debate and decide at the outset those group values that will be codified in Ends and Executive Limitations policies. The only judgment to take place in monitoring is whether reasonable persons believe that actual performance matches the preestablished criteria. Each board judgment is no longer a new ball game, but a continuation of a clarifying process in which board values are increasingly well represented in policy language. Monitoring is simpler because the value dilemmas have already been resolved in the creation of the policy. Displaying data against the policy can then be made a rather mechanical, routinized process. With monitoring thus systematized, the board can be more certain that monitoring is diligent, even without squeaking wheels or crises to compel its attention. Such systematic assurance that things are not going awry is less likely to be incomplete due to board fatigue or distraction, is more fair to all concerned, is more likely to engage the board in an appropriate level of thinking and, conversely, is far less likely to engage board members in trivia.

Methods of Monitoring

If the board adopts the discipline of monitoring only what it has already addressed in policy, its anxiety will drive it to develop all the policies needed. "If you haven't said how it ought to be, don't ask how it is," describes the principle that forces a board to monitor instead of meander. The board can then monitor each policy at whatever frequency it desires by one or more of three methods.

1. *Executive report.* The CEO makes available a report that directly addresses the policy being monitored. Unlike the common staff report, it is geared to a specific board policy. The monitoring of the financial condition, for example, would not manifest as the standard balance sheet and income statement. It would, instead, follow the format of the unacceptable circumstances spelled out in the board's policy on financial condition. The intent of so directly relating the report to policy language is that no additional interpretation is needed. Staff compliance or violation should be evident at a glance. It is the CEO's responsibility to produce data that enable a majority of the board to feel reasonably assured of performance.

2. *External audit.* The board selects an external resource to measure staff compliance with respect to a specific policy. It is important that the external party assess performance against the board's policy. If the external person judges against his or her own standards, the resulting assessment confounds monitoring and decision information. Fiscal auditors are the most common example of this method, but external audits need not be confined to fiscal issues.

3. *Direct inspection.* The board assigns one or more board members to check compliance with a specific policy. Infrequently, the board as a whole might perform this inspection. Direct inspection might require an on-site visit or inspection of a staff document. This monitoring method should not be used unless the board role and discipline are in excellent order, lest it deteriorate into meddling. Board members involved have no authority to direct anyone, nor may they make judgments on any basis but the literal policy.

"Monitoring Executive Performance" (Exhibit 6.3) was produced by Summit Pointe, a mental health organization, to ensure systematic assessment of agency performance. The board had no Ends policies in place when this policy was created, so Point 3 in the exhibit shows monitoring scheduled only for Executive Limitations policies (their "01" series). Note that the board chose to monitor two of the policies (01–005 and 01–007) with separate methods and frequencies.

The CEO's Evaluation

The CEO's only job is to make everything come out right! That translates into achieving the board's Ends policies and not violating its Executive Limitations policies. This is exactly what governance expects of the organization as a total entity. Organization performance and CEO performance are the same. Evaluation of one is evaluation of the other. Accountability is gravely damaged when the two are viewed differently.

Monitoring organizational or executive performance is a continual process. The board may wish to punctuate this continuity with an annual CEO performance appraisal. That is fine as long as the board understands that the ongoing evaluation is the most

Exhibit 6.3. Summit Pointe Policy:
"Monitoring Executive Performance."

Monitoring executive performance is synonymous with monitoring organizational performance against board policies on Ends and on Executive Limitations. Any evaluation of CEO performance, formal or informal, may be derived only from these monitoring data.

1. The purpose of monitoring is simply to determine the degree to which board policies are being fulfilled. Information which does not do this will not be considered to be monitoring. Monitoring will be as automatic as possible, using a minimum of board time so that meetings can be used to create the future rather than to review the past.

2. A given policy may be monitored in one or more of three ways:

    A. Internal report: Disclosure of compliance information to the board from the chief executive.

    B. External report: Discovery of compliance information by a disinterested, external auditor, inspector, or judge who is selected by and reports directly to the board. Such reports must assess executive performance only against policies of the board, not those of the external party unless the board has previously indicated that party's opinion to be the standard.

    C. Direct board inspection: Discovery of compliance information by a board member, committee or the board as a whole. This is a board inspection of documents, activities or circumstances directed by the board which allows a "prudent person" test of policy compliance.

3. Upon the choice of the board, any policy can be monitored by any method at any time. For regular monitoring, however, each Ends and each Executive Limitations policy will be classified by the board according to frequency and method.

    A. Semiannual Internal reports for Policy 01–002

    B. Annual Internal reports for Policies 01–003, 01–004, 01–006, 01–007, 01–008

    C. Annual External reports for Policies 01–005, 01–007

    D. Quarterly Internal reports for Policy 01–005

4. Each September the board will have a formal evaluation of the CEO. This evaluation will consider only monitoring data as defined here, as it has appeared over the intervening year.

Source: Summit Pointe.

important element. Periodic evaluations are no more than sum-
maries of the ongoing evaluation. Adding other criteria at the annual appraisal is both unfair and managerially sloppy.

There are three common ways in which boards add superfluous evaluative criteria. First, some boards allow unstated expectations to be part of the evaluation. These are criteria that the board
might have included in its policies, but did not. If a single board member is doing the evaluation, these unstated expectations might
well be those of that board member alone. Second, one of the
many generic personnel evaluation forms that can always be found
in circulation might be used. Third, CEO performance might be
compared against personal objectives that the CEO himself or her-
self originally proposed. In this case, the board is inappropriately
judging its CEO against his or her criteria rather than the board's.
These three extraneous standards of performance seriously
weaken the powerful synonymity between board policies and CEO
accountability.

Any forms developed for CEO appraisal must reflect the single
source of evaluative data. I have seen school boards create citizen
forces to design a superintendent evaluation, an action irresponsible to the public as well as to the CEO. If the boards were to do
their jobs, such games with evaluation would be unnecessary. The
only relevant questions are: What did we charge the CEO to accomplish? What did we prohibit him or her from doing? How did
he or she do against only those criteria? If the board needs public
help, it is in creating policy criteria in the first place.

Evaluating the CEO seeks to ensure that board values are truly
in place. The great utility in CEO performance appraisal derives
from its being integrated with the board's policy fabric and with
the concept of cumulative responsibility. Because of this integral
dependence on preestablished criteria, *it is impossible for the board
to evaluate the CEO when its own job has not been done.*

Keeping the Roles Separate

Without a clear difference in job contributions, the board becomes
staff one step removed. It is not unusual for a board to see its job
as "stacked" on top of staff jobs. No wonder boards have problems
distinguishing their positions from those of their CEOs! The

effective board relationship with an executive is one that recognizes that the jobs of board and executive are truly separate. Effectiveness calls for two strong, totally different responsibilities. Either party trying to do the other's job is interfering with effective operation. It is not the board's task to save the CEO from the responsibilities of that job, nor is it the CEO's task to save the board from the responsibilities of governing. Further, it must always remain clear who works for whom. The board can respect, even revere, the CEO's skills, commitment, and leadership, yet never slip subtly into acting as if the board works for him or her.

Two commonplace events in the board-CEO relationship deserve a closer look, each representing a clouding of role distinction: (1) executive recommendations to the board and (2) board involvement in executive plans and practices.

Recommendations by the Executive

Boards often wait for executive recommendations before they move. Some even believe that to move otherwise is either foolhardy or a repudiation of the CEO. As long as boards deal predominantly with staff-level material and decisions, their instincts about this matter are correct. It would be improper if the board were to make such decisions on its own. But if we clear all staff issues from the board's agenda and are left with only those that truly belong to the board, the scenario changes significantly. Now the same behavior is revealed to be the ostensible leader's waiting for the CEO to tell it what to do next. What the CEO wants the board to do may be of interest and even of some legitimate influence, but it is surely not the driving force of good governance.

Current practice is a confounding, then, of two errors. First, boards deal so predominantly with low-level issues that the CEO's *not* having a controlling influence would be foolish. Second, boards often avoid confronting genuine governance decisions by falling back on executive recommendations. When it comes to the long-term, visionary, strategic import of an agency, asking the CEO, "What do you want us to decide?" is not the language of leaders.

To help the board develop more integrity in leading, the CEO would do better not to bring the board any executive decisions. And for governance decisions, he or she can assist the board most not by making recommendations but by helping to develop policy options and their various implications. The CEO might also make spokespeople available to the board for the various policy alternatives. In this manner, the board's choice is truly the board's choice—a substantive involvement with not a hint of rubber-stamping. The vitality of the process engages the board at an appropriate level. Board members become more aware of the important currents affecting agency fortunes and futures. Members leave the board meeting knowing they have been doing the board's rather than the staff's work. This more alive and meaningful board work cannot but have a salutary effect on the quality of management.

Intrusions by the Board

Making staff decisions trivializes the board's job, disempowers and interferes with staff investment, and reduces the degree to which the CEO can be held accountable for outcomes.

Boards make staff-level decisions through any number of single motions: to hire someone, to award the painting contract to a certain contractor, to change a certain personnel rule, to switch $300 from one budget line to another, to purchase a certain computer system, to purchase new tires for the van, and so on to a level far below strategic leadership. Boards are often inexplicably unwilling to allow their CEOs to make decisions that are competently and routinely handled by persons in their daily lives. I have seen boards entrust a multimillion-dollar agency to a CEO, then prohibit that person from making expenditures greater than $5,000!

In addition to the approval process discussed in Chapter Three, boards also intrude into management by trying to help or advise staff in operational areas. Whether given by individuals, committees, or the whole board, advice to staff from the governors becomes confused with direction. In such cases, staff members have had to exercise their diplomatic skills to maintain social graces while safeguarding the integrity of delegation. When offering themselves as volunteers in tasks for which the CEO is accountable, "Board members, now wearing volunteer hats . . . are subject to the direct supervision and control of the [CEO] or the responsible staff person" (Swanson, 1986).

The board has a stake in obtaining the most return on what a CEO costs. Though I am using the CEO to make this point, other staff members are out there, eager to make decisions and to perform toward the mission. As individuals, they, like the CEO, are not hierarchically related to individual board members. It would be naive to maintain that disparate social or organizational positions can be entirely overlooked, but organizational culture can minimize their effects. When the roles are clear, it is possible for anyone to talk with or elicit wisdom from anyone with no harmful effects on the "chain of command." People operate better when they are not bound by rigid channels of human contact.

"Return on CEO" is greatest when the CEO's decision power is used to the fullest, bounded, of course, by the board's interpretation of its own accountability. The board would be irresponsible if it allowed even dazzling CEO decision making to take the organization in a direction the board did not desire or to foster activity the board considered unethical or imprudent. If a board establishes what it wants (Ends) and what it does not want (Executive Limitations), it optimizes both CEO power and board power simultaneously. The board's confidence increases as its fatigue decreases. The CEO's freedom to make decisions increases as the limitations on that freedom are made explicit. "Return on CEO" becomes "return on personnel," usually the largest single outlay of nonprofit and public resources. *Even a minor improvement in this return benefits mission accomplishment in one year more than most boards have contributed by involvement in details in their entire histories.*

Mutual Expectations

The board and its CEO constitute a leadership team. Their contributions are formally separable, and once clearly differentiated, the two roles can be supportive and respectful of each other. As in sports, the team functions only so long as the positions are clearly defined at the outset. Teamwork is not the blurring of responsibilities into an undifferentiated mass. The foremost expectation of mutual support is that each person remain true to his or her peculiar responsibility. The CEO must be able to rely on the board to confront and resolve issues of governance while respectfully staying out of management. The board must be able to rely on the

CEO to confront and resolve issues of management while respectfully staying out of governance.

Each can reasonably expect the other to exhibit leadership. If the board's job is well designed, board leadership is fulfilled by simply doing that job. But the quality of the design is paramount. Vision, values, and strategic mentality must be integral to the position. The CEO's leadership must have two components: the CEO must influence an organizational culture in which the organization's impacts on the world are at least up to board expectations and, at the same time, must set a high level of ethics, prudence, creativity, and concern for the development of people. Furthermore, the CEO influences the board toward greater integrity and capability for strategic leadership. Pressing, cajoling, and even embarrassing a board toward greater integrity are far greater gifts than pressing, cajoling, and embarrassing it toward specific content recommendations. It is unlikely that a CEO can do both well; a leader will choose the former path.

The board has the right to expect performance, honesty, and straightforwardness from its CEO. Boards can at times be understanding about performance, but should never bend an inch on integrity. The CEO has the right to expect the board to be clear about the rules and then to play by them. He or she has the right to expect the board to speak with one voice (Carver, 1992a), despite the massive currents that flow within the board's constituencies. And the CEO has the right to expect the board to get its own job done.

Next Chapter

Getting the board's job done is the theme of this entire book. In Chapter Seven, however, I focus more on ownership accountability, job description, and discipline of an effective board. These constitute the subject matter of the fourth category of board policies, Board Process.

Chapter Seven

The Board's Responsibility for Itself

The subject of this book, of course, is the redesign of the board job. How a board decides organizational results, how it controls operations, and how it relates to staff reveal much about its job design. It still remains for the board to deal explicitly with how it governs its own process, including a job description by which the board can discipline its time and action. These perspectives on the governing task itself are codified in the Board Process category of policies. In Chapter Eight, I deal with officers and committees, in other words the subdivisions of board labor; in this chapter, I address the board's accountability as a whole.

I begin by introducing the concept of ownership, the source from which board accountability derives. I then fix the onus of responsibility for good governance on the governors themselves. Next, I recognize the dynamics affecting the individual board members' ability to fulfill their responsibility as a group. I then present management of board process as a natural outgrowth of the board's products. Finally, I set forth a board job description, along with a commentary on board work beyond policymaking in support of governance responsibilities.

"Moral Ownership"

Stakeholders in a nonprofit or public organization may be clients, students, patients, staff, taxpayers, donors, neighbors, general citizenry, peer agencies, suppliers, and others. The board could be said to be accountable to all these groups, and certainly these groups all have ownership in the organization. The special class of stakeholders I call owners are those *on whose behalf* the board is accountable to others. This narrower concept of ownership embodies only those stakeholders who are situated as stockholders in an equity corporation.

Ownership as a special concept serves as the origin of board accountability (Carver, 1995b). The concept of ownership saves this legitimizing, special group from being lost in the general array of stakeholders. Surely the members of a trade association have a different order of ownership than, say, vendors or even staff members. For a city council, the municipal population occupies a position different from that of other stakeholders.

Various stakeholder groups may overlap, and, in some cases, two groups may comprise the same people. The ownership of an antique auto club is made up of club members; the beneficiaries of the club are the same people. The ownership of a community mental health center is the community at large; the beneficiaries constitute a portion of that community. The ownership of a public school system is the population of the school district; the beneficiaries are the students. Moreover, in the two preceding cases, the staffs of these institutions are members of the community at large and, therefore, also owners. Owners may either constitute a group larger or smaller than the beneficiaries. Even when the same people are involved, the organization's differing responsibilities to the several constituencies are kept straight by separating the concepts.

Ownership and *trusteeship,* as I use them, are only occasionally legal realities. It is the social obligation of trusteeship, whether or not codified in law or contract, that concerns us here. "Moral" rather than legal ownership is the basis on which a board determines its accountability. Where law requires a membership (a legal ownership), the board must determine whether the moral ownership is a larger body, far beyond the bounds of the formal membership. "The more directors agree in whose interest they are governing, the more they will feel empowered as a group" (Lorsch, 1989, p. 38).

The composition of this moral ownership can be obvious, as with a city council, or it can be obscure, as with a public radio station. Are the owners regular listeners, donors, everyone in the listening area, or all classical music buffs? For organizations that receive government and foundation grants, it is important that the grantor not be seen as owner. Ownership is not merely paying the bills, although this may be a factor. Grantors are usually best seen as high-volume customers with whom the organization makes a deal. It can choose not to make the deal. No such choice is available to the board concerning its ownership; the rightful owners do not lose their status because the board wishes to ignore it. The test for ownership is not with whom the board makes a deal, but whom the board has no moral right *not* to recognize.

The board is ordinarily a subset of the ownership, acting as a trustee on the owners' behalf. The board's trust relationship to owners *supersedes its relationship with staff.* The primacy of this relationship is easy to forget when the stream of board activity and the high visibility of organizational personnel pull the board staffward. Boards learn to speak staff language, use staff acronyms, and become involved in internal organizational issues. This understandable, intense identification with staff detracts from their being trusteeship driven. It occurs at the expense of interaction with the owners and resolution of the owners' complex interests. The mechanisms of board work must be designed to remind the board that its rightful identity is with the owners, not with the staff.

Canadian Mental Health Association, Winnipeg Region, has a policy (Exhibit 7.1) that establishes not only the composition of the ownership but also the way in which the board relates to the ownership. Note that the board has planned for communication to flow both ways.

The Board's Obligation for Board Performance

Board members, not staff, are trustees in a moral sense for the ownership and, consequently, must bear initial responsibility for the integrity of governance. The board is responsible for its own development, its own job design, its own discipline, and its own performance. Before any discussion of board process to improve governance, this responsibility must be clear to board and staff alike. Primary responsibility for board development does not rest in the CEO, staff, funding bodies, or government. These other parties doubtless have an interest in better governance. They may even seize the opportunity to affect governance quality. But they are not where responsibility for governance resides.

**Exhibit 7.1. Canadian Mental Health Association,
Winnipeg Region Policy: "Ownership."**

The "moral ownership" of CMHA, Winnipeg Region Inc. shall be perceived conceptually as primarily all persons residing within the boundaries of Winnipeg, and secondarily, all persons residing outside of Winnipeg.

1. The Board represents the moral ownership. Therefore, it shall educate itself regarding the values held by the persons it represents and shall act always under the influence of those values. The Board's education may be facilitated by (1) reviewing reports in the media, (2) studying responses in citizen questionnaires and comments by key informants, (3) discussions with elected representatives, consumers, and service providers, and (4) monitoring the demand and utilization of services.

2. The Board shall report periodically to the moral ownership on its stewardship. At least once per year, the Board shall disseminate a statement of its values and give an accounting of its financial resources and the extent to which these funds have been translated into services.

Source: Canadian Mental Health Association, Winnipeg Region.

Only responsible stewardship can justify a board's considerable authority. Board members who do not choose to accept this breadth of responsibility should resign. If they do not, it is the responsibility of other board members to structure a board development system in which such persons are, if not "converted," eliminated from the board. Being warm, willing to attend meetings, inclined to donate money, and interested in the organizational subject matter do not constitute responsible board membership. These characteristics are desirable but far from sufficient.

It is inviting to rely on the CEO to motivate a board. This scenario frequently extends further than the provision of an occasional motivation "fix." It may extend as far as spoon-feeding. No matter how well the CEO tells the board what to do and when to do it, governance cannot be excellent under these conditions. Going through the motions, even the "right" motions, is fake leadership that transforms a CEO into a baby-sitter. Only a deluded board waits for its CEO to make it a good board.

Under these conditions, public-spirited and ethical CEOs prod the board to do and say what they think a responsible governing body should do and say. With time, observers of such a situation may question the need for the board to be responsible: "If everything turns out well, what is the fuss? Getting the board to be truly responsible may be pedantic and perhaps unrealistic. After all, board members frequently are 'just' volunteers; how can a part-time, outside group of largely nonprofessionals presume to tell a professional or technical staff what to do?" This litany impedes any further inclination to motivate leaders to lead.

The preceding unhappy scenario is the *up*side! What if the CEO is not public spirited and ethical? The improprieties resulting from lackadaisical governance are easy to imagine. I have observed boards whose laissez-faire rubber-stamping came to an abrupt end upon discovery of misconduct. Most nonprofit boards are too private or too small for public embarrassment to be a realistic threat. Yet they must endure their own awareness of having been asleep at the throttle. Their failure may not have been in misjudging a specific issue, but *simply in not having realized that the throttle belonged to them.*

Boards are responsible for their attendance, discipline, governance methods, development, agendas, and ability to envision the future. Others can help. Surely the CEO should even be required to help. Helpers, however, can only assist a body that has assumed full responsibility for itself; helpers can only marginally compensate when ostensibly responsible parties are not taking responsibility.

The board of the Ohio College of Podiatric Medicine has set the standards to be met in the conduct of board affairs (Exhibit 7.2).

Diversity and Dynamics

As a board sets out to fulfill its trusteeship, its most immediate responsibility is to deal with the implications of being a group. Individuals must understand their individual obligations and how those aggregate into a group obligation (Carver and Carver, 1996b). Indeed, the hurdle of moving to a true group responsibility can easily keep a board from attending to critical duties. Boards are fraught with extensive interpersonal dynamics, as is any other group of

Exhibit 7.2. Ohio College of Podiatric Medicine Policy: "Governing Style."

The board will govern with an emphasis on (a) outward vision rather than an internal preoccupation, (b) strategic leadership more than administrative detail, (c) clear distinction of board and chief executive roles, (d) collective rather than individual decisions, (e) future rather than past or present, and (f) proactivity rather than reactivity. The board will:

1. Deliberate in many voices, but govern in one.

2. Cultivate a sense of group responsibility. The board, not the staff, will be responsible for excellence in governing. The board will be an initiator of policy, not merely a reactor to staff initiatives. The board will use the expertise of individual members to enhance the ability of the board as a body, rather than to substitute the individual judgments for the board's values.

3. Direct, control and inspire the organization through the careful establishment of broad written policies reflecting the board's values and perspectives. The board's major policy focus will be on the intended long term impacts outside the operating organization, not on the administrative or programmatic means of attaining those effects.

4. Enforce upon itself whatever discipline is needed to govern with excellence. Discipline will apply to matters such as attendance, preparation for meetings, policymaking principles, respect of roles, and ensuring the continuity of governance capability. Continual board development will include orientation of new members in the board's governance process and periodic board discussion of process improvement. The board will allow no officer, individual or committee of the board to hinder or be an excuse for not fulfilling its commitments.

5. Monitor and discuss the board's process and performance at each meeting. Self-monitoring will include comparison of board activity and discipline to policies in the Governance Process and Board-Staff Linkage categories.

Source: Ohio College of Podiatric Medicine.

human beings. People differ in their comfort with confrontation, inability to express feelings, and in the personal defenses they bring to an interaction. People differ in fears, hopes, optimism, and excitement, all of which contribute to the interpersonal aspects of board operation. These aspects exist quite apart from models, rational structures, and job designs.

This book does not set out to deal directly with the interpersonal dynamics of governing groups. The abundant and useful literature on small-group process obviates the need for such discussion here. I do, however, recognize the powerful influence interpersonal processes have on governance and point to a few phenomena peculiar to boards. Most of all, I want to persuade the reader that taking time to design a sound board process, before the process becomes personalized, is the greatest safeguard against the debilitating effects of unfortunate interpersonal dynamics. The only other preventive measure that comes close is to ensure that all board members are intelligent, communicative, assertive, and mentally healthy! Alas, even emotionally "together" Renaissance people cannot compensate for an inadequate governance process.

Designing areas of board job performance carefully will profoundly channel the interpersonal process of a board. For example, job design influences the types of conflict that will be experienced and members' decision to follow a commonly proclaimed discipline or their individual disciplines. Diversity is directed toward some areas and muted or eliminated in others. Clarifying tasks and off-limits topics helps to depersonalize subsequent struggles over the appropriateness of an issue for board discussion.

A sound, codified board process can ameliorate jockeying for power, individuals' controlling the group through negativism, and the board's digressing into unrelated topics. Dealing with the dysfunctional behavior of a board member is far more difficult if the board has not previously determined what constitutes appropriate behavior. This proposition has quite helpful applicability to the occasional "renegade" board member (Carver, 1994c). Without board-developed guidelines, the matter will be considered a clash between personalities, and the issue of acceptable board behavior becomes lost in ill feelings.

The board of Glendale Elementary School District No. 40 showed unusual character in adopting "Board Members' Code of

Conduct I" (Exhibit 7.3). (This board has a separate "Code of Conduct II" policy for the usual conflict of interest provisions.) As a group, the elected board members determined to protect the school system from themselves as individuals, a commendable and bold action. Many elected boards I've dealt with recoil from getting tough with themselves simply because, as independently elected officials, they have no authority over each other. This board decided to find a way.

Effectively dealing even with appropriate diversity requires a discussion of process prior to the specific disagreements. Diversity must somehow be funneled into a single position. Not all ideas can prevail, and if members approach disputes personally, there will be winners and losers. Simple compromise is not necessarily a responsible solution; either of two very different approaches may be far better than a compromise between them. The challenge can be side-stepped by delaying decisions or by squelching dissent as being too painful, too impolite, or too impolitic. Indecisiveness and unanimous votes often result from the desire to avoid confrontation.

As the family members did in *Who's Afraid of Virginia Woolf?* (Albee, 1962), boards sometimes deliberate on inconsequential issues to avoid dealing with a difficult, unspoken issue. What appears as a preoccupation with trivia may be fear of confronting the larger issues in a group setting. Small wonder; we are not very good at confronting central issues, even as individuals. Moreover, board members deprived of trivia might not know how to spend their time. A board member once asked me in all sincerity, "What would be left for the board to do if detailed review and approval of staff plans and procedures became unnecessary? If we do not do staff work, what will we do?" This organization had for years avoided a searching exploration of its mission. The board continued to hide behind the manufactured busyness and apparent conscientiousness of its demanding, staff-driven agenda.

Another way to escape confrontation with diversity is to use board committees, heavily "assisted" by staff, to make recommendations. Operating largely from CEO recommendations is a similar dodge. Conflicts among board members are thus avoided, as is any questioning that might be interpreted as lack of faith in the CEO. Instead of judiciously resolving differences, the board ignores them or smooths them over. Rather than eliciting and embracing their

Exhibit 7.3. Glendale Elementary School District No. 40 Policy: "Board Members' Code of Conduct I."

The public is represented by the school board acting as a body. Consequently, the school system is answerable to the board as a body, not to individual board members. The board fails to be accountable to the public if it allows any breach in this principle. Therefore, individual board members are committed to proper use of their authority and to decorum consistent with maintaining the integrity and discipline of board leadership.

1. While the board as a body cannot exercise authority over individual board members, the board is responsible for the organization's exposure to members acting as individuals. To that end, the board can exercise authority over the superintendent's response to individual members and can enumerate its expectations for individual member discipline.

   A. While the board expects individual members to be given common courtesy, it does not require the superintendent and staff to heed any individual member's opinions or instructions.

   B. Regardless of any individual member's dissent from a decision of the board, he or she must support that the superintendent is bound by directions given by the board as a whole.

2. Individual board members may not attempt to exercise authority over the organization unless explicitly set forth in board policies.

   A. Individual members' interactions with the superintendent or staff must recognize that individual members have no authority over staff or to insert themselves into staff operations. (Nothing contained in section 2.A. is intended to restrict or discourage normal and open communication between the governing board, staff and community.)

      i. No board member can place himself or herself between staff members in their disputes or negotiations.

      ii. No board member can serve on staff committees, engage in solving staff problems, or interpret anything to staff.

      iii. No individual board member may be in the schools except a) when engaged in organized board visitation or monitoring of system performance, b) after notifying appropriate staff, and c) when fulfilling a role distinct from being a board member, such as parent or invited volunteer.

   B. Although all members are obligated to register differences of opinion on board issues at the board level as passionately as

Exhibit 7.3. Glendale Elementary School District No. 40 Policy: "Board Members' Code of Conduct I," Cont'd.

desired, individual members may not direct their differences of opinion to staff in a manner which would create dissension or polarization in the organization or undermine a decision of the board majority.

C. Members' interactions with public, press, or other entities must recognize that individuals have no authority to speak for the board unless specifically authorized by the board.

D. Members will not individually render judgments of superintendent or staff performance apart from compliance with board policies as monitored by the board as a body.

Source: Glendale Elementary School District No. 40.

differences, board members are embarrassed or even frightened by them. This is a pity, particularly for boards that represent the public, for such differences partly define the nature of "public."

When boards choose to recognize and handle differences, they find that they need a mutually agreed-upon system to keep the group on task. Without a good system, personality becomes the dominant characteristic of any confrontation. Our points of departure may be ideas, but interaction can easily deteriorate into issues of feelings and control. As people form alliances and experience personal power, the person who expresses an idea becomes more important than the idea. And feeling rebuffed or vindicated may become more important than judging the merit of the idea.

Governing can thus be shaped by personalities rather than issues. Overpoliteness and power-based confrontation, seemingly opposite, both spring from valuing personal aspects more than the issues. Once the calm surface has broken, interpersonal dynamics that squelch dissent transform into personal confrontation. The opportunity to develop productive confrontation around issues dies, people are hurt, and the governance experience leaves a bad taste. If the system is poor, even well-meaning people bore or bite each other to death.

The chairperson bears a peculiar responsibility with respect to board process; however, more cogent to this discussion, the entire board cannot avoid its share of responsibility. In other words, the existence of a chairperson does not relieve other board members from contributing to the integrity of the process (Carver, 1992a, 1996h). If the board as a whole does not accept responsibility for board process, the best the chairperson can achieve is superficial discipline. As Jerry Kerr of Nepean, Ontario, puts it, "It is everyone's obligation to make meetings work, even those who are not in charge."

One way in which the board participates in good process is by placing explicit policies concerning the topic into the Board Process category. The chairperson can then maintain the process by referring to board policy, which is easier than invoking disciplinary measures on the basis of his or her individual sense of what should be. Board members expect too much of the chairperson when they ask him or her to save the board from being held hostage by its most controlling member. Each member has the right to want to run things or never to budge. But, as a body, the board does not have the right to allow individual proclivities to destroy the process.

The Cincinnati–Hamilton County Community Action Agency board incorporated its strong resolve to keep board discussions on target into Points 4 and 5 of their policy (Exhibit 7.4). They decided that some topics are simply off-limits during the board meeting.

Process explicitly designed can produce a discipline controlled more by the will of the board than by individual inclinations or exigencies of the immediate dynamics. When board process is derived from the job to be done, it will be aptly shaped by the planned products. There always lurks the danger that the products of governance will turn out to be merely the random aftereffects of an unplanned process.

Board Products: A Job Description

Construction of Board Process policies begins with consideration of the board's overall reason for existence, because the ultimate test of process is whether this reason is fulfilled. The board's "megaproduct" (as opposed to the organization's mission) is the bridge built between those to whom the board is accountable and those who are accountable to the board.

Exhibit 7.4. Cincinnati–Hamilton County Community Action Agency Policy: "Board Meetings."

Board meetings are for the single task of getting the Board's job done (see Board Job Description).

1. Meetings will be open to the public except when executive session is officially announced by the president. Executive sessions will only be used when the subject matter is related to litigation, personnel, or contemplated real estate transaction.

2. Any member may request an executive session, but:

   A. The reason for the session must be stated.

   B. The Board may include no one else or anyone else it chooses.

   C. Authority to declare the session is vested in the President unless overridden by simple majority vote.

   D. Where possible, announcement of executive session should be on the published agenda.

3. Agenda Control: The Board is the sole authority over its own agenda. The President will exercise this control on behalf of the Board, though any board member—with a majority agreeing—can add or delete business from the agenda. Normally, material related to the agenda will be given to board members with adequate lead time for preparation.

4. Agenda Content: Only those issues which are within the board's chosen areas of responsibility (see Board Job Description) shall consume Board time. That is, the Board will work only on the Board's job, not on the staff's jobs, though the Board may review staff performance against Board Policies at any time it wishes.

5. Board members are obligated to prepare for meetings and to participate productively in discussion, always within the boundaries of discipline established by the Board.

Source: Cincinnati–Hamilton County Community Action Agency.

An effective board process, then, must start by clarifying the specific contributions of this bridge between owners and producers. Before we can design board process intelligently, we must ascertain what the board exists to accomplish—"Form follows function." Appropriate practices are determined on the basis of the accomplishments expected. The board job description is thus the central factor in board process.

Conventional job descriptions are detailed lists of job activities. Their emphasis is on job means rather than job products. I use a more powerful, succinct format that omits activities and that focuses on why activities take place—the intended outcomes. This method, convincingly argued by Reddin (1971), yields a job description that, in effect, states the "value added" by the position. How is the organization different because this job exists? What does this job contribute? In describing job contributions, I speak of job "products" simply to keep before us at all times the output aspect of work rather than the activity.

Boards can contribute any number of products to an organization. Only three products cannot be delegated, an irreducible trio applicable to all governing boards. The board's role as a bridge between ownership and staff produces three mandatory products.

Core Board Products

The board must contribute whatever legitimate link the organization has with its ownership. The board's first direct product is the organization's *linkage to the ownership*. Furthermore, the board has the obligation to fulfill fiduciary responsibilities, guard against undue risk, determine program priorities, and generally direct organizational activity. We have seen that a board can be accountable yet not directly responsible for these obligations by setting policy.

The board's second direct product is *explicit governing policies*. These policies should be the ones I describe as Ends, Executive Limitation, Board-Executive Relationship, and Board Process—in each case developed to whatever level of detail the board chooses.

Finally, the board is obliged to ensure the staff's fidelity to the board's policies. If the CEO continually fails to fulfill these explicit expectations, the board itself is culpable. The board has no choice but to take the steps necessary to remedy the situation. The board's third direct product is *assurance of executive performance*.

These three undelegable job contributions are the *unique responsibilities* of a governing board—unique because only the governing body can contribute these products. The board may add other products to this list, but it cannot shorten it and still responsibly govern.

Optional Board Products

Although all other contributions to the organization beyond the core three may be delegated to the CEO, it does not necessarily follow that the board should delegate them. The most common additional board products involve fundraising and legislative action.

Should a board be responsible for fundraising? The answer depends on the kind of organization and its circumstances. From the perspective of governance concepts per se, one can only say that fundraising may be either delegated or retained, at the board's discretion. If a board assumes this responsibility, it should define the contribution well enough that there is no confusion between staff and board responsibilities. "Fundraising" is an activity, not a result. Using results language forces the board to confront the task it has taken on and its expectations of staff. Does the board merely make philanthropic contacts and leave to the staff responsibility for actually bringing in the money? Is the board responsible for the funding level, that is, everything up to and including the goal amount? Or does its responsibility lie somewhere between? Wasteful conflict about the roles of the board (or its fundraising committee) and the CEO (or the CEO's director of development) can be reduced, perhaps avoided, by defining the job in terms of the expected result rather than the means used to attain that result.

With respect to legislative action, the same points apply. Does the board wish to assume responsibility for legislative strategy? For network notification? For "personal presence" at hearings? Remember, too, that board members can offer themselves as volunteers under staff direction without complicating the board's job itself. For example, the board might hold the CEO accountable for certain legislative impact, but guarantee to supply board members as informed volunteers to participate in testimony under the CEO's direction. With this approach, there is no need to add legislative results to the board's job, yet board members are still providing a valuable contribution. It must always remain clear who has authority and responsibility for the strategy and mechanics necessary to achieve the legislative results. In this instance, the CEO is in charge even though board members are involved. Board members work for the CEO, or the CEO's designee, when engaged in activities for which the board holds its CEO accountable.

Whatever the board decides about assuming more than the basic three responsibility areas, the matter must be made explicit and all further board activities must be made consonant. It is important that because the initial three core areas cannot be delegated, they should be given primacy. No board should add items unless it is sure that its allegiance to the first three will not be diluted.

Some might say that fundraising is the chief responsibility, even the raison d'être, of a board. I disagree. Fundraising by the board may be critical to a given organization, but it is more important that the organization be *worth raising funds for.* That worth is what the three areas of basic governance are designed to ensure. I do not mean to denigrate board fundraising in cases in which the board has made sure the agency is worth the donors' money. To the contrary, I applaud it and hold both the skills and the dedication involved in great respect. There is no reason a board cannot attend quite well to the basic three products plus fundraising, but this wholeness is ill served by lopsided attention to fundraising as the chief board responsibility.

The Basic Board Job Description

The irreducible minimum contributions of governance are restated below. Note that these constitute the board's specific job *responsibility,* but if accomplished, ensure the board's overall *accountability* as well. This responsibility/accountability aspect of managerial job design saves the board from acting as if everything is its job. The board creates a limited responsibility list, but constructs it so that the board's accountability for the total is not circumvented in the name of simplicity. Here is a summary of the board's job products:

1. *Linkage to the ownership:* The board acts in trusteeship for "ownership" and serves as the legitimizing connection between this base and the organization.

2. *Explicit governing policies:* The values and perspectives of the whole organization are encompassed by the board's explicit enunciation and proper categorization of broad policies.
3. *Assurance of executive performance:* Although the board is not responsible for the staff's performance, it must ensure that staff members meet the criteria it has set. In this way, its accountability for that performance is fulfilled.

Each of these three products is a job output, not a job activity, though any number of attendant activities are implied. The board job, however, is neither built on activities nor evaluated on the completion of activities. Within each area of responsibility, the board can set objectives to guide its short-term work. Although the board need not set objectives for staff work, it surely must for its own work.

The Ramsey Action Programs board adopted the basic board job products in its policy (Exhibit 7.5). Optional outputs were considered and not chosen, so there are only three parts. Executive Limitations appears here as "Administrative Constraints," Board Process as "Governance Process," and Board-Executive Relationship as "Executive Linkage." These variations in references to policy categories are immaterial.

The Board's Hands-On Work

The three job products are intended to capture the reason the board exists. In those organizations in which the board wishes to add more outputs to its basic three, the additional job products must be reflected in the job description. In any case, subsequent board work is channeled into activities designed to fulfill these intended outcomes. Previous chapters have dealt with principles and actions pertinent to job products 2 and 3. Let us now consider some aspects and activities of job product 1 and briefly note the work involved when the board adds areas.

Direct Work: Linkage with the Ownership

The identity of ownership and perhaps the favored channels for connecting with it are deliberated and then set forth in the Board

**Exhibit 7.5. Ramsey Action Programs Policy:
"Board Job Contributions."**

The job of the agency is to achieve the mission in a prudent and ethical way. The job of the board is to make certain contributions to the total which are unique to its public trusteeship role and necessary for proper governance and management of the corporation. Consequently, the "products" of the board itself shall be:

1. Connection between the agency and its "ownership," the community at large.

2. Written governing policies that concern:

    A. Ends (what benefits, which needs, what cost)

    B. Administrative constraints (prudence and ethical limitations binding upon the staff)

    C. Governance process (how the board carries out its task)

    D. Executive linkage (passing of power and measurement of its use)

3. The assurance of staff performance (through control and evaluation of the executive director).

Source: Ramsey Action Programs.

Process category of board policies. That explication is, like all policy-making, a verbal undertaking. Making the linkage real, however, is likely to require action.

The board should continually struggle to define and link with its ownership. It should do so with the same vigor it would have if owners were organized and looking over the board's shoulder. "'Community' ownership," Ewell (1986) wrote of hospitals, "is not clearly defined, and the community does not voice its opinions or require reports on hospital performance as rigorously as industry shareholders do." It is only in rare cases that such owners are organized. In the case of nonprofit organizations, it is even likely that most owners have no idea that they are owners. Any ownership voice that becomes audible is doubtless the voice of but one segment of ownership. Although the board owes that segment its ear, it owes the silent segments the recognition that one group does not represent all. Elected boards seem particularly vulnerable to the error of listening to segments as if they were the whole. I have seen city councils, library boards, school boards, and utility commissions be unintentionally unjust to those owners who were not vociferous. Allowing lengthy floor time for a few faction spokespersons makes boards feel democratic but may cheat the broader mandate. Linkage to the ownership requires a more affirmative outreach than holding open meetings and entertaining spokespeople from the floor.

Linkage with the ownership can be viewed as attitudinal, statistical, and personal. The first, simplest level of obligation is attitude: board members behave with the belief that they are moral trustees for the owners. This intention establishes a frame of mind that, if not particularly schooled, at least leads the board to appropriate considerations and loyalties when resolving value issues. At a second level, the board gathers statistical evidence of the owners' concerns, needs, demands, and fears. Techniques include surveys, interviews by third parties, and statistical data. The third level is more personal; it engages board members in direct contact with owners and owners' representatives. Interviews, focus groups, public forums, invited presentations at board meetings, dialogue with other boards or public officials, and other intimate exchanges might be employed.

Maintaining the attitude of linkage may require no overt action. Developing a board informed with respect to the pure data on ownership and its desires may require no more than study. But the third level, personal contact, requires overt action by board members. They must go forth, sit and listen, make conversation, and struggle with communication. The board may choose to take these actions as a whole, in committees, or as individuals.

The board's status as a subset of the ownership is a built-in mechanism of linkage. Board members do not constitute a random subset, however, as they are selected because they can best fulfill the trust of governance. Because nonrandomness is a factor, boards must ensure that the selection process does not impair the most visible connection to ownership—personal similarity. Persons similar to the ownership in color, income level, geographic location, gender, and other characteristics are obviously connected to the ownership. But it is unwise for an even meticulously representative board to consider its ownership linkage thus discharged. Whether a black person can "represent" blacks or a woman can "represent" women is questionable. The superficial characteristics indicate that specific groups have not been excluded, not that they are adequately represented. Tokenism might suffice for the former, but only an adequate, ongoing linkage to ownership will ensure the latter.

The board can delegate to committees or individual members the responsibility for parts of the linkage task. A committee might meet with a focus group or a delegation from the ownership in partial fulfillment of a board objective relating to the quality of linkage. This means that the board's objective on linkage should be clear, as should any limits on the activities involved and the expected time for completion. In other words, the usual elements of delegation apply to a board's assignment of tasks to subgroups. The board has this option of delegating to a committee or to an officer, just as it may delegate to the CEO, but delegation to board members is a more slippery process. Because the board has much better control over tasks delegated to the CEO than those given to board members, it is propitious to keep the board's self-delegations to a minimum. The more there are, the more care must be taken to ensure that the objectives are actually achieved and that there is no overlap with tasks for which the CEO is accountable.

One way for boards to link with the ownership is to connect with organs of ownership. In communities, many boards allegedly speak on behalf of the general public. Yet boards in the same community have virtually no dialogue with each other. Their staffs may interact, but at the governance level, there is virtually no systematic interaction. Were they more attentive to their linkage with ownership, boards would realize that they have much to discuss with one another inasmuch as they have overlapping if not identical ownerships. For community boards that truly see themselves as wedded to the larger context, over 25 percent of board effort spent dealing with other boards would not be out of line. The cross section of community leadership thus linked holds the promise of making a real difference in the fabric of the community.

Direct Work: Optional Responsibilities

If philanthropic funding, public image, legislative impact, or other delegable performance areas are made board responsibilities, the board must organize to perform. The board has the option of operating as a whole, in committees, or through individual assignments. In any event, it becomes the responsibility of the board, not the staff, to develop and use whatever means are necessary. If the board wants the staff to carry out and be responsible for the outcome of a specific task, then that task should not be part of the board's job. Policy control by the board will suffice. To the extent that a board adds direct responsibility areas to its job, the situation increasingly approaches that of the workgroup board mentioned in Chapter One. The risk of diluting attention to the core governance responsibilities also grows accordingly, as does the risk of confusing board and CEO roles.

The optional areas of responsibility listed in the preceding paragraph enjoy a rich literature concerning ways to organize for optimal performance. I do not presume to add to that body of knowledge here, except to point out how important it is that the board clarify the tasks it has assumed. Taking on an *activity* is not rigorous enough. The board's responsibility in any of these areas is not activity—however busy and impressive—but results. It is both more powerful and more incisive to define the responsibility in results terminology at the outset.

Next Chapter

In the organization of board work, officers and committees emerge as official subdivisions of the whole board. Strategic leadership is best served when this division of labor does not jeopardize the board's wholeness. In Chapter Eight, I discuss roles and rules for the board's officers and committees.

| **Officers and Committees**

Once the board role is clear, we can make sense of the parts into which a board divides its labor. Officers and committees are the mechanisms by which a board partitions its job. Establishing officers and committees is a delicate undertaking because subdivisions endanger board wholeness. Preservation of "one-voice" governance and integrity of board-to-CEO delegation are both threatened.

I consider the problems and principles involved in establishing officers and then committees. In each case, I examine the topic with respect to three factors: minimalism, preservation of the CEO role, and board holism. Finally, I comment on typical committees in light of the governance principles espoused here.

Officers

I assume that the board has decided to name as CEO its top paid executive, not the unpaid board chairperson. Further, to simplify this discussion, I do not consider the CEO to be a board officer. Commonly, boards establish the chairperson, vice chair, secretary, and treasurer, though it is not rare to find more than one vice chair and often a chair-elect.

Minimalism

Structure is best kept to the minimum necessary to accomplish the task. Establishing more officers than needed increases complexity with no compensating gain. Consequently, a board should start with the minimum number of officers required by law and add more only as they are needed. In many states, nonprofit boards can get by with two officers, a chairperson and a secretary.

From the minimalist standpoint, it is often hard to justify more officers. The office of vice chair usually exists only so that someone is readily available to fill in for an absent chairperson; however, a board can simply rotate temporary chairing duties in the absence of the chairperson. The treasurer is an unnecessary office in organizations with over twenty or so staff, and in many that are smaller. The CEO can, in many jurisdictions, double as secretary. The point I wish to make here, however, is not which officers are justified, but that establishing the fewest officers required by the task will result in clearer rules and a smoother process.

Preservation of the CEO Role

Accountability is best when delegation is traceable, unitary, and balanced with respect to responsibility and authority. For delegation to be traceable, each link from superior to subordinate must be clear to all parties. To be unitary, assignment of responsibility to and subsequent evaluation of any person must occur through a single channel rather than multiple channels. If the boss is a board, the principle of unity requires that several persons speak as one, to preserve the single channel.

If the CEO must answer to one voice only, no individual board officer can have any authority over the CEO or other staff. Conversely, the CEO must answer to the board as a whole, not to individuals on the board. As board member Dawn Oparah of Peachtree City, Georgia, put it, "We will deliberate in many voices but govern in one." Most violations of this principle involve the chair or treasurer, each of whom has been known to assume authority over staff functions. The board-CEO connection is interrupted as much by an officer who assumes individual authority over the CEO, as by any other board member who does so. The executive either works for the board as a whole or does not.

If the board chair has no authority over the CEO, who tells the CEO what the board expects? The board does. When the board speaks with one voice in explicit statements, what can the board chair legitimately add? If the chair presumes to represent the board to management, he or she either is acting unnecessarily (if nothing is added) or abusing authority (if something is added). Moreover, an executive who is obliged to acquiesce to what the chair adds is now (1) working for the chair alone and can no longer be called CEO, or (2) working for both board and chair, which is untenable because it is not unitary.

A similar flaw in delegation is commonly found in the treasurer's role. A board holds its CEO accountable for fiscal integrity. The CEO is given commensurate authority to do whatever is necessary (establishing fiscal methods, keeping records, adjusting budgets) to maintain whatever level of fiscal safety the board finds acceptable. Yet, more than half of the bylaws I have encountered state that the treasurer of the board is charged with the books of account, disbursement, and a host of other fiscal management activities.

If the treasurer is responsible, then an integral part of management accountability has been taken from the CEO. The case can be made that the CEO role, thus dismembered, no longer exists. Does the treasurer have the authority to carry out this role? If not, then responsibility and authority are not matched. If so, does that mean the treasurer has authority over fiscal staff, perhaps over the CEO? Does the CEO then work for the treasurer as well as for the board? On the other hand, if the CEO is the one accountable to the board for fiscal purity, how can the bylaws assign the job to the treasurer?

The office of treasurer in such an organization is like a vestigial organ. It may have been needed when the agency was so small that the board treasurer truly did fulfill the fiscal function. Or, perhaps that never was the case, but legal counsel inserted a boilerplate provision in the bylaws despite its meaninglessness. In any event, boards, executives, and staff fiscal officers across the land wade through wasteful nonsense every month pretending that the treasurer role makes sense.

I often encounter the following process. The fiscal officer and CEO confer with the treasurer prior to a board meeting. At the meeting, the freshly briefed treasurer recapitulates what he or she has been told. The treasurer looks informed and the board feels secure because the ritual continues. Substituting finance committee for treasurer in this scenario, by the way, does not make the pretense any more reasonable.

Some boards slightly alter the treasurer issue by creating assistant treasurers who are staff members involved in finance. In this version, bylaws give the treasurer the usual overstated responsibilities, but allow the treasurer to delegate any number of them to assistants. Now there is delegation from a board officer not only to the ostensible CEO, but also to the CEO's subordinates. Just who is responsible for what and to whom in these convoluted circumstances?

The truth is, in the presence of a CEO, there is *no role* for a board treasurer that is both necessary and legitimate. If an unnecessary role is manufactured, great care must be taken that it is legitimate. One reasonable, albeit still manufactured, role would be to monitor financial performance; however, this role is illegitimate if the treasurer monitors fiscal performance against criteria other than those embodied by the board's policies. When the board's criteria are clear and when monitoring information precisely answers to these criteria, an expert interpreter is rarely needed.

Board Holism

A holistic board is a single organizational position and must officially behave as one. Consequently, board officers exist to help the board do its job, not as powers unto themselves. For the minimum two officer positions, I suggest the following job descriptions, stated in the job product style:

CHAIRPERSON: Responsible for *the integrity of board process*
SECRETARY: Responsible for *the integrity of board documents*

These job responsibilities serve the wholeness of governance. They do not interfere with unitary delegation to the CEO. The chair is not responsible for the functioning of the organization, nor for the quality of the CEO. The chair is responsible for the functioning of the board, which ordinarily proves to be job enough! Using the board job description from Chapter Seven, the chair can trust that if the board works well, CEO performance will follow.

If the chair's job product is integrity of board process, selection of a chair should be based on ability to achieve that output. The chair's job requires skilled handling of group process, an ability to lead a group fairly but firmly, to confront and even to welcome its diversity, and to adhere to agreed-upon rules for board conduct. Boards should take great care in choosing chairpersons who can develop the leadership that often lies dormant in the group. Rather than foisting a heavy-handed discipline, the good chair incites the board to generate all the rules it needs out of its own wisdom. The chair merely calls forth the board's own statements of discipline when needed, as if he or she has no choice but to deal with the group the way the group itself has decreed. The David M greeting card sentiment penned by Monica Sicile to describe friends aptly describes good chairpersons as well: "Friends sing your song when you forget the words." The good chairperson demonstrates the optimum combination of discipline and group responsibility when, with as much affection as firmness, he or she confronts the board with its own song.

The quality of governance often depends on the skill of the chairing party. The better the board, the more judiciously it chooses a chair; but, ironically, the more responsible the board is as a group, the less the chair makes a difference in the near term. Boards only denigrate their mission when they choose chairs on the basis of length of service or availability. It is better to obtain a good leader who can invest three hours a month than a marginal leader who has thirty hours to give. Many a CEO has seethed under a chair who had time to spare.

The chair's responsibility to board holism extends to his or her ex officio role with the public and press. When interviewed, the board chair does not have the authority to venture beyond what the board has actually said. "Representing the board" means stating only what the board has stated unless the board has specifically granted further authority. One workable way to carry out this function is to apply the same delegation principle applied to the CEO, except within the Board Process and Board-Executive Relationship policy categories. This approach allows the chairperson to make decisions about board process and mechanics as well as specifics of the delegation and monitoring process so long as she or he is within the board's broader pronouncements on these topics. The chair cannot, however, interpret Ends and Executive Limitations. To do so would be to instruct staff and, thereby, to be in conflict with the authority the board has given to the CEO.

While the chair is guardian of what the board *is doing*, the secretary is guardian of what the board *has done*. If the secretary's job product is "integrity of board documents," selection of a secretary should be based on ability to make that contribution. Responsible for no one else's behavior but his or her own, the secretary need only be compulsive about correctness, accuracy, and appearance. The secretary's job may have little to do with taking minutes, but will have much to do with the official record of process and actions. He or she certifies the evidence of board action, including board policies and minutes.

The policy of the Planned Parenthood of Metropolitan Washington board carefully focuses the jobs of officers (Exhibit 8.1). Note that the treasurer role is retained, but defined so as to be consistent with the board's relationship to its executive director. Note, too, that the vice president has been made responsible for maintaining the monitoring system. Board members thought that this role would be excellent training for the person who might next assume leadership of the board.

Minutes constitute the most basic record of board action. Even the all-important board policies are created and altered only when the authority of the minutes so instructs. What any board "says" includes only those statements passed in an official process. Detailed, narrative minutes (more than what the board has *officially* said) are unnecessary and detract from the board's "one voice," as well as loading the record with material of negligible official significance. In long minutes it is almost impossible for the writer to render an unbiased record of the board conversation. If the minutes are wrong, someone has been misrepresented; if they are right, it does not matter anyway, because only official motions that are passed represent board action. A record of official motions and members' statements suffices for minutes in almost any board situation.

Committees

Board committees are *to help get the board's job done, not to help with the staff's job*. Like officers, committees should be established consonant with due care for minimalism, reservation of the CEO role, and holism. Have no more committees than absolutely needed. Do not compromise the clear accountability linkage between the board and its CEO. Disturb board wholeness as little as possible.

Exhibit 8.1. Planned Parenthood of Metropolitan Washington Policy: "Officer Responsibilities."

Officers of the Board are in the service of the Board. As such they are bound by Board wishes and by limits of Board authority. The officers may meet as a group with the Executive Director for purposes of preparing agenda and other pre-Board work (as defined by its policy on Committee Process), but they may not act in place of the Board, except as it specifically delegates.

1. *President:* The President is to assure the integrity of Board process including effectiveness of meetings and the Board's adherence to its own rules. The presidential succession, in cases of temporary absence of the President is the Vice President, the Treasurer, and the Secretary. In the absence of the President, the term "President" shall be construed to apply in due turn to this succession of officers.

2. *Vice President:* The Vice President will act in the absence of the President. The Vice President also will monitor the consistent operation of the monitoring system.

3. *Treasurer:* The Treasurer is to perform duties in connection with finances of the agency as may be required by the Board. Duties of the Treasurer will neither lessen nor add to the Executive Director's accountability to (and only to) Board policies on fiscal conditions and budgeting.

4. *Secretary:* The Secretary, by affixing his/her signature, shall attest formally to the legitimacy of Board documents. The Secretary also is responsible to the Board for reporting on and noting any inconsistencies of Board actions.

Source: Planned Parenthood of Metropolitan Washington.

Minimalism

Traditionally, we speak of boards and committees in the same breath. Boards are supposed to have committees, aren't they? Boards have told me they determined their size on the basis of how many members were needed for committees! And these were governing boards with nothing to do but govern; they did not need or use committees to make up for lack of staff. Committees can serve a useful function, but the propitious path is to start with *no* committees and add them only when clearly needed.

Even then, the choice to establish committees, no matter how intelligently made, is not simply a decision about ideal structure. There are no "right" committees to have, no list of correct subdivisions for getting a job done. None of the common committees is indispensable. Subdividing the board to get a job done is the personal preference of board members at the time. A particular mixture of persons may work better or worse in subgroups, depending on the people's personal characteristics.

Preservation of the CEO Role

Board committees are established to aid the process of governance, not management. This simple rule safeguards the board-CEO accountability relationship. When board committees are assigned tasks that make them essentially oversee, become involved in, or advise on management functions, it becomes less clear who is in charge of these activities. Personnel, executive, and finance committees are habitual offenders. The CEO role deteriorates as a result of these committees' well-intended, official interference. The board's ability to hold the CEO accountable deteriorates apace.

Unfortunately, many board committees are actually designed to be involved in staff-level issues. This is bound to occur when the boards themselves are involved below their level. The problem seems even greater in committees than in full boards because of the belief that committees should be involved in details and because of the traditional committee assignments.

Level of Work

It is widely accepted that committees should delve into more detail than the board as a whole. To boards that insist on acting on staff-level issues, forming a subgroup to work through the details may well make sense. To the extent to which boards extricate themselves from staff work to do board work, this need evaporates. If the committee is to help the board do its work, having the committee work at the lower level is neither appropriate nor helpful.

Committees should work at the board level. With respect to policymaking, the best contribution a committee can make is to prepare truly board-level policy issues for board deliberation. With respect to the nonpolicymaking aspects of a board's job (for example, linkage to ownership or fundraising), committees may deal with details, but not in areas that have been delegated to staff.

Topics

As in policymaking, there is no reason for boards to form subgroups in categories that are appropriate to administration. When boards create committees with titles that duplicate staff functions, those committees can be expected to drift into staff work. Personnel committees automatically work at the staff personnel officer level. Finance committees usually slip into a comparable trap. A service committee dealing with a specific program will likely find itself dealing with staff-level management issues concerning that program.

When a committee works at the staff level, the crisp board-CEO-staff chain of accountability disintegrates. Look at the relationship between the committee and affected staff. For whom does the staff work—the committee or the CEO? If the staff works for the CEO, then it cannot take direction from the committee (otherwise, the CEO can hardly be held accountable for the outcome); yet such direction, more or less subtle, does take place. If the staff works for the committee, then there is no true CEO because the board has chosen to delegate to staff through more than one channel.

Some boards have protested that such committees exist only to advise staff, thereby making good use of the special skills of board members. But advice to staff by committees—or even by the full board—is suspect. Although offering advice may be an honest intention, the staff members are seldom so sure. In most of the cases I have observed, the first time this matter was explicitly considered was when I raised it. That is, the board had not seen fit to define committee-staff relationships. Boards may easily overlook the lack of clarity, but staffs rarely escape its consequences. Staff members are loath to treat committee input as they would real advice.

What does one do with advice from the boss? If it is truly advice, there is no obligation to pay attention. If it is truly advice, advisees are within their rights to dispense with one set of advisers and select another or no one. If it is truly advice, the staff members may, by not attending meetings or reading reports, effectively disband the committee. If it is truly advice, the board will not think ill of its staff for these rebuffs. If the board has made Ends and Executive Limitations clear, evaluation of staff members—even informal evaluations—on the basis of their acceptance of advice is not only superfluous but pernicious.

Advice should be totally within the control of advisees. Staff members who want advice should obtain it however they deem best and from anyone they choose. Staff may ask board members for advice, but the advice mechanism should not then be confounded with board authority. Board members can advise freely as long as that counsel is not misconstrued as subtle orders because they are still wearing board hats. Establishing formal, official board committees to advise staff is not only unnecessary but damaging.

Joint board-staff committees can be legitimate when they prepare options for the board to consider. This activity should be undertaken only when the respective roles are crystal clear. The joint committee must think at the board's level, not at the staff's. By no means should the committee make either board or staff decisions. Board committees need never relate directly with staff except to gather intelligence for use in subsequent board deliberations.

Board Holism

No common practice so threatens board wholeness as the traditional approach to committee work. Let us consider how committees' work can be useful to a board at minimal cost to its unity.

Traditionally, boards with a great many decisions to make have found it natural to divide their labor. Several committees working simultaneously can digest and form solutions for several times as many problems as can the board working as a whole. Each committee works as a board in microcosm, studying, debating, formulating, and finally arriving at a course of action and recommendations for adoption by the board.

What does a board do with recommendations originating from its several committees? It can review each committee's entire process so that all board members understand and participate in the problem-solving experience; however, to do so would unnecessarily duplicate committee work and, in fact, obviate the need for committee work. So, by and large, committee recommendations are accepted. To avoid feeling like rubber stamps, board members may ask a few questions and put the committee "on the spot" before they give approval. Most board members accept that they do not know as much about issues handled by committees of which they are not part. Unless there is reason to believe the committee is incompetent or biased, they accept the recommendations.

In reality, then, the board does not aggregate its values across a wide range of governance topics. It aggregates the values within committees on one topic at a time: the values of Liza, Erin, and Hannah about personnel; the values of Rachael, Martin, and Richard about finance; the values of Terry, Buckley, Tanya, and Jennifer about . . . , and on and on. On the surface the board is fulfilling its obligation to speak with one voice, but, except for a relatively perfunctory approval vote, there is no board. There is only a group of congenial miniboards, inappropriately importing into governance a method that is quite rational in a workgroup.

The governing responsibility is to create a holistic, integrated set of connecting values that, taken together, "cradle" or encompass the nature of organization. Proper governance is not a piecemeal endeavor. Whole-board decision making tends to illuminate those "dark corners" where staff or board members can exercise undue power by pushing an idiosyncratic agenda. *The only way a board can create unified policies is to do so as a whole.* Fortunately, when a board attends to the larger policy issues and refrains from prescribing executive methods, its job becomes manageable and the board can make decisions as a whole. The quality of the policies thus created reflects the value coloration of the entire governing body across all topics.

Consequently, board committees, when they are needed to assist the board in decision making, should do *preboard work, not subboard work.* They may work on matters before the board does, but at the board level. They should not work below the board level or at staff level. But if bringing a recommendation to the board is not supportive of board holism, what then is effective "preboard" work? In boards that govern by policy, most committee work relates to board decisions on policy. A minor part of board work is "doing" rather than "saying," and in these "doing" instances, committees can be used to accomplish an objective as long as their work does not overlap with that of the CEO. For this discussion, I consider only what committees can do to help boards create policy.

If a board is to deliberate and adopt a policy position, it will do a better job if several options are available. Having only one option is a flaw inherent in the recommendation practice. The availability of several alternatives, however, will not necessarily lead to an intelligent choice unless the board is aware of the implications of each option. In other words, the board needs to know the choices and the consequences of these choices. Only then can it ponder, debate, and vote intelligently.

A useful "preboard" job product of a committee is just such a recounting of policy alternatives and their implications. To produce an alternatives-implications product for the board, the committee must proceed through several careful steps. Assume that some problem, opportunity, or situation has arisen. The matter may have been assigned to the committee by the board or the committee may have come across it in the course of related work.

The committee's first task is to clarify just what the board-level issue is. Determining the appropriate question makes it possible to search for optional answers. The committee must be certain that it is addressing the correct issue, for it is not uncommon to spend prodigious time probing the wrong issues. Issues are incorrect when they belong to someone else or when they have been inadequately formulated. The former situation occurs when an issue has an inappropriate breadth. The committee then seeks the alternative value positions or perspectives available to the board in answer to the issue. What are the optional policies to be considered? Next, the committee investigates the cost, public relations, productivity, and other implications of each policy option.

Relevant implications will form the basis on which the final policy is formulated, so they must be approached thoughtfully. Staff may be called to assist, not in selecting a course of action but in ensuring that available options and important implications have not been omitted. External help may prove useful as well; the board's auditing firm, for example, may have helpful input regarding implications for specific fiscal constraints under consideration. The committee's product, then, consists of policy options and their implications.

With this product in hand, board members discuss, persuade, and vote. There is no committee choice to rubber-stamp, nor does the board redo what the committee has already done. No recommendation is necessary. The committee may communicate its preferred option to the board, but it would be of little utility. In this process, the committee job and the board job are sequential and separate. It is greatly significant with respect to board holism that a member not on the authoring committee is just as capable of casting an informed vote as anyone on that committee. Using a clearly presented survey of options and implications, the board makes a choice *as a board.*

Remember that boards that govern by policy need not deal with a flurry of never-ending details and low-level issues. They have the time to make fewer, though broader, decisions reflectively. Though they deal with massive value conflicts, these are not boards that react to every staff crisis or that feel nothing should go on that they do not know about. Boards that govern by policy can afford adequate preparation and wide-ranging board consideration of strategic interests.

The Bissell Centre board policy (Exhibit 8.2) protects the executive director's relationship with the board. Note that the policy attempts to prevent committees from becoming overidentified with any single area of organization.

This approach to the policy role of board committees places a high value on the wholeness of board action. It values board-integrated oversight of large issues more than participation of segments of the board in narrow slices of organization. With this approach, the bromide "real work takes place in committees" no longer holds true. The board meeting is the place of action. It is not the place for ritual voting or for carrying out the unnecessary business that clutters most board agendas. It is where leaders come together to make leadership decisions.

Legitimate Committees

If board committees should not be tied conceptually or physically to the specific divisions of staff labor and topics, to what should they be related? Which committees might a board use? Recall that the policymaking job is divided into four discrete categories. One option might be to structure committees around these categories. One committee does preparatory work for board choices about Ends, a second prepares for choices about Executive Limitations, a third prepares for policies about Board Process, and a final one prepares for policies on Board-Executive Relationship. As the categories are exhaustive, the committee topics are exhaustive. If ad hoc rather than standing committees are desired, committees can be established whenever a special need arises, and then disbanded.

Exhibit 8.2. Bissell Centre Policy: "Committee Principles."

The board may, from time to time, establish committees to help carry out its responsibilities. To preserve board holism, committees will be used sparingly, only when other methods have been deemed inadequate. Committees will be used so as to minimally interfere with the wholeness of the board's job.

1. Board committees may not speak or act for the board except when formally given such authority for specific and time-limited purposes. Such authority will be carefully stated in order not to conflict with authority delegated to the Executive Director.

2. Board committees are to help the board do its job, not to help the staff do its job. Committees will assist the board chiefly by preparing policy alternatives and implications for board deliberation. Board committees are not to be created by the board to advise staff.

3. If a board committee is used to monitor organizational performance in a given area, the same committee will not have helped the board create policy in that area. This is to prevent committee identification with organizational parts rather than the whole.

4. Board committees cannot exercise authority over staff, and in keeping with the board's focus on the future, board committees will ordinarily have no direct dealings with current staff operations. Further, the board will not impede its direct delegation to the Executive Director by requiring approval of a board committee before an executive action.

Source: Bissell Centre.

In either case, the nature of preboard work would be the same. When proper principles for committee work are maintained, the actual structuring is of less import. The structure may change as the board's need for subgrouping evolves.

Comments on Traditional Committees

The approach to board committees presented here differs substantially from conventional wisdom. To underscore this model's departure from governance as usual, let us look at several frequently encountered committees in light of the new concepts.

Personnel committees. There is no justification for the existence of personnel committees. After assisting the board on one or two policies, personnel committees have no place to go but into staff work. A board with a CEO *never* has a managerially legitimate reason to establish a personnel committee. But what about hiring a new CEO and handling grievances? If these tasks are so great as to require a standing committee, the board has a problem that will not be addressed by the establishment of a committee.

Executive committees. An executive committee tends to become the real board within the board, with debilitating effects on holism. An insider-outsider division among board members is not an uncommon result, as the executive committee "becomes the 'in' group of the board, with a corresponding loss of interest and attention of other trustees" (Haskins, 1972, p. 12). If the board is reduced to governable size, an executive committee as usually defined is not needed; however, circumstances peculiar to a given board may unavoidably impose a large board size, and an executive committee may become necessary in order to get business done. When not established because of board size, an executive committee ordinarily arises because of a lack of clarity in the board's delegation of authority to the CEO. Therefore, executive committees (1) make or approve executive decisions that could otherwise be left to the CEO, (2) assume prerogatives that should be left to the board, or (3) do both. In other words, executive committees authorized to act must take power either from the board or from the CEO. Establishing an executive committee to make board decisions between monthly meetings is specious. Board decisions will not arise that often if the board is proactive and delegates properly.

Program committees. If the program committee is involved in staff implementation decisions, it can be dropped with no loss. If, however, it is preparing truly board-level issues for discussion, then it is in order. Program committees can be legitimate, as described earlier, doing preboard work with respect to Ends. Most program committees I have encountered, however, are involved in program means rather than program results and relate their work directly to current and near-term staff operations.

Finance committees. There is scant justification for finance committees. These are much like personnel committees. They could assist the board in developing a very few Executive Limitations policies on financial matters. After that, they have no place to go but into staff work. Sometimes, legitimate board work in fundraising is assigned to a finance committee, though the two functions are vastly different. In such cases, it would be better to rename the committee (for example, "Development") so as not to invite it into inappropriate activity. With adequate financial Executive Limitations policies and the kind of pointed systematic monitoring described in Chapter Six, boards with CEOs have no need for finance committees.

If, however, the board has retained the function of safeguarding endowment or reserve funds, then a "Doing" committee might well be used to carry out that task. In this case, the board job description would include a fourth item such as "safety and return of reserve funds."

Nomination committees. The nominating committee does not exist to help the board create policy, but to replenish itself or its officers. This committee is part of the system that empowers individuals to serve as governors or officers. It is a proper governance committee and is the only board committee that may need to be described and empowered in the bylaws, particularly if it acts as a membership committee, selecting nominees for the board.

Traditionally, committees and officers are often used to monitor staff performance. The discussion in Chapter Six argued for monitoring only against the criteria formulated by board policies. If the criteria exist and monitoring takes place as described, the need for committees or officers to monitor is all but eliminated. A group is needed only when the criteria have not been set forth or have been set forth unclearly. If monitoring reports are *precisely aimed* at policies being monitored, boards can end the wasteful practice of using board time in meetings to determine whether criteria were met. Officers and committees can then cease their unnecessary work and attend wholeheartedly to helping the board put its strategic leadership in order.

Next Chapter

Codifying board values and processes is a necessary element in enabling board leadership to be all it can be. Chapter Two made a case for governing by policy, but using a new technology in the approach to that task. Subsequent chapters described four categories of board policies along with implications for the board as a whole, board officers, and board committees. Policies presented in the foregoing chapters illustrated discrete policy topics in the final form their authors created. In the next chapter, I demonstrate the flow of creating policies from their global level toward more detailed levels, that is, how policies are "grown" through a number of graduated levels.

Chapter Nine

Policy Development by Levels

Policies in Policy Governance are not monolithic documents. They are statements carefully assembled by level. The concept of policy "levels" has already been explained as a spectrum from the most inclusive, global statements to the most specific, focused ones. Policies created in this way have a distinctive architecture—an outline format where the preamble carries the most global meaning, with narrower statements appearing under it and further outline subparts cascading when necessary to fulfill the policy's intent.

Form and Function

In previous chapters, you have seen examples of this kind of policy format as it occurs in the four policy types, each borrowed from a number of real organizations. In this chapter, I display a series of sample policies in order to demonstrate the sequence in which these policy levels are created.

Ground Rules

Because of the verbal nature of the board's task, the use and even the arrangement of words are important factors in governing. Here are a few ground rules for developing and displaying the board's words.

• *Participation and voting.* The board can invite anyone to participate in its task of policy creation. Staff members, outside experts, persons from other boards, or anyone that the board feels can help it make wiser choices is free to play a role in debate. Although it is important for the board to be open about this phase, it is just as important for it to guard its own right to make the choice. That is, anyone can participate, but only the board will vote.

• *Decision information.* In Chapter Six, I described the differences among information for decisions, for monitoring, and for incidental purposes. As the board prepares to create policy, its single-minded focus should be on decision information. Decision information is of whatever nature and comes from whatever source the board finds appropriate. For example, Ends decisions will require demographic data, needs assessment data, owner testimony, staff input concerning operational capabilities and costs, and information about what has been possible in similar organizations.

Boards developing Executive Limitations policies might call for information from financial, risk management, or other experts. These experts are in a position to understand what can go wrong and, therefore, what to prohibit by policy. Because such outside experts may be accustomed to traditional governance, not Policy Governance, they may need educating before they can help effectively. One straightforward approach, however, might be to ask the expert, "If you were on this board—not in charge of the staff function managing this issue—what would you be worried might happen?"

Board Process and Board-Executive Relationship policy development are directly related to the board's own means. Consequently, the board needs to gather information on just these topics. Adopting a fully developed conceptual model of the board's job answers many questions, but gathering information about how other organizations function within that model is still a useful exercise. In all policy categories, decision information is that which increases the board's wisdom to address decision making.

• *Everything in its place.* When the board creates policy, it does so within one of the four categories of board policy: Ends, Executive Limitations, Board-Executive Relationship, or Board Process. Policy is not to be created that either (1) falls outside these categories or (2) crosses these categories. Either flaw would reveal that the board is not rigorously defining its task. Any legitimate single governance issue can only be in one of the categories, not several.

Furthermore, there will often be a need for board members to translate the organizational issue they want to address into a higher level before dealing with it. Normally, policy issues are not generated from events in the organization, but from the board's studied consideration of its leadership task. That is, although the board would normally create policy proactively, on infrequent occasions it would do so in reaction to considerations it had overlooked until it was stimulated by some current event.

• *Proceeding top-down.* Because the board will address policy issues beginning at the global level and will only then proceed to more detailed levels, the written policies will reflect this progression. Thus, a policy may consist of only a single sentence. Or it may consist of the single sentence that forms a preamble, followed by one or more statements-substatements (as an outlining convention, I'll number these), each of these standing alone or followed by further indented statements-substatements (as is conventional, these will be designated by letters). Theoretically, there is no limit to how far this sequence can go. Pragmatically, the limit is encountered rather quickly, for as the board goes into greater detail, the workload involved—carefully gathering information, then debating and voting each step of the way—grows geometrically.

Format

The policies shown in this chapter demonstrate the hierarchical structure in which the broadest principles are voiced first, while those addressing a greater level of detail come in descending order. This physical layout of board policies follows from the theory of expressing board values from larger to smaller. This format can help boards create clear, adequate organizational policies. It encourages a way of thinking about organizational concerns from the conceptual top down, starting with large issues, working down toward the small ones, and leaving the rest of the decision-making field free. In this free field, the CEO can make choices about Ends and Executive Limitations policies and the chairperson can make decisions about Board Process and Board Executive Relationship policies. Let's look at how language is shaped into policies that leave only the amount of ambiguity the board intends.

Examples of Policy Expansion

I will demonstrate the sequence of expansion from a global policy to ones of greater detail, first in Ends, then proceeding through the remaining policy categories. I will assume that the hypothetical board has decided to use serial numbers for its policies. A serial number approach is a matter of convention, one chosen to make policy designations simpler to handle. In the scheme used here, the prefix indicates the policy category. Quite arbitrarily, 1 indicates Ends, 2 indicates Executive Limitations, 3 indicates Board-Executive Relationship, and 4 indicates Board Process. Therefore, the most global Ends statement, for example—that which corresponds to the mission—is numbered 1.0.

As the board expands policies in each category, it assigns decimal suffixes. A policy just a bit more narrow than the broadest Ends policy might be 1.1, while another policy no more narrow, but on a separate subtopic might be 1.2. Just as a matter of policy maintenance, I suggest adding a letter suffix to subsequent versions as amendments occur. For example, if the board decides to change the insurance provisions in Policy 2.3 (see Exhibit 9.7), the new version would be 2.3a. Quick checks of board members' board books can ascertain whether everyone has the most current policies.

Ends Policy Development

To illustrate this sequence of policy growth, Exhibit 9.1 shows where a progression of Ends development in a cancer research organization begins. You may not agree with the content of this policy. For example, you might understandably feel that this "mega-Ends" statement is so ambitious as to be ludicrous. After all, Ends are intended to be doable, not blue-sky dreaming. My point in this demonstration, however, is not the content of these policies, but what the board does with its chosen content. At the broadest or most global level in this example, the board's wording qualifies as a mission statement, though clearly one constructed with the discipline required for Ends. The rule, remember, is that the CEO is empowered to use any reasonable interpretation of the board's words.

As an aside, notice that the policy is titled "Purpose." The policy title is meant to be helpful in referring to the policy. It is not

Exhibit 9.1. Sample Ends Policy: "Purpose, Serial No. 1.0."

The mission of Hope Cancer Fund is a world with sufficient knowledge for the radical reduction of death by cancer.

part of the body of the policy, and therefore has no substantive role to play. My clients have chosen "Mission," "Basic Purpose," "Macro-Ends," and other titles of their choice for this first Ends policy. Whatever seems fitting to the board is acceptable, for it is the substance of the policy that matters.

If the board stopped at the level of Ends policy development shown in Exhibit 9.1, it would be leaving a wide range of CEO prerogatives, indeed! The rule, remember, is that the CEO is empowered to use any reasonable interpretation of the board's words. Put another way, the board is obligated to accept as successful any achievement that can be considered a reasonable interpretation of the board's policy language.

Exhibit 9.2 shows that the board has expanded upon its broader language. As an amended version of the original Policy 1.0, this one is serialized as 1.0a. The board would have amended the policy simply because not doing so would have, in its opinion, left an untenably wide range of choice to the CEO. Note that the numbered parts are parallel issues, each a level of abstraction below the statement that stood alone before, but is now a preamble. This hypothetical board has taken the opportunity to give a sense of its priorities with these four second-level Ends statements. If the board had chosen not to state some priorities, the de facto priorities would have been any reasonable interpretation of priorities the CEO wished to use.

These points of greater detail are a bit removed from the previous range of allowable CEO interpretation. Of course, at some point, the board has no choice but to leave remaining judgment to its CEO, but within a field of interpretation that the board finds palatable. Let's trace the next step, assuming that the board wishes to exercise further control over the meaning of Items 1 and 2 of Policy 1.0a, those dealing with producing basic knowledge and with methods of making laboratory findings clinically applicable.

As to format, the board could simply continue the outlining format on the same page, putting more material under Items 1

Exhibit 9.2. Sample Ends Policy: "Purpose, Serial No. 1.0a."

The mission of Hope Cancer Fund is a world with sufficient knowledge for the radical reduction of death by cancer.

1. The highest-priority result area will be basic knowledge of the chemical, molecular, and cellular biology of cancer.
2. The second-highest-priority result area will be methods of making laboratory findings clinically applicable to treatment and prevention.
3. Delivery technology will be capable of mitigating social, psychological, and economic effects of cancer patients and their families, though at the expenditure of no more than 10 percent of resources.
4. Lifestyle behaviors will be consistent with the prevention of cancer.

Exhibit 9.3. Sample Ends Policy: "Basic Knowledge, Serial No. 1.1."

The highest-priority result area will be basic knowledge of the chemical, molecular, and cellular biology of cancer.

1. Knowledge of why normal cells become cancerous—the priority result before 1999.
2. Knowledge of causes of growth and spread.
3. Knowledge of factors that increase risk—no more than 5 percent of resources.
4. Knowledge of genes that can prevent cancer—the priority result after 1999.

Exhibit 9.4. Sample Ends Policy: "Applicability of Findings, Serial No. 1.2."

The second-highest-priority result area will be methods of making laboratory findings clinically applicable to treatment and prevention.

1. Effective clinical protocols for chemotherapy.
2. Effective clinical protocols for radiation—major emphasis.
3. Effective clinical protocols for hyperthermia.

Exhibit 9.5. Sample Executive Limitations Policy: "Global Executive Constraint, Serial No. 2.0."

The CEO shall not cause or allow any practice, organizational circumstance, activity, or decision that is either imprudent or in violation of commonly accepted business or professional ethics.

and 2. That is certainly workable, but for ease in handling the policy documents, my clients have usually found separate sheets preferable. In this format, whichever numbered point of Policy 1.0a is to be expanded is simply taken to another page and used as the preamble of a policy dealing with only this subtopic. I use this separate page method to show the expansion in Exhibits 9.3 and 9.4.

Of course, the board could also create Policies 1.3 and 1.4. Or it can go into even further detail with any of these policies, creating, say, 1.2a, then at some later date 1.2b. The depth and content will vary from board to board. The only constants are the principles of governance followed through every step.

Executive Limitations Policy Development

Executive Limitations policies begin with a prohibition broad enough to cover all possible circumstances and activities that the board would find unacceptable. After that point, Executive Limitations policies follow the same path of development as shown for Ends. But it all starts by couching the global statement carefully, perhaps as in Exhibit 9.5. While the board can stop at this level if it is willing to accept any reasonable interpretation of these words by the CEO, I have never seen a board do so.

This policy is almost always expanded to cover more detail. Exhibit 9.6 illustrates an expansion into the second level, focusing more detailed description on six subtopics. Because it amends 2.0, I name it 2.0a. The board could stop at this level of detail, if it is willing to allow its CEO to use any reasonable interpretation of these narrower words.

Using the same separate sheet format as in my Ends example, let us now see what happens when the board expands its policy-making into a third level of detail. Exhibits 9.7 and 9.8, using as preambles Points 3 and 4 of the earlier policy, proceed to give the CEO even less room for interpretation. Yet there is still considerable room for CEO interpretation. For example, by leaving the language as depicted in Parts 2 and 3 of Policy 2.3, the board allows the CEO to determine how much is "material" and how much is "unnecessary."

As with Ends, the board can expand any parts of any policy, as long as it (a) proceeds from the global policy (2.0), and (b) moves toward more detail only one level at a time.

Exhibit 9.6. Sample Executive Limitations Policy: "Global Executive Constraint, Serial No. 2.0a."

The CEO shall not cause or allow any practice, organizational circumstance, activity, or decision that is either imprudent or in violation of commonly accepted business or professional ethics.

1. Paid staff and volunteers shall not be subjected to unfair, undignified, or unsafe treatment or conditions.

2. Budgeting any fiscal year (or remaining part) shall not deviate materially from board Ends policies, risk fiscal jeopardy, or fail to be derived from a multiyear plan.

3. Assets may not be inadequately maintained, unnecessarily risked, or unprotected.

4. Actual financial conditions and performance shall not incur jeopardy or compromise the board's Ends priorities.

5. Staff compensation and benefits shall not deviate materially from market.

6. Board information will have no significant gaps in timeliness, accuracy, or completeness.

Exhibit 9.7. Sample Executive Limitations Policy: "Asset Protection, Serial No. 2.3."

Assets may not be inadequately maintained, unnecessarily risked, or unprotected. Accordingly, the CEO shall not

1. Fail to insure against (a) theft and casualty to at least 80 percent replacement value and (b) liability losses to staff, organization, and board members to at least $2,000,000.

2. Unnecessarily expose the organization, staff, or board members to claims of liability.

3. Allow unbonded persons access to material amounts of funds.

4. Receive, process, or disburse funds with controls insufficient to meet the standards of the board-appointed auditor.

5. Invest or hold operating capital in insecure instruments, including bonds of less than AA rating and uninsured checking accounts, or in non-interest-bearing accounts, except where necessary to facilitate ease in operations.

Exhibit 9.8. Sample Executive Limitations Policy: "Financial Condition and Activities, Serial No. 2.4."

Actual financial conditions and performance shall not incur jeopardy or compromise the board's Ends priorities. Accordingly, the CEO shall not:

1. Expend more funds than have been received in the fiscal year to date.

2. Incur debt beyond normal accounts payable in amounts that cannot be repaid with sixty days.

3. Conduct interfund shifting in amounts that cannot be restored within thirty days.

4. Fail to settle payroll and debts in a timely manner.

5. Allow tax payments or other government-ordered payments or filings to be overdue or inaccurately filed.

Exhibit 9.9. Sample Board-Executive Relationship Policy: "Governance-Management Linkage, Serial No. 3.0."

The board will link governance and management functions through a single chief executive officer, titled executive director.

Board-Executive Relationship Policy Development

In like manner, the board policy that sets the stage for the governance-management relationship is a global statement. In Exhibit 9.9, Policy 3.0 establishes the fundamental pathway between governance and operations: the CEO. The CEO can have whatever title the board chooses, but the nature of his or her job is crucial to really being a CEO.

Policy 3.0 sets the stage, but is almost always further augmented by second-level statements such as those that show up in Exhibit 9.10. Since the policy category is Board-Executive Relationship, the board chairperson will be granted the right to interpret the board's words.

To illustrate expansion of this category into a third level of policy detail, Exhibits 9.11 and 9.12 depict Policies 3.1 and 3.3, respectively.

It is easy to conceive of slight variations in the formatting of Policies 3.1 and 3.3. For example, Section 4 of Policy 3.1 (Exhibit

Exhibit 9.10. Sample Board-Executive Relationship Policy: "Governance-Management Linkage, Serial No. 3.0a."

The board will link governance and management functions through a single chief executive officer, titled executive director.

1. All board authority delegated to the operational organization is delegated through the CEO, so that all authority and accountability for the operational organization is considered to belong to the CEO.

2. The CEO is accountable to the board for achieving provisions of the board's Ends policies and avoiding provisions of the board's Executive Limitations policies.

3. Monitoring data that disclose the degree of organizational performance upon Ends policies and Executive Limitations policies will be systematically gathered by the board and considered to be the only evaluation of CEO performance.

4. Individual board members may have whatever relationship with the CEO or staff members that is acceptable to the CEO, except that they can never carry the instructive authority of the board, nor can they waive requirements set out by the board.

9.11) could be more obviously shown with subsections 'a' and 'b' in outline form. Similarly, Section 2 of Policy 3.3 (Exhibit 9.12) could more clearly demonstrate visually that a fourth level of policymaking has been entered.

Board Process Policy Development

This category, dealing as it does with the board's own job, begins with a global description of the role like that shown in Exhibit 9.13.

Remember that the chairperson is granted the authority—and given the obligation—to interpret and further fulfill the board's words in this category. In fact, that role is set out in Exhibit 9.14 as the board expands upon its global policy. In this amendment of Policy 4.0, there are seven more-defined explanations of the original policy.

As in the previous examples, let's examine two extensions of this policy. Sections 4 and 6 are selected to be shown here as Policies 4.4 and 4.6 in Exhibits 9.15 and 9.16, respectively. And, of course, the board can expand (or contract) any of these policies at any time.

Exhibit 9.11. Sample Board-Executive Relationship Policy: "Delegation to the CEO, Serial No. 3.1."

All board authority delegated to the operational organization is delegated through the CEO, so that all authority and accountability for the operational organization is considered to belong to the CEO.

1. The board will direct the CEO to achieve specified results, for specified recipients, at a specified worth by establishing Ends policies. The board will limit the latitude the CEO may exercise in practices, methods, conduct, and other "means" by establishing Executive Limitations policies.

2. As long as the CEO uses *any reasonable interpretation* of Ends and Executive Limitations policies, the CEO is automatically authorized to establish all further policies, make all decisions, take all actions, establish all practices, and develop all activities.

3. The board may change its Ends and Executive Limitations policies, thereby shifting the boundary between board and CEO domains. But so long as any particular delegation is in place, the board and its members will respect and support the CEO's choices. This does not prevent the board from obtaining information in the delegated areas.

4. Only decisions of the board acting as a body are binding upon the CEO. Decisions or instructions of individual board members, officers, or committees are not binding, except in rare instances where the board gives specific authorization. If board members or committees require information or assistance without board authorization, the CEO can refuse such requests that require— in the CEO's judgment—a material amount of staff time or funds, or that are disruptive.

Policy architecture goes beyond the merely cosmetic. It is an important device, a "terraced" policy format that keeps clear at all times how broadly and how narrowly the board has expressed itself on various topics. It follows, then, that the process of developing policies of this sort is itself an important skill of board leadership. Although this book is devoted to the concepts of the Policy Governance model, *Reinventing Your Board: A Step-by-Step Guide to Implementing Policy Governance* (Carver and Carver, 1997) is written to guide a board through the step-by-step sequence in arriving at its own tailored versions of policies.

Exhibit 9.12. Sample Board-Executive Relationship Policy: "Monitoring CEO Performance, Serial No. 3.3."

Monitoring data that disclose the degree of organizational performance upon Ends policies and Executive Limitations policies will be systematically gathered by the board and considered to be the only evaluation of CEO performance.

1. A given policy may be monitored in one or more of three ways: (a) *Internal report:* disclosure of compliance information from the CEO to the board, (b) *External report:* discovery of compliance information by a disinterested, external auditor or inspector selected by and reporting to the board, and (c) *Direct inspection:* discovery of compliance information by the board as a whole, or by a board member or committee if duly assigned.

2. Any policy can be monitored by any method at any time the board chooses. For regular monitoring, however, the board will classify each Ends and Executive Limitations policy according to frequency and method: (a) *Quarterly internal reports* for Policies 4.3, 4.4, 4.7, and 4.8, (b) *Annual external reports* for Policies 4.4, 4.9, 1.1, 1.3, and 1.4, (c) *Semiannual direct inspection* for Policy 4.10, and (d) *Annual internal* reports for Policies 1.0, 1.2, 1.3, and 1.4.

3. Each September, the board will have a formal evaluation of the CEO, considering only these monitoring data.

Exhibit 9.13. Sample Board Process Policy: "Purpose of Governance, Serial No. 4.0."

The role of the board, on behalf of the citizens of Jefferson, is to assure that Employment Counseling Service (a) accomplishes what it should, and (b) avoids unacceptable activities and conditions.

Exhibit 9.14. Sample Board Process Policy: "Purpose of Governance, Serial No. 4.0a."

The role of the board, on behalf of the citizens of Jefferson, is to assure that Employment Counseling Service (a) accomplishes what it should, and (b) avoids unacceptable activities and conditions.

1. The board will engage in structured contact with citizens of Jefferson to represent their diversity.

2. The board will define in Ends policies what is to be accomplished in terms of benefits, recipients, and their relative priorities. It will define in Executive Limitations policies those activities and conditions it considers unacceptable. The board will delegate performance on these matters to a CEO.

3. The board will carry out its job with discipline, emphasizing strategic rather than short-term issues, policy rather than single events, and group rather than individual decisions.

4. The chairperson is charged to make decisions on issues of Board Process and Board-Executive Relationship within board policies.

5. Conduct of board members will be consistent with their fiduciary responsibility and with the discipline adopted by the board.

6. If board committees are necessary, they will assist in the board's job only, never interfering in the direct link between the board and CEO, and never fragmenting the wholeness of the board's job.

7. The annual cycle of the board will conclude with reestablished Ends policies just prior to CEO construction of a new annual plan and budget.

Exhibit 9.15. Sample Board Process Policy: "Chairperson's Role, Serial No. 4.4."

The chairperson is charged to make decisions on issues of Board Process and Board-Executive Relationship within board policies.

1. The purpose of the job is to see that the board behaves consistently with its rules and those imposed upon it from outside.

   A. The content of meetings will only be issues that clearly belong to the board to decide, not the CEO.

   B. Deliberation will be fair and open, but also efficient, timely, and orderly.

2. The chairperson is authorized to use any reasonable interpretation of the provisions in Board Process and Board-Executive Relationship, except where the board specifically delegates portions of this authority to others.

**Exhibit 9.16. Sample Board Process Policy:
"Committee Principles, Serial No. 4.6."**

If board committees are necessary, they will assist in the board's job only, never interfering in the direct link between the board and CEO, and never fragmenting the wholeness of the board's job.

1. Board committees are to help the board—not the staff—ordinarily by preparing policy alternatives and implications for board deliberation. Board committees will not advise staff.

2. Board committees may not speak or act for the board except when formally given such authority for specific and time-limited purposes. Their authority will not conflict with authority delegated to the CEO.

3. Board committees cannot exercise authority over staff.

4. Board committees are to avoid overidentification with organizational parts rather than the whole. A committee that has helped create policy on a topic will not monitor performance on that topic.

Next Chapter

After designing a technical framework to meet the governance challenge, a board must confront the hard part: making it work with real human beings in real situations. Too often, board dreams are shaped, constrained, and thwarted by meandering, crowded, and pressing agendas. Board dreams, unhappily, are too often regulated, if not determined, by their agendas. In Chapter Ten, I will consider how governing board members can ensure that their agendas and discussions serve their dreams.

Chapter Ten

Making Meetings Work

In striving for excellence and struggling to conserve time, boards are compelled to use their energy and talent more precisely. The central resource in governance is the wisdom with which board members enter the boardroom. Eliciting this wisdom on the right issues, at the right time, and in the right form is not easy. Crowded agendas, scattered foci of discussion, and all the familiar weaknesses of group discipline conspire against the efficient use of board energy.

Like the parent of a two-year-old, the governing board knows it has the power, but never quite feels truly in charge. Because of inadequate information, the changing rules of external authorities, a staff more knowledgeable about organizational activities, and time constraints, the board appears to be the seat of organizational power in theory more than in fact. The traditional mechanisms intended to make board members feel they are more on top of things and more involved can themselves drive boards even further afield.

In this chapter, I look at what it is like to restrict a large job, built almost entirely on the use of words, to a small amount of time. I then discuss the care a board must exercise in selecting subject matter, and include instances in which outside expectations dictate ill use of board time. Next, I explore the formal, planned use of board time as manifested in agendas. Having dealt with economy in the use of time, I turn to the central goal of this discussion—transforming diverse voices into a single voice. I end the chapter with a brief consideration of board meetings conducted according to the new model.

Managing a Talking Job

Governing boards have precious little time in which to do their jobs. Even a liberal average of six hours per month yields less than two regular work weeks in an entire year. There is little room for inappropriate or wasteful activity when a year's governing must take place in such scant time. Even in small organizations, the number of possible items for learning, discussion, and decision is far greater than the available time will allow. Just because a topic is important is not reason enough to deal with it; there are too many important topics.

To complicate the use of time further, each board member has favorite interests to explore or points to make. In large boards, the process can slow to a crawl so that all members have their say. It is not uncommon for boards to adopt unstated strategies that deny members this right, not because anyone seeks to throttle them, but because giving members this leeway consumes too much time. As conventional board agendas are wide open to topics of staff means, board actions can easily become a laundry list of individual members' operational interests.

Boards fall prey to the same "clean-the-desk" syndrome that afflicts individuals. In the face of overwhelming choices among competing and profound values, it is attractive to back off and do menial work. For an individual, that may entail nothing more harmful than the diversion of cleaning the desk; for a board it is likely to mean dabbling in details. Damaged delegation aside, the distraction robs precious board time, the more so because boards are able to convince themselves that such diversions constitute being "involved."

There are always staff members eager to use board time for show-and-tell. Diversion is particularly inviting because the topic seems legitimate. Staffs are proud of their work and want to talk about it. Attracting praise or even notice from the board can be very rewarding. Tradition fails to warn boards that faithfully listening to staff reports may not be governance at all.

External authorities demand board time. They do so sometimes for legitimate reasons, but often because of a dysfunctional construction of governance. An example is the raft of inappropriate actions demanded of local school boards by state legislatures and demanded of many private social service agencies by their certifying bodies. For public and nonprofit boards receiving public money, the lawfully required wastes of time not only plunder the resource of board talent but also jeopardize the tenuous psychology of strategic thinking.

In the few hours that remain after such diversions, a board's expression of visionary leadership is—let us be frank about the probabilities—*thoroughly unlikely.* Tradition, time, and available diversions are stacked against real leadership. "Surely," observes Gene Royer, speaking of boards of education, "our forebears . . . did not envision our taking on all these combined chores and cramming them into a two-hour meeting once or twice a month" (Royer, 1996b, p. 61). This budget needs to be approved. This grant must be signed and sent right away. Financial reports are to be reviewed. A roof needs to be repaired. An aspect of the group insurance needs to be changed. Staff cost-of-living increments and merit raises must be sanctioned. Time's up. Perhaps we can get around to strategic leadership next year. A surfeit of insistent demands makes a mockery of boards' yearning for the long view.

Choosing the Issues

The board's job is a verbal task. The school board coaches no basketball teams. The county commission constructs no bridges. The hospital board cures no patients. The symphony board conducts no music. The board's job is not to coach, construct, cure, or conduct. The board talks. Debating, clarifying, and enunciating values are talking tasks.

Words are the board's tools. When the job is one of words, there must be discipline in the talking. That discipline involves *what* is talked about, *how* the talking occurs, and *when* it is done. It is not acceptable to talk about any issue that might come up. It is not acceptable to talk about an issue in whatever way desired. It is not acceptable to talk about an issue at an inappropriate time. Boards, as trustees for the interests of others, have no more right to converse randomly than employed lathe operators have to cut whatever piece of metal strikes their fancy. When boards wander aimlessly, they are as negligent as the professional shortstop who decides that right field is a nicer place to be today. Boards cannot simply address any topics in any way they wish at the moment and hope to excel.

Screening Form Before Content

Screening issues prior to board discussion brings process criteria to bear on board meetings. Boards can resolve the question "What will we allow ourselves to talk about?" before specific issues arise and their enthusiastic sponsors obscure the discipline that could have been exercised. The board needs to address the matter in a Board Process policy. Instituting such a policy enables a board to judge the appropriateness of an issue against criteria before including it on the board agenda. It is important that no one start speaking to the content of the issue before dealing with its form. The first screening question is "What category issue is this?" Is it an issue of intended effects in the world? An executive means issue? An issue of the governance job itself? Or an issue of board-executive linkage? Answering this screening question concretely labels the issue as, respectively, one of Ends, Executive Limitations, Board Process, or Board-Executive Relationship.

The second screening question is "Whose issue is it?" If the issue belongs to this organization at all, it should be clearly "owned" by either the board or the CEO. If the issue belongs to a staff member other than the CEO, as far as the board is concerned it belongs to the CEO. So the question before the board is, simply, "Is this issue yours or mine?" Finding that an issue is "yours *and* mine" bespeaks unclear criteria or an issue yet to be disentangled. Beware of "shared" responsibility; shared is likely shirked and almost certainly sloppy. In a good system, there are no orphan issues. They all belong somewhere.

The third screening question is, "What has the board already said in this category and how is the issue at hand related?" This question looks not only at the content of existing board policy, but at the breadth or level of that policy. Content is inspected to determine (1) whether the board has already dealt with the issue and, if so, in what way, and (2) whether the issue at hand is several levels of abstraction below current board policy or simply the next level lower. If the board has already addressed the matter, then the only relevant question is whether the board wishes to change what has already been said. If the issue at hand is several levels below the current board policy level, the task is to reframe the issue so that it is conceptually adjacent to previous policy.

One way to do this is to ask, "What is the broadest way to address this issue so that it is still 'under' the board policy we already have?" And, having answered that question, the board should ask, "Will that suffice to deal with our concern?" If *not*, the board then repeats the process. For example, let's say that the board has a policy prohibiting the CEO from paying staff compensation that is "materially greater than market." This policy would itself fall just under, or would be "conceptually adjacent" to, the broadest policy of the Executive Limitations category: "Allow no practice or circumstance that is unethical or imprudent."

Let us assume that a board member expresses concern that "market" can mean local or national or a special segment, such as professional. Perhaps there is a worry that, with respect to clerical salaries, political problems will arise if the organization is out of line with local governmental scales. Although the board member does not want to limit the CEO to the local market in seeking people nationally, the member is convinced that "market" is unacceptably broad in light of this political worry. A majority of the board may feel comfortable enough with the broader level of proscription already set forth. If a vote reveals that the majority is satisfied, then there is no issue. If a majority agrees with our concerned member, the compensation policy might be amended to read: "No compensation may materially exceed the applicable market. Local units of government will constitute the market for job classifications that local governments employ." The board would have, in effect, come in at a lower level, although the policy is still only two sentences long.

These screening checks take surprisingly little time if the board uses the configuration of categories and levels described in previous chapters. The total registry of board policies creates a "value map," which the board uses to navigate through the otherwise confusing array of established and potential policy issues. Determining the placement of any organizational issue with respect to other issues and with respect to board and CEO "territories" is relatively easy.

It is out of order for board members to talk about content before the form is settled. And if the board has decided that options and implications are needed for informed deliberation, it is out of order to begin problem solving before these adequate data have been developed.

Being Ready for Discussion

Obtaining adequate data before creating policy can be a reasonable cause of delay. There is a danger, however. Boards, like individuals, have a tendency to put off doing something acceptable and to wait forever to do it perfectly. Complete information is rarely available, so boards, like all managers, must learn to take action with incomplete data. The peculiar situation in this case, however, is that the option to put off policy is often an illusion. A board cannot wait until later to create policy, for even as it waits, the existing *implicit* policy is overtly in effect. A board can delay changing a policy but it cannot delay having one.

Executive action continues whether or not the values and perspectives on which it is based are stated. If those actions are consonant with a previously stated board policy, they remain unchanged until the board alters the policy. If the board does not mind that, then a delay causes no harm. If, however, the board is not happy with certain actions even though they are consonant with the old policy, a delay merely prolongs the period in which such actions must be deemed acceptable. In such cases, the board may adopt a tentative policy that approximates a "final" board position. Although this policy may change soon, it is official.

I have many times led boards through a rapid policy development exercise, a process demonstrated in a forthcoming book (Carver and Carver, 1997). These policies need no more subsequent revision than policies that have taken much longer to develop. In fact, policies formulated after months of work are, in some ways, worse. Boards are reluctant to alter policies that take so long to develop! So the more quickly developed policies are just as good and, as it turns out, more flexible. Once board members grasp the idea of policies as values and perspectives, they are able to turn their worries and intentions into governing documents with little difficulty.

Rubber-Stamping Responsibly

It is hard to find champions for rubber-stamping. It enjoys de facto popularity while enduring rhetorical derision. Rubber-stamping is the relatively automatic approval of another's plan or performance. Exactly what that means, however, is not as clear as it might appear at first.

For example, if a board believes that whom department directors hire as their secretaries is staff business, it follows that the board should not be involved in the hiring. Most persons would not consider such delegation as rubber-stamping. If for some external reason—let us say the law requires it—employment of secretaries must be sanctioned by the board, then it follows that the board will be asked to approve a hiring decision. What if the board feels as it did before? Would the board now be rubber-stamping if it approved the new hires without debate and, in fact, without even reading the names? Most persons would call this rubber-stamping. But the same degree of governance responsibility was exercised in each scenario.

Even good delegation appears to be rubber-stamping when a delegated action passes across the agenda. School board agendas would shrink if the boards were to delegate sensibly. Antiquated, ill-devised laws and tradition *require* that unnecessary items be on the agenda. Because those items are on the agenda, school boards feel compelled to probe, study, and publicly comment on a great deal of trivia, even though doing so makes no managerial sense. Not to do so would subject them to charges of rubber-stamping.

When board members have an uncomfortable feeling that they are rubber-stamping, they dig in and study the offending issue, ask questions, and stimulate discussion. Such behavior is conscientious and is often the wise response. But not always. Sometimes, the more effective, system-improving response would be to question why the issue is on the board agenda. Certain items on the agenda *should be rubber-stamped* because the right to make the decision in question ought to be the CEO's. The telling question is how a CEO decision gets on the agenda in the first place.

Tradition and Law

Tradition brings personnel procedures, budgets, plans, and program designs to the board for approval in most organizations. For some organizations, the list extends to hiring, job descriptions, organizational design, and even more mundane matters. These practices are often demanded by accrediting bodies because these bodies are merely following tradition themselves. Some states require that boards of agencies funded by state money approve all payment vouchers. Local governmental boards, such as city councils, county supervisors, and school boards, must conduct extensive reviews of staff operations. Both tradition and law embody a "meat-ax" approach to accountability: to ensure order, virtually all staff activity must be passed before the board to be belabored and blessed, even when the activity has already occurred! This myopic version of accountability justifies disproportionate attention to fiscal and legal jeopardies over program outputs. It serves accountants and attorneys who would avoid jeopardy far more than it serves dreamers, creators, and leaders who would add value to the world. This kind of accountability sways boards into spending more time looking over their shoulders than toward the horizon.

Mindless rubber-stamping of true board prerogatives is a dereliction of duty. Rubber-stamping of decisions that should have been management prerogatives is not. What are management prerogatives? They are *whatever* means the CEO chooses in order to accomplish board-dictated Ends that are *within board-dictated Executive Limitations.* If the CEO is within these boundaries, then what reason would the board have for not approving? Disapproval would mean that the board had not seriously constructed its boundaries in the first place. On the other hand, if disapproval is *not* seriously considered, why is board time needed for approval?

When board approval is imposed externally, the board is justified in *intentional* rubber-stamping. That is, it can go ahead and approve as it is required to do ("rubber-stamp") and move on. *If the board has truly done its homework* and is fully convinced that its responsibility has been faithfully discharged, it need not take the approval seriously, only as a matter of empty formality, for empty formality is exactly what it is.

This tactic is similar to the "consent agenda" that many public boards use to speed routine items. It differs in two ways: in its origin and in the mechanics and meaning of removing items. Conventional consent agendas are intended to isolate routine, noncontroversial actions so that less board time is consumed. The consent agenda suggested here has nothing to do with the controversality of an issue or with its routineness. It concerns prior delegation and might more accurately be termed an *automatic approval agenda.*

Issues placed on the CEO's automatic approval agenda are among the many decisions that the board has already determined are in the CEO's domain. They may not be routine and they may be controversial, but *they are not board decisions.* Unlike conventional consent agenda items, these items may not be moved from the special agenda to the regular agenda by a single board member's request. They are on the automatic approval list not to save time but because the board has made a conscious decision that these items not come to the board at all. They have shown up as board business only because some authority to whom the board is beholden said they must. Therefore, no single board member can have the right to *un*delegate the matter, that is, to have the item moved from the special to the regular agenda. The board as a whole, of course, does have that right.

Finally, a word about rubber-stamping done to coddle executive indecisiveness. There are CEOs who do not want the responsibility of decision making. To such CEOs, a tradition that transfers their responsibility to the board is quite comforting. They enjoy hiding behind "the board's decision." Boards collude with these CEOs, thinking that it is kindhearted to let them off the hook on "hot" decisions. It is sloppy management design to differentiate board and CEO decisions on the basis of the CEO's preference. This practice contributes to diffusion of roles rather than to clarity. If the CEO does not or cannot make decisions, the board has good reason to question whether it has the right CEO. As a rule, the board need never make a decision solely because the CEO does not want to make it. When the CEO is not both enabled and *expected* to make CEO decisions, the board is wasting a powerful tool and much of its own valuable time.

Planning the Agenda

Boards must continually struggle with agenda content: "What do we *have to do* this month?" There is an element of passivity in this statement, a hint that boards will put on the agenda whatever the exigencies of their worlds put there for them. The spokesperson for those pressing circumstances is most often the CEO. And, as some hapless boards have discovered too late, he or she who can be oracle for the gods assumes a commanding position even without malevolent intentions.

It is common for boards to defer to their CEOs on agenda sequence and content. To the extent that a board is needlessly entangled in staff practices, it is compelled to get its signals from persons intimately familiar with staff issues and timetables. Boards become so dependent on their staffs to fill agendas that many would find themselves adrift without such guidance. "Of course," they say, "our CEO provides most of our agenda content, because she or he is the one *who knows what is going on around here*." The problem is circular: boards are trapped in staff-level issues and, therefore, need staff input as to what those issues are. Staff members are called on to generate board agenda and, therefore, board agendas are composed chiefly of staff-level material. Through these actions, the board job is thereby defined as a reviewer of staff material, not a creator of board material. In fact "board material" traditionally comes to consist largely of staff material to be reviewed. In these circumstances, board and staff lose sight of just what a board issue looks like.

Tying Agendas to the Long Term

Boards are often subject to a zigzag phenomenon in agenda content. Without staff guidance the problem is usually worse. More than we would like to admit, agendas are developed around rituals, reactions to immediate stressors, and last-minute approvals for external consumption. Suppose a board has carefully eliminated business it does not need to do. It will have disposed of meaningless actions and will have sufficiently empowered the CEO to save it from staff decisions. Yet it is still faced with the concrete, real-time problem of this month's agenda. The board cannot then fall back and have the staff supply enough items to keep it busy. The leaders cannot ask the followers to tell them what their job is.

Board work need not come to a screeching halt. When confronted with an ambiguous or bewildering task, we need only retire to the next higher level of thought to get our bearings. If we lose our way on wooded paths, we can reestablish confidence by hovering over the forest for a few moments. What we cannot do physically, we can do mentally. The board needs to hover a while, to shift its attention from the immediate agenda to the year's agenda and, if that is insufficient, to the perpetual agenda. This is what wise chairpersons do when, in the midst of confusion, they suggest looking at "the big picture."

The perpetual agenda comprises the basic board job contributions and any optional ones the board has added. These outputs belong to the board; they are not merely a summation of staff work. This perpetual agenda was discussed in Chapter Seven as a board job description. To gain control over its own agenda (so that the outcome will truly be *the board's* agenda), the board must begin with the nature of governance itself. What does this board exist to contribute?

Remember that the unique and continuing contributions of the board—its perpetual agenda—include (1) linkage with ownership, (2) explicit governing policies, and (3) assurance of executive performance. A board looking for a starting place would do well to begin with the second contribution—creating all four policy categories. Linkage with the ownership occurs only after the board has established and expressed—in a Board Process policy—who the ownership is and how the connection will be made. Executive performance cannot be ensured before Ends, Board-Executive Relationship, and Executive Limitations policies are established, as these policies contain the delegation, monitoring, and performance criteria.

In short, the board should get its policies in order before undertaking any other task. With a perpetual agenda, the board has a starting place from which it can plan major board work in the immediate future. Hence, the perpetual agenda leads to a more specific, time-framed agenda that is neither long term nor near term. The most useful time segment for planning board meeting agendas is often about one year.

The board establishes objectives for the ensuing year within each of its responsibility areas. The board might determine to forge a dialogue with other boards or to enhance communication with its ownership through public or private media. It might improve policy integrity through more systematic inclusion of financial experts or dissenting programmatic viewpoints. It can upgrade its assurance of executive performance by making the monitoring system more rigorous or less costly. If the board has adopted other contribution areas, such as securing philanthropic funds, it can set objectives for these responsibilities.

Establishing board objectives for the midterm, then, yields a sequence of single-meeting agendas and between-meeting work. Weekly, monthly, or quarterly meetings are thus integrally derived from the larger process. Officer or committee expectations are drawn from the same schedule. Note that the board's annual establishment of the agenda, although open to staff input, *is not staff-dependent*. Because of this, the board is able to move two steps forward in terms of taking responsibility: not only does it produce "answers" without executive ventriloquism, but the board generates the questions as well and, hence, exhibits a significantly greater level of leadership.

This approach to agenda setting makes three major contributions to rational board process. First, it avoids the zigzag agendas set from meeting to meeting. Second, the board is in greater control of its own agenda and less dependent on its CEO to tell it what to do each time. Third, the rightfully dominant board concern with Ends is less likely to be lost in a sea of lesser issues.

Using Ends to Justify the Meetings

I have found that policies in all categories except Ends are rather stable. Mission—the broadest, most inclusive Ends policy—may hold relatively still, but further explication of beneficiaries and benefits seems to change enough to require continual attention. This should not be surprising. In a business for profit, constant awareness of customers and products is the key to success. The late 1980s explosion of concern over quality relates chiefly to a continual, systematic obsession with *customers'* requirements, a parallel to the nonprofit and public duty concerning Ends.

For the public or nonprofit board, one eye should be on customer-equivalents and one on ownership. In other words, one outcome of a good governance system is that the governors are free to concentrate on the mission and on those in whose behalf the mission is pursued. Relative value stability in other policy areas and the strategic importance of Ends lead the board to work on two compelling concerns each year: (1) "How can we connect with even more integrity with those on whose behalf we serve?" and (2) "Given new information, new wisdom, or new possibilities, what good for which people at what cost should we strive to do in the years ahead?" In other words, the majority of board energy is expended on the first element of its job (linkage with ownership) and the first part of the second element (explicit governing policies concerning Ends).

Although improvement in ownership linkage need not be constrained by specific time periods, specifying Ends is subsequently tied to time-sensitive staff actions such as writing budgets and planning programs. It is therefore subject to more "punctuations" in the flow of time. As the board's Ends work is strongly tied to these administrative time lines, for most boards *the annual agenda is best constructed around a yearly cycle of exploring and restating Ends policies.*

The board selects an external event to which the organization directs itself. For some, this is the budget submission date of the major funder. For others, it may merely be the annual meeting of the membership, the start of a fiscal year, or the completion of an election cycle. In any event, the date selected is when executive planning must either go into effect or be publicly announced.

To give the CEO ample time to prepare for that deadline, the board's annual update of all Ends policies is set two or three months earlier. To update, the board restudies its mission and all subsidiary Ends policies in light of new information and possibly new dreams. Then, working backward from the due date, the board calculates a year of agendas to lead it to that point. It uses the same technique to establish completion dates for committee tasks, should the use of committees be needed. Other board needs can and are considered, but the central organizing factor is the never-ending focus on mission and other Ends policies.

The board plans its dialogue with other representatives of the ownership (other boards, councils, and commissions), examines its assumptions about environmental factors, and structures discussion of the implications with the CEO and other staff. The board may entertain speakers on competing viewpoints or on the division of social labor among the various agencies in the area. Board-to-board dialogue and other work designed to enlighten vision may take more time than the board has. Or, too much leadership influence may be needed to bring other boards along. At any rate, the work is sufficient that in the first year a board will not accomplish all these steps. Several annual cycles are required before the board comes near its potential in visionary leadership.

Board members cannot go through this process, particularly early on, without stumbling. But it is ever so much more defensible to stumble over mountains than over curbs. The leadership involved in persuading boards to converse seriously about the effects they are seeking for their beneficiaries is a breakthrough itself. Even small successes are a giant leap from poring over budget lines or probing into sick leave procedures.

After the annual changes or reconfirmation of the Ends policies, the CEO begins to plan. The CEO embodies the first year's portion of the board's longer-range vision in a programmatic plan and budget. In doing so, the CEO must adhere to all other applicable board policies as well. The board is not responsible for this balancing act; the CEO is. Except for its normal monitoring, the board's annual work is completed when it reconfirms the Ends policies.

In summary, the board begins to gain control over its agenda when it accepts total responsibility for the agenda. Individual meeting agendas are derived from the larger picture of the board's goals for the midterm—say, one year. These midterm goals are derived from the board's perpetual agenda. The board governs by plan instead of shooting from the hip, thus avoiding the floundering that invites a rescue by its CEO. The board moves further away from a short-term mentality by tying everything to the long-term challenge. Board time is to be spent largely on creating the future, even beyond the two-thirds proportion argued by Mueller (1974). The regular agenda is designed to develop strategic vision, not by inserting an orphan agenda item (or even a retreat) on strategic planning, but by being formed around and infused by a long-range mentality.

Getting Started

The first year's agenda involves a great deal of start-up activity. For example, no matter how long an organization has been in existence, its board may well find that few true policies exist. Most "policies" are either staff documents improperly elevated to governance status or actual policies generated out of staff, not board, values. Moreover, the board will likely have conceived of its job as a collection of traditional activities rather than outputs. It is important to recognize the magnitude of change in concepts and behaviors needed before a board embarks on the path to Policy Governance.

Gaining Commitment

The first step is to gain board members' commitment to strive toward the new model. This involves discussing the model itself and the changes that it portends. It is important to include the CEO in the process and, as far as possible, to optimize all variables that will affect the board's subsequent success (Carver, 1984a). When the decision to pursue Policy Governance is made, it should be captured in Board Process policies, similar to, perhaps, the "Governing Style" and "Board Job Contributions" policies shown in Chapter Seven (Exhibits 7.2 and 7.5, respectively).

As pivotal an act as this massive alteration of roles and rules will be, as much consensus as possible is in order. The board will be leading in a new order, inviting all the hurdles and detractors Machiavelli warned of. This decision, like all policy decisions, should not be delayed until full agreement is reached. Practices of the past need not cast the deciding vote. Moreover, board discussion should lead not only to a choice as firm as if it had been unanimous, but to a clear understanding that *all* members are obligated to help make the resultant choice successful.

Establishing a Sequence

In most cases, the board should write policy before either linking with ownership connections or ensuring CEO performance. These latter tasks are better defined when the policies are established.

A board may wish to review all its old policies to see what it can translate into the new format, but this course of action is greatly discouraged. Except in very rare cases, the resulting material takes more time to organize and results in a poorer product than if the board had started from scratch. It is at this stage that boards come to realize how inadequate traditional policymaking is, even when done well. The confounding of means prescriptions, activities, results, high- and low-level values, single-event (nonpolicy) decisions, and violations of good delegation principles in previous documents often constitute a Gordian knot.

In building policies from scratch, the board should proceed according to the principles given in Chapter Three and illustrated in Chapter Nine; they should start "thin" in all categories and then carefully expand. In expanding into narrower policies, many boards find that the best sequence is Executive Limitations, Board Process, Board-Executive Relationship, then Ends. Policies are to be developed by the whole board, not by a committee. If the latter method is necessary, the committee must have the board's mandate and must keep the board informed with respect to the process.

Implementing the Plan

What are the broadest statements for the four categories? These constitute the board's "starter set" on which all remaining policy is expanded. The following examples differ in exact wording from those shown in Chapter Nine, but they are—and this is the important factor—model consistent:

Ends	The purpose is stable employment in our community, achieved at an efficiency normal in the industry.
Executive Limitations	The executive director may allow no practices or circumstances that violate commonly accepted business and professional ethics or common business prudence.
Board-Executive Relationship	The board will relate officially to staff only through the executive director. The executive director is accountable for the entire organization's attainment of Ends and compliance with Executive Limitations.
Board Process	On behalf of the total community, the board will govern with one voice through written policies with an emphasis on long-term Ends.

As simple as these statements seem, formulating them involves some struggle. To decide the meaning of "stable employment," for example, the board would have had to discard "broad base of employers," "high personal income," and other alternatives. They may even have gone a round or two over "community" versus "town" or "county" or "region." They should have compared their optional missions with others in the community. How does their mission relate to the mission of the Chamber of Commerce or the goals of the city planning department?

Expanding the Policies

Following the sequence recommended earlier, the board returns to Executive Limitations and generates "worry areas." Each worry area evolves into a policy topic, as discussed in Chapter Five. These negative policies are dealt with first, to eliminate the board's anxieties. If its worries about budgets, financial condition, risk, and personnel can be relieved, the board can relax and attend to building the future.

Next, the board works more on its own process. Remember that self-examination is where this process began, culminating in one or two policies. Now the board checks back to make this category complete. The reason for isolating part of Board Process earlier was simply to get the sequence started. Now the board can deliberate the remaining topics that deal with its methods of governing. Then it will be prepared to establish the ground rules of delegation and CEO functions by creating the Board-Executive Relationship policies.

Last in this start-up sequence, the board comes to Ends policies. It might seem that the board should deal with Ends first, and, in a new organization, that would be best. But in organizations that are already operating, Ends may be dealt with last for four reasons. First, Ends are the most important policies and the board will now have considerable experience, having "practiced" on the others. Second, the other policies not only prescribe the board's role with respect to Ends, but go far to remove impediments that block the board's attention to Ends issues. Third, the *implicit* Ends remain in place until the board confirms or changes them with written Ends; the organization is already aimed somewhere. Fourth, when the board arrives at the Ends challenge, it stays there forever. Ends work constitutes the bulk of the board's perpetual engagement.

Managing the Transition

The process just described takes from several months to a year or longer, depending on the board's commitment, agility, fear, and reluctance to make the necessary changes. If the board is professionally guided, all the foregoing policies except Ends can be developed in one or two meetings. When national organizations with far-flung board members use a special task force for initial policy writing, it ordinarily takes longer. On the other extreme, a community organization with a relatively agile board can finish in six hours. Adjusting previous board and CEO patterns of behavior takes longer. When this initiation process is complete, the board begins to establish the annual planning cycle, as already discussed in this chapter.

During the transition, it is important to balance the need to maintain momentum with the need for the entire board's involvement and understanding. The longer the transition takes, the more likely it is that the changeover will not be completed, for the old ways pull hard. Staff can play an important role while the board retrains itself. The CEO should take care not to bring the board material that is inappropriate for its new role. Furthermore, the CEO must actually use the power the board delegates. With the new policies in place, monitoring under the new regimen should start immediately, both to quell board worries and to convince board and CEO that the board stands behind its new rules.

At this point, boards usually have to struggle to remain focused on criteria rather than reports. It is easier to think about familiar reports (balance sheets, overdue accounts list) than the criteria for which disclosure data are to be received. During the transition, boards often experience something like withdrawal symptoms from giving up their old traditional role. Accustomed more or less to flying by the seat of their pants, boards must learn in this early period to be comfortable with more sophisticated systems. A jumbo jet cannot be flown using the cockpit technology of a crop duster.

E Pluribus Unum

Whatever the agenda content, the central interpersonal challenge to the board is to convert divergent views into a single official view.

It is as important for the board to have multiple minds as for it to have a single voice. To weaken the multiplicity of viewpoints would be to rob the board of its richness of wisdom. To weaken the unity of voice would be to rob the board of its opportunity for effectiveness. On any issue, the board must elicit as much divergence as possible and resolve it into a single position.

Pursuing *Pluribus*

Divergence occurs without prompting in many boards. In others, members must be given explicit permission, perhaps overt stimulation, to diverge. Whether an immediate need for disagreement exists or not, all boards should discuss and adopt a policy that fosters and manages diversity. The discussion and the resultant policy help ensure that social rewards operate in support of diversity. Are dissenters looked upon askance? Is it socially safe to disagree? The chair should assertively pursue differing viewpoints. The behavioral message is that disagreement not only is tolerated but also is necessary to the health of the process. Furthermore, a board can reach outside to seek opposing viewpoints. The board should be so eager to widen its lens that it imports adversaries to invigorate the process!

The board is thus perceived as a forum of churning debate and exposure, an exciting place. This debate and exposure, of course, must concern the big questions rather than the small ones, the results rather than the methods. This is definitely not staff work, though staff members will undoubtedly have ideas to contribute. In fact, involving both board and staff here causes no problem. As long as roles are clearly defined, the board can invite staff to join in the fun. The board is not being pulled downward to staff-level concerns; rather, the staff members are stretched upward to board-level concerns, though as guests in the process, not as its masters. As thinking, caring human beings, staff members have much to contribute to the dialogue, and everyone profits by their being invited to do so.

Pursuing diversity has implications for the practice of CEO recommendations. As already discussed, most nonprofit and many public boards unquestioningly use CEO recommendations as a point of departure for board action. In fact, boards often do not "depart" very far from this starting place. In the approach presented here, the CEO is a participant and may well include staff in the process. But he or she does so to provide a variety of viewpoints, not to support some prepackaged CEO recommendation. Staff input to the governance process does not need to be homogenized by the CEO if the input is about appropriate board issues. When the board does its job and allows and requires the CEO to do his or her job, exciting opportunities for "bigness" open up.

Ultimately Reaching *Unum*

Where do we go with all this richness? It is used chiefly to increase awareness, to decrease smallness (choosing furniture just does not have the same allure anymore for board members), to reveal new ways of looking at the world, and to sharpen the issues. This richness helps boards pose new, more penetrating questions. It guarantees that boards will henceforth operate a step ahead of staff, rather than a dependent step behind. Boards stop trying to be the *final authority* and become instead the *initial authority*.

This healthy, provocative divergence still must be reduced to a single official position. Disagreement is best resolved from the conceptual top down. In other words, the board should elicit agreement first on the broadest position.

For example, it would be much easier to get a majority to support "Human beings deserve a high quality of life" than "Business should be allowed to fail in that more efficient economies increase overall quality of life." The larger the question, the more likely that differences can be resolved. This is one reason the policymaking process suggested here starts with the broadest application. It is not that the broadest level is without controversy, but that (1) it must be resolved, in any event, before the board deals with subsidiary issues, and (2) it probably will be associated with fewer wide swings in value.

Note that this approach requires the articulation of policy parts discussed in Chapter Three. That is, the board should not debate a page of monolithically constructed mission and priorities. It should debate the very brief mission first, then the next level of issues, then the next. Running them all together makes wise translation from diversity almost impossible. Even in single-policy statements, there can exist at least a couple of levels, the first represented in the preamble and the others in the body of the policy. Should the amount of diversity require it, the board can resolve the preamble level first, and then work on the parts one at a time. This process is only slightly slower and it is a far more accurate way of turning board values and perspectives into hard copy. Furthermore, policies produced in this highly articulated (almost outline) form are easier to modify later through amendments. Remember that the implications of the various policy alternatives will have been sought, so the board is not simply flying by the seat of its passionately held opinions.

Making the policy decision, in the final analysis, means taking a vote and declaring a position. Consensus, if honestly achieved, is certainly workable, but requiring a consensus before taking action is a prescription for either mediocrity or dishonesty. Koontz (1967) felt that the tradition of unanimity poses a major danger to board effectiveness wherein vociferous members can "tyrannize the majority" (p. 54). When the vote is taken, the official pronouncement is as firm as if there had been no disagreement at all. Healthy governance requires that board members agree up front that any position resulting from a fair process is, *and of right should be,* the position of the board. This agreement on process is embodied as a policy in the Board Process category. Individual freedom of opinion, however, need not be sacrificed. There is no reason the members of a board should pretend they agree on content after the vote when they did not before. But they should agree on and support procedural integrity. Supporting the process only when one wins the vote is not supporting the process.

In fact, recurring unanimous votes are suspect. All persons on a board may agree on a given issue. But if the voting record of a board is regularly or predominantly one of unanimous votes, we must question whether dissent is being squelched or if the issues are simply not important enough to disagree about. Either possibility calls for examining board process. Brian O'Connell, executive director of INDEPENDENT SECTOR, contends that boards try too hard for harmony and compromise. He welcomes occasional split votes, finding it better to have split votes, even charged debate, than to water everything down so it is mush that offends nobody but about which nobody gets very excited either (personal communication).

Collecting Board Wisdom

Nonprofit and public boards are not good specimens of institutional memory. Some board members have a long memory of the organization's traditions and evolution. Some long-term staff members carry similar memories. But the board as a body may have a hard time remembering deliberations of only a few years ago. Staffs often wonder if such an entity as a "board" exists, except in the most ephemeral way.

Turnover has much to do with this, but there is more to it. I have seen boards behave as if they did not have responsibility for previous board positions. The board as an organizational position goes on, regardless of individual turnover. An individual person becomes, upon induction, a part of a body that has existed for some time. The body's obligations and commitments do not change just because the new person joined. The new member mounts a moving train, not one that leaves the station just as the last passenger gets on board.

Turnover and short memory are good reasons to use an explicit, brief policymaking approach. With succinct policies, the board's values and perspectives are accessible, allowing new members to catch up more quickly. They know what their board stands for and with which of its positions they disagree. They "get on board" more quickly because they are not befuddled for two years before understanding what is going on. Institutional memory may still be foggy, but the accumulated value positions are not. Board values and perspectives at their current state of evolution can be found in a few pages. The vessel for better institutional memory is in place.

When explicit policies have been produced over a long period, an organizational "value history" is retrievable from the sequence of amendments. As opposed to sequences of events and personalities (the "story" history), value histories trace shifts in the organization's values and perspectives over time. This type of documentation provides a sense of history without perforce binding anyone to tradition.

Consider the collection of values and perspectives in everyday situations. In the conduct of board meetings, a great deal is said but not seized. I see little to recommend the standard narrative minutes with all their detail, but I do commend the practice of capturing apparent consensus, majority feelings, or unresolved conflicts as they emerge randomly in discussion. Much wisdom is often expressed and has no place to go. Unless the comments are directly related to a policy under consideration at that moment, spontaneous board sentiments are lost.

I once consulted with an elected public board that "developed" most of a policy on the disposal of surplus real estate while they bantered during a break. They did not realize they had set forth the elements of a useful policy until I showed them my notes on the informal discussion. Such gems can be collected through a simple mechanism that does not detract from the topic at hand. The board secretary might persuade certain members to stay alert for such commentary. These positions can simply be noted for later review, for further focusing, and perhaps for consideration as policy or change in existing policy.

If several board members are frightened by a news report of another agency's bad fortune and express their fear during a board meeting, what should be done? The board goes to the policy manual. Does policy address the worry? If not, how can it be made to do so? If policy does address the worry, is the monitoring system working? If it is working, does it assess performance closely enough or frequently enough to allow the board to relax? This step-by-step sequence not only diminishes board anxiety but results in a stronger policy position. Jacqueline Jackson, of Palo Alto, California, calls this the "heartburn strategy: I determine what's bothering me, see if the policy covers it, put it in writing" (personal communication). When resolving the problem, the board must remain *focused on the policies.*

With a well-designed system, the board that takes care of its policies finds that the policies take care of it. Truly, *making* the policy system work is the way to make a board work. If worries are not dealt with forthrightly and in the self-correcting manner just narrated, they destroy the system, bottleneck board and staff, and crowd out time already critically short for mission development. Handled well, worries provide an opportunity to reconfirm that the system works and that expressing fears is a healthy part of the process.

The Character of Meetings

Let us consider how this process looks and feels. Perhaps the most obvious characteristic of this process is a short agenda. Instead of facing a plethora of issues, the board encounters a much shorter, though deeper, list. The board comes to see a lengthy agenda as a sign that something is wrong. Board time is treated as a non-renewable resource; it must be used with care and made to count.

Attendance is high. Board meetings are not considered optional. Members attend because the meetings are interesting and they feel that they can *accomplish something*. There is an atmosphere of bigness and acceptance of diversity; the board is a forum to embrace diversity more than to homogenize it. Yet there also exists a businesslike awareness that the board is a deciding body, not a debating society. Meetings are worth board members' time. The members may have less exposure to interesting staff operations, but this loss is more than replaced by the active stream of contacts and issues generated from the ownership. At the forefront of the board's mentality is whether the dream is big enough, focused enough, visionary enough. There is a refreshing conception of the board as part of a family of boards that form an inspiring stratum of leaders. Agendas and discussions increasingly reflect that the organization and its mission are integral to the larger context. In short, the board *lives* strategic leadership.

Next Chapter

The essentials of Policy Governance have now been covered. The final chapter provides both challenges and counsel for attaining and maintaining successful strategic leadership in the governing board. Six strategies are presented; the first five are old friends to us all, but are couched in principles of the new governance. Let us consider, finally, strategies for board leadership.

Chapter Eleven

Redefining Excellence in Governance
Strategies for Board Leadership

In this final chapter, I synthesize more than summarize. The following six strategies cut across various aspects of the Policy Governance model and challenge board members to move from paradigm to performance.

Be *Obsessed* with Effects for People

It seems obvious that the board's primary concern should be the benefits for people. But in the usual routine, programs, projects, activities, and methods demand so much attention that boards virtually neglect the benefits for people that justify the organization's existence in the first place! The never-ending struggle with organizational Ends, according to Richard J. Peckham, formerly of the Kansas State Board of Education, "ought to consume us" (personal communication).

Don't Ponder Ends, Attack Them

"Passion, commitment, and fire for what we are doing must start at this table," pleads Donna Chavez, commissioner for the park district in Naperville, Illinois (personal communication). Being obsessed with Ends demands that the board tackle the difficult questions by mobilizing board time, mechanics, and concern around what good is to be done for which people at what cost (Carver, 1992d, 1996c). The board cannot forget these questions, even for one meeting.

All other policy categories are easy compared to this one; they are more quickly resolved and stable for longer periods. Adequate development of Ends requires a long-term commitment. The board will forever be involved with Ends issues; the struggle is never completed.

The rigorous focus of this process opens up new insights into what the proper Ends should be. To make Ends policies about poverty in a community action agency, the board is forced to develop a new understanding of the nature and perpetuation of poverty. To make Ends policies for a public school system, the board must become more sophisticated about the skills needed for personal and social success in the world to come. To make Ends policies for a Third World development agency, the board must learn about the nuances of development and underdevelopment. A board that recognizes that such learning is going to occur will not behave as if only the answers evolve. The protocols of debate must enable deliberation of the questions as well as the answers. New questions will emerge over time and transform the degree and substance of the wisdom itself.

Moving mountains an inch often appears less active than moving molehills a mile. Boards who would be strategic leaders must move at a more deliberate pace than their staffs, but with issues far more momentous.

Keep the Mission Out in Front

As powerful as a good mission statement is, its predominance is a fragile commodity. It is easily transformed from a compelling authority into mere words and, ultimately, becomes hard to locate and impossible to remember. Purely mechanical practices, such as printing the mission on all correspondence, on the reverse of members' name plates, and on the front of the policy manual, can help.

Brian O'Connell (1985) called for keeping the dream alive in board meetings. The leadership must keep the dream out in front so members always see the relationship of mundane things like budgets and audits in the context of the "glorious outcomes" that the board members have convened to achieve.

Testing everything against mission becomes the standard check of organizational direction. This mentality is best achieved when every board meeting has some mission-relevant conversation. No board meeting should go by without a debate or presentation on some facet of the Ends development process. The central reason for meeting at all is the mission and mission-derived Ends policies.

Invigorate the Ends Debate

There is no more exciting topic than Ends. An Ends dialogue that is boring should be considered a symptom of poorly designed Ends work. Atrophy is easily avoided (Carver, 1996f). A quick solution is no further away than the staff. Even a small staff will harbor divergent, enthusiastically held ideas about the priority of outcomes. Encourage staff to develop arguments for competing viewpoints. Invite them to be passionate rather than coldly analytical.

Beyond the staff are even more sources of divergence. Some constituents do not believe your organization should exist at all. Listen to them. If your organization is in the public eye, there will doubtless be factions that think your priorities are all wrong. These factions do not agree with each other. Much can be gained from their debate. Rather than avoiding dispute, elicit it. The board should be the forum for public debate in its chosen area. It is, as the Rhode Island Board of Regents agreed to be, the "boiling cauldron" of whatever controversy is afoot.

Of course, none of these invigorating avenues is available if the board neglects to foster acceptance of diversity within its own membership. The board must value, even crave disagreement within its ranks if it expects to be comfortable with the lively dissent outside. A board that believes it must vote as a block in order for its pronouncements to carry weight fails to signal that its one voice *always* grows from and in spite of diversity. Strategic leadership is big enough to embrace diversity and wise enough to be enriched by it.

Divergence is not the only source of richness in the Ends dialogue. Much of the vigor comes from allowing leaders to dream. In the short term, there is scant place for dreaming, for one must choose between being taken seriously and being visionary. In the long term, however, leadership cannot afford to overlook the wisdom of dreams, even the wisdom of playful dreaming. Vision that bounds higher than the barriers that confine us often springs from earnest playfulness.

Drive an Ownership Ends Dialogue

The board derives its identity and legitimacy from its ownership. Some ownerships (such as the general public) are broad enough to have trusteeship vested in multiple boards. Board service to the ownership need not be confined to the specific organization being governed. The board may well reach out to other organs of ownership, that is, other boards. In this extended arena, strategic leadership can be of momentous effect. Bringing the Ends dialogue to the community of boards not only provides leadership to the whole, but infuses the organization as well. It is more exciting and farsighted to be part of an exciting and farsighted whole.

It is important that interboard dialogue focus on the results each pursues in the interests of the shared ownership (Carver, 1990a). Organizations commonly meet on more operational issues, an undertaking appropriate for staff. Boards could profit from discourse on their respective missions and the community-related issues they have uncovered in framing missions. Does the sum of their missions accomplish the aggregate outcome that this cross section of leaders would want? Leaders in such an interaction feel a closeness with the abstract ownership that often eludes them in their separate board meetings. Their minds are stretched beyond the familiar home boardroom.

Don't Be Seduced by Cost Control

The quality of organizational results is best served by devoting unswerving attention to greater quality, not to ever more stringent cost control. "An obsession with cost reduction produces narrowness of vision. . . . It actually hurts as much as helps," argues Skinner (1986). Crosby (1979, 1984) and Deming (1986) forcefully maintain that costs will decrease when quality increases, although focusing on the reduction of costs does not increase quality. The concept of quality used by these authors concerns fulfilling customer requirements with minimal waste, rather unlike the means-oriented professional use of the word *quality* typical in many nonprofit and public agencies.

Dare to Be Bigger Than Yourself

Demand daring. Bring the bigness of this invigorated debate into the boardroom. It need never be small again, for there will be neither time nor toleration for smallness. Conscious strategy is necessary because it is so easy to be more aware of the immediate and near at hand than the unbounded, distant horizons.

Keep Trusteeship up Front

Trusteeship carries compelling obligations, which are obvious to public boards that operate in the limelight. But not-so-public boards, which operate *as if* in trusteeship for the public, are not always known by that public. As a busy public, we do not run around to oversee those who operate in our name, though many a beleaguered school board or city council may think otherwise. Social service and hospital boards operating as nonprofit, private corporations still see themselves as owned by the public, a public who often forgets that it is owner. For such boards, there is less public pressure, though there is a greater moral challenge. How does a board act as agent for principals who are unaware of the relationship? The board that would respond to its leadership opportunity cannot avoid confronting the problem. If it is to be more than an academic consideration, the nature of trusteeship must be a frequent board topic.

Lead Leaders

With respect to the staff, it is pivotal that the board not only lead, but that it lead leaders. Bigness must be passed on. Leading leaders calls for a mentality that allows others to make decisions. The board should never give the message, by trying to intervene in every potential mistake, that to err is unacceptable. Emphasizing the avoidance of errors rather than the creation of breakthroughs propagates not leaders but followers. It encourages not decision makers, but bureaucrats. Leading leaders requires tolerance of risk, because leaders do not remain in the safe, old ruts. They try and sometimes fail.

One approach is to view governance as *empowerment.* The board passes power to others and expects them to use it as assertively and creatively as they dare. The board will have both the circumspection and the mechanism to empower *toward* something definitive (the impelling criteria of Ends) and to empower *within* something definitive (the boundary criteria of Executive Limitations). The *amount* of risk is thereby controllable. Empowerment is not carte blanche, for delegation need not dissipate into abdication.

Furthermore, the board's ability to keep its own eye on the horizon is prodded by mental bigness in the executive staff. Having leaders work for us is a gift, indeed, for they ally themselves with that which is big in us, save us from distracting side issues, and urge us on toward still greater leadership.

Respect Your Words

If saying what you mean and meaning what you say is difficult for individuals, for a group the task becomes formidable. Boards have a tendency to write words that quickly become disjointed from their authors, as if the speakers and the spoken are unrelated. Some new board members are delayed in getting "up to speed" because it takes time to learn where all the relevant words are to be found and, after locating them, to learn which words mean something and which do not.

One solution is to use fewer words. When a board's verbal product is voluminous, there is no way board members can fully embrace it. It is common for public school board policies to be several centimeters thick. When a board has that many policies, for practical purposes of governing it has no policies at all. It is far better that a board generate few words after much thought than many words after little thought. Part of the problem arises, of course, when the board acts as if it must approve or adopt all staff documents. Most nonprofit boards should get nervous when their total official paperwork increases beyond fifty pages. There is nothing magic in this number and it may not apply to all boards, but the minimalist sentiment is the same in all cases.

The second greatest source of volume is duplication. Stating the same board value or perspective in different places increases the volume. There is less of a need to read carefully because the material will probably be repeated. The words at hand, therefore, lose some importance. Board utterances cast in the format of traditional administrative topics restate or imply the same values repetitively, for relatively few values run across all topics. Perversely, if the values are only implied rather than expressed explicitly, in repetition they may be weakened rather than reinforced. Voluminous words, reliance on inference, inconsistency, or any factor that weakens the clarity of board values in their written form impairs the ability to speak with one voice. A greater volume of board words makes board values less clear.

When the board's policies are explicit, concise, and unrepetitive, it is still necessary to observe them scrupulously. The integrity of board documents, hence the integrity of the board's word, requires that the board never violate its policies nor create conflicting policies. This mandate would seem too obvious to state, but it is regularly ignored. It occurs when the board creates policy and then lays it aside, as if once done it may be forgotten.

Because existing board values can always be found in the single repository of board policies, a board would never consider a new action without relating it to the existing policies. Living closely with the policies enables any interpolicy conflict to be cleared up in the normal course of business. The policies thereby evolve as a consistent expression of board values and perspectives. Not only are they consistent, but they increase in quality, for the monitoring process reveals finer points or new information with which the board can hone its language still further.

Hence, every contemplated board action is pressed against the record of what the board has already said. The compendium of policies will be short and explicit enough for this to be done easily, so the board need not be a collection of librarians and lawyers. To ensure the continuing fidelity and usefulness of these policies over time, the board must constantly use them or it will surely lose them.

Finally, a board's respect for its policy language may be heightened by cosmetics. Board policies, in this model, constitute a document as condensed as it is consequential. Presenting these few policies in a way that reflects their critical importance helps the board keep their importance in perspective. Therefore, the essential governance declarations should not be typed on plain paper or photocopied. Use special printed forms with color, if possible, and the organization's logo. Make them look like the momentous, center-stage statements they are.

Invest in Selection and Training

Performers—human or machine—can perform only up to their capability. That capability can be diminished or improved, so it is a variable that deserves care. The concept of investment is crucial, for the board can choose to see training as a troublesome cost or as an opportunity to reap a return.

Recruit Those Who Will and Can Govern

Raw material makes a difference. If the board is able to select its own new members, it should start with a well-deliberated set of qualifications. If the members are selected by others, the board should enroll appointing authorities to use the board's desired qualifications whenever possible. Aggressive recruiting involves not only selling prospective members on board membership, but excluding those who do not fulfill the requirements.

Entrusting recruitment to a nominating committee can be useful, but integrity is maintained only if the board as a body has decided what types of people it desires. Nominating committees are too often left completely to their own judgment. They cannot help but develop implicit criteria, but rarely develop explicit criteria prior to becoming entangled in the personality-loaded interactions of recruiting. Even if they were to use a distinctly two-step process (a good idea if the board defaults), the board itself will not have been party to this matter that is critical to future board performance.

If the nominating committee has board-stated qualifications in hand (recorded as a Board Process policy), it can render better service. The board should phrase its committee charge (also in the Board Process category) so that finding the right people is given greater priority than filling vacancies. "We don't do a very good job of assessing prospective board members," said Edward Able, executive director of the American Association of Museums. "We tend to do it in the whole nonprofit sector in a very superficial way" (Blumenthal, 1988). Arthur Frantzreb, consultant in McLean, Virginia, claims that the biggest failure is "inappropriate construction of membership—many boards have the wrong people on them" (Blumenthal, 1988). Indeed, boards would do well to tolerate a few more empty seats instead of rushing to fill them. Recruiting would be more diligent if it were made known that membership in this board is an honor. After all, the board is selecting those who will bear the privilege and burden of trusteeship.

What qualifications are important? These vary, of course, but with governance construed as I have designed in this text, a few universal characteristics logically follow. To be sure, members "must be knowledgeable, sophisticated, and politically mature" (McGowan, 1987). To be more specific, we must start with the job to be done, so we begin by consulting the Board Process policies on the board job description and style of governing. Members need to have the understanding, skills, and willingness to contribute to the governance task the board has so carefully set forth (Carver, 1996h). For the degree of strategic leadership championed in these pages, five qualifications, among others, are necessary.

1. *Commitment to the ownership and to the specific mission area.* As agents of the organization's ownership, board members must be committed to that trust. Commitment to the mission is important, though less so, for the mission is largely if not wholly a continuing creation of the board itself. Therefore, fidelity to those in whose name mission is created is more essential than fidelity to the current mission.

2. *Propensity to think in terms of systems and context.* Some people focus quickly on parts. Whatever the relationship of whole to part might be, these persons more readily focus on the part itself for inspection, discussion, and decision. Such persons, with all good intentions, place distractions, if not massive roadblocks, in the way of strategic leadership. Prospective members more comfortable with parts have a valuable gift, but one that can more usefully be shared as a volunteer adviser to staff, not as a board member. The board needs members who are cybernetically aware, drawn naturally to the harmony of the whole.

3. *Ability and eagerness to deal with values, vision, and the long term.*
The members who make the best contributions are those who have
a natural propensity to look not only beyond the stream of single
events, but beyond systems to the values on which they are based.
It is only a small step from divining today's values as they currently
are to planning tomorrow's values as they should be.

4. *Ability to participate assertively in deliberation.* Productive board
deliberation depends on bringing the foregoing characteristics to
the governance struggle. Boards are overly tolerant of members who
fail to share their capacities in a way that enhances the deliberative
process. It is not enough to have the potential to be a good board
member; the potential must be manifested through participation.

5. *Willingness to delegate, to allow others to make decisions.* Board
members, with respect to each other, must be able to share power
in the group process and, with respect to staff, must be able to delegate. Board members who are loath to delegate will impair the
board's leadership by constantly bringing small issues up for consideration. They will impair staff by denying them the opportunity
to grow.

The pithiest counsel for choosing board members may be that
of O'Connell (1985, p. 25), who was "pained to see others pre-
occupied with the buzz word 'expertise.'" If he had to rely on one
characteristic, he "would single out the ability to start and end
every analysis and evaluation with the standard of what is right."
What stronger argument can be made that a board member's
greatest gift to enterprise is educing, weighing, challenging, and,
frequently, fighting over values?

Some prospective members are required to attend board meetings prior to assuming membership. Others are chosen from a
pool of persons already familiar with board operations. These are
useful tactics. At minimum, a board should determine that a
prospective member understands the board's governance model,
bylaws, policies, current condition, and suspending issues. Frankly,
a prospective member who fails to ask about such things is probably not a good candidate. Selection of the most qualified members deserves careful thought and design. "Qualified," as is clear
from the foregoing list, need not refer to academic credentials or
high position. It need not relate to gender, color, or income. It is

more likely to relate to grasp, mentality, connectedness, and commitment. As an assessment of *past* selection, consider this test: if fewer than half the board's members would make good chairpersons, the selection needs improvement.

Prepare New Members

Orienting new members can help institutionalize the board's governance process and prepare new members for immediate participation. Excellence can be lost simply through the influx of new members who have not agonized through the process of improvement. As they bring in their expectations about governance from other settings, they may cause a regression to the norm. Institutionalizing the hard-won process calls for helping new members understand the governance already reached by their colleagues. It is crucial that new members learn the principles of Policy Governance (Carver and Carver, 1996a) as quickly as possible. When this has been done, says Nash Williams, executive director of Southeast Georgia Regional Development Center in Waycross, "new board members can start making meaningful contributions almost immediately." Orientation is important enough to be a mandatory step rather than an optional exercise. The bylaws can require that a new member complete orientation prior to a vote. That members who are ignorant of the organization are regularly given a voice in board decisions is an absurdity that only familiarity can explain.

Part of the problem lies in the word *orientation,* which may smack of learning where the lavatory, the coffee pot, and the desk supplies are located. Adequate preparation to shoulder the burden of strategic leadership requires something a bit more substantial. What is called for is job training, though the term may be offensive to new members who are accomplished in their occupations or in other board service. In any event, proper preparation of new board members requires that they become thoroughly familiar with the process and the current values and perspectives of the board they are joining.

Present board members are the best persons to impart this training. Staff can certainly acquaint new members with operational matters. "Acquaint" is the distinguishing word inasmuch as new members' primary need is not for operational information.

Such information may help members form impressions of the whole and even to ask good, board-relevant questions, but operational information is the domain of management, not of governance. No matter how well this information is presented and learned, it still will not equip the new member with the tools he or she needs to participate constructively in the board process. New member training must be built primarily around preparation for strategic leadership.

Consider Knowledge as an Investment

All jobs require continual updating of skills and refurbishing of understanding. Turnover would perpetuate this need, even if it were capable of being met for all time for a given group of persons. Greater skills and understanding may often be bought without the expenditure of dollars. If dollars are necessary, the outlay is best approached from the standpoint of investment rather than cost; instead of depicting training as an irritating cost, see it as an investment made for its expected return.

Consequently, return-on-investment criteria are applied. Although the return in terms of more effective governance will always be subjective, because quantification is difficult, the idea is the same. Boards would learn that education per se is not the issue; it is education about the *right things*. Moreover, decisions about board skill building would give appropriate consideration not only to the cost of training but, as Ronald P. Myers, a New York management consultant, points out, to the cost of ignorance as well (personal communication).

Surmount the Conventional Wisdom

Until the prevailing understanding of governance changes, leaders must be aware of the deleterious influence of conventional wisdom. Current norms drag down boards that aspire to a higher standard. A board must continually overcome regressive pressures from the general expectations people have of boards, the requirements foisted by funders and authorities, and even the well-intended advice of experts.

Influence of Those Who Expect

When observers see a board behaving atypically, they are surprised, maybe bewildered. Their discomfort with deviation has little to do with whether the departure from the norm is productive. When members of a national association watch their board or members of the public scrutinize an elected board, they may be confused, suspicious, and even angered.

In the public sector, the ownership's commitment to a better system is largely rhetorical. We do not petition our public boards to create more effective systems; we assail them for some small instance of implementation that offends us. So the board that would create a better system will find few committed supporters among the onlookers. A survey of what lobbyists lobby for would indicate what aspects of a system truly command our attention. We pursue "fixes" of the element that concerns us, not more integrity in the process itself.

Rituals and symbols of responsible board behavior have grown over the years. Observers (not to mention board members themselves) have come to expect a responsible board to *look* a certain way: it approves budgets, monthly financial statements, and personnel "policies." It might adopt long-range plans, but these are expected to originate from staff recommendations for board reaction and revision. Observers have come to believe that boards that skip these steps are mere rubber stamps for staff wishes. They have seen occasional excesses and even disasters. So there is every reason to believe that boards who follow the prescribed route are responsible and those who do not are not. A board that forges new symbols does so at its peril. The unmasking of empty symbols rarely receives as much attention as their absence.

Boldness and inclusion are keys to success in overcoming these impediments. Boldness is needed to do anything new against the pressure to conform. Inclusion of all relevant parties in the adventure helps to defuse opposition. In other words, the board can seek to include observers throughout its discussion of governance principles and during its adoption of a new model. Those included might be journalists, advocacy groups, unions, lawmakers, and any other relevant stakeholders.

Influence of Those Who Demand

Those who have power over the board constitute a special class of observers. Funding bodies, regulatory agencies, and lawmakers incorporate the conventional wisdom into their demands. After all, in the development of federal or state regulations, statutory language, association certification, and standards of accreditation, there is little but traditional concepts of governance to guide the authors. Consequently, even vastly improved governance can run afoul of accreditation or law because of the improvements themselves. Mediocrity can pass tests that excellence fails.

It is not uncommon for standard-setting bodies to be very prescriptive about what constitutes "good" governance. National associations might dictate that a local board have a certain set of committees, particular officers, or monthly meetings. Federal legislation and regulations might dictate that grantees meet similar requirements. Hospital accreditation may require the board to go through certain approval procedures. State law requires school boards to take action on a host of personnel and expenditure matters. Houle (1989, p. 93) muses that "many a school board member has wondered whether it is possible to get through a single meeting without becoming an outlaw."

Often, little can be done beyond the consent agenda ploy suggested in Chapter Ten. If possible, a board would be well advised to interact with funders, regulators, and accreditors in a manner that takes the threat to their authority into account as compassionately as possible (Carver, 1994d, 1996j). Sometimes it is possible to maintain a good governance model while giving the controllers what they are looking for, that is, evidence that they are in control and will not be viewed as lax by those who evaluate them. Enrolling them in the board's adventure in governance innovation may be one approach. Another may be to proceed through the ritual behaviors expected, but not to take them seriously (Carver, 1996c). The consent agenda can be a handy device.

Influence of Those Who Help

Vast experience and expertise are available in the literature and from educators and consultants. Competent help can be obtained on strategic planning, financial oversight, fundraising, endowment building, administrative controls, audits, bylaws, corporate restructuring, and on and on. As part of their ongoing education as well as for specific issues that arise, boards should avail themselves of this body of knowledge.

Because expertise is available and helpful formats have been developed within the conventional governance framework, the board must be a wise consumer. Texts, academic courses, and advice from consultants are likely to be topic-specific. The board needs assistance with its *peculiar conceptual segment* of budget, personnel, or planning activities, not with all budget, personnel, or planning activities. The board role can be more easily confused than helped when the board becomes smarter about administrative or programmatic topics in their entirety, because the board can expend itself learning how to do the wrong things better.

The challenge facing boards is to take advantage of accumulated knowledge, yet to reframe that wisdom so that it contributes to better governance within a conceptually useful model, not simply to more information within an impaired model. Some helpers can adapt to this challenge quite well, but boards should not expect adaptation to be either automatic or voluntary. A conceptual struggle might be involved, not to mention a little ego. Staff members, for example, may find that their training advice is not as useful to a board that is fulfilling an appropriate role. Although staff members may have expertise in many areas, governance is not typically one of these areas. To adapt their expertise to what the board needs to learn, staff must have an understanding of advanced governance. That understanding is not so widespread that boards can expect to find it, even in skilled educators and consultants.

Help helpers to be helpful by querying them about competing value issues in the area under discussion. Rather than seeking their recommendation as to what a selected value might be, draw them out on the range of value alternatives available and what they see as implications for options within that range. Implications are not only the predictable consequences but also the "industry averages" with regard to others' experience in making certain choices.

Particularly with regard to developing Executive Limitations policies, helpers can bring a great deal to a board's struggle in setting the ranges within which staff members are allowed to act. They can assist the board in discovering, debating, and deciding what the conditions of jeopardy might be in, say, financial condition or personnel management. On these two topics, accountants and labor lawyers can be extremely enlightening if their counsel is taken in a way that relates to the board's proper role in such matters. Do not expect accountants or attorneys to know the proper board role, for they, too, will be operating from the conventional view. Following the "raw material" advice of an accountant or attorney can, indeed, result in poor governance. The use of consultants has always been an important skill; good consultees are made, not born.

Perpetually Redefine Quality

Just as the board's work on Ends policies is a perpetual task, so is its pursuit of excellence in the governing process itself. The definition of quality never stands still. What constitutes quality governance grows as we do, yet always remains a little beyond our grasp. The constancy of change can be unsettling. Ferguson (1980) said that it is not change itself so much as "that place in between we fear. It's like being between trapezes. It is Linus when his blanket is in the dryer. There is nothing to hold onto."

One solution is to give up the chase and settle for the status quo. A second is to continue the pursuit at the expense of feeling not good enough all along the way. The first trap is always present in human events. The temptation to settle for the norm is strong in public and nonprofit organizations because they are not forced to show results per dollar. The second trap is well known to people who learn fast and continually. They have only to look back a little to see the last thing they did that, in light of the new learning, now looks unwise. Their standards of wisdom and quality move forward, and advancing standards can be an unspoken indictment of the past. Hence, in addition to the direct cost of working toward higher ideals, there is a psychic discomfort that accompanies continual improvement.

View the Past as Inspiration, Not Impediment

Continual improvement may be viewed as harsh treatment of tradition. Organizations with long histories can cherish their past without being beaten into inactivity by it. Organizational history, particularly a value history rather than a narrative history, can serve the purposes of renewal and recommitment by reminding members of what the organization represents. Traditions can even ignite a secular revival if treated as a gift, not a chain from the past. Traditions are not to be discarded, but built upon. Glendora Putnam, Boston, chairperson of the National Board of the YWCA, spoke of her board as "moving ahead against long and revered traditions" (personal communication). When tradition boxes us in and mindlessly determines who we are, it is no longer to be revered but escaped. The board is, after all, creating tomorrow's traditions with the actions it takes today. Leadership compels us to be truer to tomorrow than to yesterday.

Pursue Excellence Rather Than Solving Problems

Commitment to excellence produces change that is more creative than reactive. Institute change to grow closer to an ever receding standard of quality. Such change is not characteristically driven by problems. It is not problem solving as much as it is ideal creating. It aims to fill the gap between what is and what can be, more than it seeks to escape what has been. It is a "solution" of the future rather than the past.

"If it ain't broke, don't fix it" loses its charm as a guiding principle because it delays improvement until it is necessary to move. Imai (1986) points out that if we do not fix the "unbroken," someone else will—with predictable market advantage. Peters (1988, p. 3) has altered the old bromide to, "If it ain't broke, you just haven't looked hard enough." For "broke" is not a property of the thing itself, but of its sufficiency in our ever changing world. What was not broken comes to seem broken simply by virtue of new expectations and new possibilities.

Realize That Good Begets Better

The easiest and best time to improve is when things are already going well. Incorporating better systems is easier when it is not perceived as discipline of an errant member or as initiating a power struggle. When problems are rampant, almost any correction will be personalized. Thus, systematic monitoring of executive performance is best installed when the board and its CEO have a trusting, respectful relationship.

Remember That Excellence Begins in the Boardroom

Boards can be successful strategic leaders if they nurture their group responsibility. That responsibility must be accepted by every board member, not just officers. All members must participate in the discipline and productivity of the group. All members must be willing to challenge and urge each other on to big dreams, lucid values, and fidelity to their trusteeship. All members must cherish diversity as well as an unambiguous, single board position derived from diversity. All members must strive for accountability in the board's job, confident that if quality dwells in the boardroom, the rest of the organization will take care of itself. For in the long run, as surely as excellence ends with clients, patients, students, or other customers, it begins with governance.

"To rule is easy," counseled Goethe, "to govern difficult." The greatest difficulty may lie in shifting from old to new paradigms. "Just as managerial ability is distinct from technical expertise," said Elaine Sternberg in an apt comparison, "so the qualities needed for being a director are not the same as managerial skill" (Sternberg, 1994, p. 228). Successful strategic leadership demands powerful engagement with trusteeship, obsessive concern over results, enthusiastic empowerment of people, bigness in embracing the farsighted view, and the commitment to take a stand for dreams of tomorrow's human condition. Re-creating governance can generate a zestful new genre of strategic leadership in the boardroom, to be sure, but the effects go far beyond. Douglas K. Smith pointed out the compelling occasion to provide leadership through modeling: "When leaders are learning and growing, everything about them communicates the same opportunity to other people. They're excited, they do things differently. One of the most profound—and unusual—experiences people can have on the job is to see their leaders grow" (D. K. Smith, 1996, p. 27).

Varieties of Applications

The model of governance set forth in this book was developed to be generic, applicable no matter where or what boards govern. It is meant to encompass most organizational variations comfortably within a general theory of governance. Adapting the model to profit-based corporations, which have not been the subject of this book, requires only slight modification. Public and nonprofit boards face special circumstances that make adaptation appear—and in rare cases be—difficult.

I have had the opportunity to interact with board members from every populated continent. Naturally, the boards across the world span vast cultural differences, yet the rather fundamental precepts of Policy Governance garner an enthusiastic response. In this continent, for example, I have worked with native North American groups, all of whom found the concepts culturally compatible.

Still, each organization likes to feel that it is different, as each has its own history and personality. It has been said that consultants think all organizations are alike, while organizations think they are all different. Even so, boards would do well to resist focusing prematurely on their peculiarities, and to look first to generic principles of strategic leadership in governance. These principles, rather than detracting from the uniqueness of an organization, make its distinctiveness possible.

So it is that a board must deal with its peculiar conditions by first ignoring them. The peculiarities should be viewed through a framework of general principles. Amazingly, boards often find that they are not so different after all. The real payoff lies in their being able to apply powerful, generic principles even when they are lured away by an illusory atypicality.

"Governance is governance is governance" may not be the whole truth, but it is not a bad place to start. Special circumstances do matter, but to deal with them effectively, a board must have a sound footing in the basics. Here are a few examples of how the generic model applies to special situations. It is not my intent here to address all the varieties of organizations, but only to comment on the applicability of Policy Governance to their board work.

City Councils

Four peculiar conditions apply to city councils: (1) council members are elected individually; (2) councils have police power or coercive authority over a geographic territory (not just over their own staff); (3) councils are tightly regulated by state or provincial law as to powers and methods; and (4) when an independently elected mayor serves statutorily as CEO, the board-CEO structure does not pertain. In these cases, the relationship is more like that of the Congress and president, each having separate powers.

When each member represents a separate constituency, working together for the whole can be difficult. Furthermore, electorates tend to expect officials to attend to the smallest of concerns, rather than the sweeping, momentous ones. City councils have a particularly hard time distinguishing between owner concerns and customer concerns (Carver, 1992i, 1996g). A citizen is more likely to complain about a garbage collection incident or stop sign placement than about the city's long-term maintenance of infrastructure. Police power gives the council authority over third parties, and thus creates a unique area of governance statements beyond the four policy categories of the model, *ordinances,* or, in Canada, *bylaws.* State-prescribed structure and procedures sharply cramp the latitude available in a council's governance and delegation. Moreover, councils resort to hands-on control so frequently that their time is always overcommitted, which severely strains council members. But the greater political consequence, as stated by Ron V. Houser of the City of Grande Prairie, Alberta, is that "Society is often unable to attract the best candidates with the necessary vision and talents to lead . . . due to [the job's having been defined as requiring such exhausting] time and financial sacrifices" (personal communication).

These conditions make it difficult, but not impossible, to apply good governance principles. Condition 4 (an independent CEO) introduces a major difficulty in fully applying the model. Even then, however, a council can use some of the same policymaking principles. In the pure council-manager form, this problem does not arise. With only minor exceptions, then, Policy Governance is applicable.

School Boards

Local boards of public education have one of the most difficult tasks among public and nonprofit bodies. They face four peculiar conditions: (1) individual board members are often elected; (2) school boards are tightly regulated by state or provincial authorities; (3) school boards preside in the public spotlight over an emotional topic; and (4) everyone thinks he or she is an expert because, after all, we all went to school. Condition 1 is similar to the first situation confronting city councils. Condition 2 is so oppressive that school boards misuse *most* of their time in trivial pursuits. Condition 3 intensifies Condition 1 inasmuch as the emotional electorate can be unyielding and irrational. Condition 4 simply makes the job a little more difficult. The generic Policy Governance model, however, is thoroughly applicable.

Boards in State and Provincial Government

Peculiarities range broadly because of the wide variety of statutes establishing and charging such boards. Boards of government departments, depending on the jurisdiction, have greater or lesser control by the governor or other executive authority and greater or lesser independence from other organs of government. They also have various degrees of authority over their respective CEOs and departments. Across these boards, the generic Policy Governance model ranges from largely to totally applicable. What these boards do have in common is their intimate relationship to legislatures and legislation.

When describing such boards' jobs, legislators have a tendency to write enabling statutes that conflate powers, prescribed activities, and outputs. As the conceptual framework used by state boards does not disentangle these managerially distinct concepts, much leadership potential is wasted. There often appears to be a subtle legislative intent that the board not truly govern, but just as often the problem is simply an instance of naive design. An example of poor design is the Georgia State Board of Education. The board has various approval authorities over the state superintendent and the Georgia Department of Education, yet the superintendent is an independently elected official. It is no wonder that vehement conflicts arise with such a foolish arrangement.

According to B. Christmas, as quoted in the *Atlanta Journal-Constitution* (Oct. 3, 1996, p. B4), no matter how much everyone seems to focus on the personality conflicts that flare up, "Unless that is fixed, the same conflicts are going to keep happening over and over." Legislative traditions predate the development of twentieth-century management, so it is no surprise that legislative action often transpires as if principles of modern management never developed.

Foundation Boards

The only peculiarity is that foundation boards (excluding "operating" foundations) give away money rather than run their own programs. Thus, they are like relief agencies, the United Way, the Community Chest, and government funding agencies. The generic model is entirely applicable.

Church Boards

Where the church board is actually the church governing body, the model is totally applicable (Carver and Clemow, 1990; Carver, 1995c). When this is not the case (for example in Catholic parishes), the variety of arrangements makes a single comment difficult. For example, some local church boards are merely advisory to a larger hierarchy, while others are advisory to the clergy, and some are in charge, but only of nontheological aspects of the church. In these latter cases, the generic model is partially applicable.

Hospital Boards

Hospital boards have one peculiarity—the "third power" relationship with physicians. Doctors granted privileges to practice in the hospital constitute an organized body called the medical staff. Unlike employed personnel, medical staff do not work for the board, though there may also be salaried physicians who do. The administrative and clinical people operating under the CEO do work for the board and often find themselves caught in the middle between board and medical staff. Occasionally, the medical staff is directly represented on the board. Even so, boards can completely apply the generic model, usually by treating the medical staff organization as a body advisory to the board on the quality of medical practice and practitioners, while still honoring a fully empowered CEO role.

Multicorporate systems in which hospitals are often involved may have an additional peculiarity. It is common to find a parent-subsidiary structure and roles that are artifacts of government payment schemes, not designs based on optimal health care delivery. Multicorporate structuring is more recently waning, however, as cost reimbursement fades into history.

Boards of Associations of Organizations

In this configuration, otherwise separate organizations have formed another tier of organization, a separate nonprofit corporation to which the constituent entities yield some of their powers for a common purpose (Carver, 1996d). The peculiarity of the federation form lies in the nature of the ownership, ordinarily a membership composed of individual organizations. Like city councils, association boards have great difficulty distinguishing their members' ownership role from their customer role (Carver, 1992i). Improved governance by the association board must be accompanied by greater understanding of governance and some degree of "buy in" by the broader group, because better governance calls on the membership to exercise control more responsibly, that is, to be responsible owners.

Because such groups often use the association to impose standards on themselves, individual organizations in the membership frequently try to end-run the ownership's mandates, placing the association staff in the middle. This phenomenon is particularly insidious when the person leading the end run is also a board member. Power struggles and the ownership's reluctance to be governed even by its own rules ensue and can deteriorate into bizarre entanglements. Association staffs often see member organizations as more provincial and less concerned with the esoteric issues. Constituent agencies see the association staff as running out of control and perhaps even hoodwinking the association board (Carver, 1995g). All manner of patchwork, politically motivated structure, and process can grow up around these problems, none of which resolves the fundamental governance flaws that spawned them. Even so, the generic Policy Governance model is totally applicable.

Holding Company and Subsidiary Boards

The parent-subsidiary arrangement of boards is an upside-down version of the federation. In this case, the single, central board owns the multiple boards (see also Carver, 1996e). The holding company structure has long existed in the profit sector, but is a relative newcomer to nonprofit organizations. Four peculiar conditions exist: (1) the ownership of subsidiaries usually comprises a single voting member, the parent corporation; (2) there is often a direct, supervisory link between the staff of the parent and the staff of the subsidiary, bypassing the subsidiary board; (3) the chain of successive staffs and boards up through the hierarchy can become a channel of repetitive approvals, taking the power away from the subsidiary boards; and (4) in some cases, the parent never intends that the subsidiary board govern, only that it provide legal window dressing. None of these conditions causes a problem in application and, in fact, Conditions 2 and 3 are considerably improved by the application of better principles. The generic model is applicable except when Condition 4 exists, in which case the model must be adapted.

Civic Club and Homeowners' Association Boards

The peculiarity is the absence of staff, so these comments apply to any board that has no staff or almost no staff (see also Carver, 1993e). The board and members who can be rounded up are the only "staff" in sight. If the board remembers to wear its governance and workgroup hats separately, the only operational peculiarity lies in the nature of delegation. The board essentially delegates to subgroups of itself or to officers. For the purely governance portion of the board's job, the model is fully applicable, though not nearly as necessary as in larger organizations.

Advisory Boards

Advisory boards or committees can most influentially advise about Ends issues. To influence Ends responsibly, a body must do virtually the same things it would do if it were to govern Ends. So, in that sense, advisory groups can use precepts of the model to give counsel within the latitude available to the advisee. In many cases, advisory boards are merely collections of advisers, which means that many voices, not "one voice," are heard. In this role, neither group decisions nor formal meetings are necessary. The roles an advisory body assumes depend solely on the person or group seeking advice. The model is partially applicable to stretching the visionary breadth of the advisory body and of little use with the collection of individual advisers.

Business Boards

For the most part, business boards are free of the market-surrogate obligation faced by organizations operating in the muted market. They still, however, must determine ends, delegate some degree of latitude to the CEO, and decide how they will best represent investors. To the extent that corporate boards actually represent owners and hold CEOs accountable (remember the skepticism of Geneen, 1984), their need for better governance is almost as great as that in nonprofit and public boards. Drucker (1989) has observed that business boards have much to learn from their nonprofit cousins on this score. The model presented in these pages, with only slight alteration, is completely applicable to the governance of business corporations.

Legislatures and Congress

There are vast differences, of course, between the bulk of nonprofit and public boards and the political "boards" of our state or provincial governments (legislatures) and federal government (Congress or Parliament). Probably the most important structural difference is that, as in some cities, the CEO (governor, president, prime minister, premier) is not subordinate to the board. In the absence of a hierarchal relationship out of which separate roles and authority can be generated, legislative and executive powers are separated in chartering documents.

Still, an examination of legislative behavior using principles of corporate governance is a tempting exercise (Carver, 1991b, 1992g). Controversy over micromanagement receives frequent attention, as do legislative excursions into executive investigative areas perceived to have political appeal. Budgeting on an annual basis for gargantuan agencies of government strains credulity, the more so when compounded by the perennial lateness of the budget process. The long-term mentality of government is severely hampered by such budget policy.

The inability of legislative groups to deal well with their own members' individual impingements on the executive process (intervening in grants, influencing procurement) bespeaks an irresponsibility of momentous proportions. In the United States, the "Keating Five" and Housing and Urban Development scandals of the early 1990s were instances of congressional interferences that went too far even for Congress's lax standards.

By "coaxing, flattering and occasionally threatening federal agencies to meet constituent needs" at the rate of more than three million cases each year (Kiernan, 1989), members of Congress "try to solve the nation's problems one at a time" (Nader, 1989), rather than forcing self-correction in the systems that produce these anomalies. In politically self-serving displays of power, individual legislators damage (or, at best, fail to improve) effectiveness in the very systems their legislation created. Members of Congress were offended when a former Housing and Urban Development administrator suggested that members use oversight power, instead, to ensure proper administrative operation (Felton, 1989).

Former Senator Howard Baker (1989), speaking of the Congress as "a kind of national board of directors," said that body should represent the people on major policy decisions. Its calling is "not to manage the federal establishment to the last detail. We have an executive branch . . . to do that. Congress could do its job better if it did less of it." Nevertheless, the most august of assemblies, shrouding actions in pomp, can do very silly things.

In the words of H. G. Weisman of the Georgia Department of Labor, we "cloak irrelevance in prestige" (personal communication). We have coasted a long time on the design of our founders; arguably, no conceptual breakthrough in republican governance has been created for American government in two hundred years. Perhaps it is time that government gained a new understanding of governance. The Policy Governance model is partially applicable.

Bylaws

This book speaks more to the process and focus with which leaders can better lead than to the initial, enabling mechanism. Yet, mechanics cannot be entirely ignored, even when one deals predominantly with principles and concepts (see also Carver, 1995e). For all nonprofit and many public boards, bylaws create the kind of organ that the board itself is to be. Bylaws, therefore, may help or hinder governance as conceived in these pages.

Bylaws are located in the middle of the hierarchy of documents. The first level is the establishment document, which, for nonprofit organizations, is the articles of incorporation or letters patent and, for public agencies, is a statute or other governmental order or charter. The third level comprises pronouncements of the governing body; in the model presented here, these would consist almost entirely of policies. Bylaws, the middle document, connect this artificial creature of the state to real human beings. These real beings, acting as a board, for practical purposes *become* the artificial person called a corporation.

I offer the following guidelines concerning characteristics of the bylaws.

- *Length.* Bylaws are best kept lean. Include only those items that establish the basic structure and empowerment of the board and its members. Whatever can legitimately be put into policy should be omitted in the bylaws.
- *Membership.* Not-for-profit statutes call for a "corporate membership" to which the board is accountable. The members are the nonprofit equivalent of stockholders. For many groups, such as chambers of commerce and service clubs, membership is a prag-

matically useful concept. For others, such as community health clinics, membership is a confusing entity. It is not comprehensive enough to be the moral ownership referred to in the text. Yet it is usually larger than the board and, thus, constitutes a separate body to be dealt with. Some organizations make use of membership in a ceremonial way, conducting annual meetings and board elections as a ritual. For most, however, it is best to nullify the membership in practice by simply constituting the board as the only membership, thus satisfying law and simplicity simultaneously.

• *Board size.* With respect to board size, the simple rule is to justify any number over seven. There is nothing magic about this number; however, as boards grow progressively beyond this size, they pay an increasingly higher price in awkwardness, discipline, and unfocused energy. Large boards have more than their share of flaws. Such boards are easier to manipulate. Members of large groups tend to assume less responsibility as individuals. Large boards have more difficulty setting meeting dates, deliberating about issues, and staying on task. Nason (1989), speaking of foundation boards, found that the feeling of unity, common purpose, involvement, participation, and responsibility for the organization is greater in smaller boards. But he also felt the range of viewpoints and judiciousness of final consensus are enhanced by larger boards. Taking these opposing factors into account, I would promote as the guiding principle that a board should be no larger than the task of ownership linkage requires.

• *Quorum.* Set the quorum no lower than 51 percent. A surprising number of nonprofit boards establish the quorum at one-third or, on rare occasions, even lower. They usually do so because of attendance problems and bitter experiences in not making the quorum. But a quorum set low is an open admission that attendance does not matter. A board would do better to struggle with expected board member behavior than to hide the issue in a low quorum.

• *Attendance.* One way to deal with the quorum is to require attendance. Public boards have far fewer problems with attendance than nonprofit boards. In the latter, it is not uncommon to find an attendance requirement, but with two fatal flaws. The first error is acknowledging a difference between excused and unexcused absences. In practice, there is no difference, for it is the rare board that can determine if an excuse is good enough. So "excused" comes to be defined as notification that one will not be present. This fulfills the requirement for courtesy, not for attendance.

The second flaw is that termination of membership is not automatic, but dependent on a vote. A motion must be made that Rosemarie or David be kicked off the board. No one wants to do that, so the attendance provision is not enforced. A workable, though slightly softened provision can be written: "Any member absent from three meetings in succession or four meetings in any twelve-month period is automatically terminated. If such a member requests reinstatement within two months, the board may reinstate the seat, though this provision may not be used for any member more than once per term."

- *Officers*. Keep the number of officers minimal and describe their jobs in terms of output areas and authority. Unless the board chooses to name its chairperson as CEO, do not describe the chair's job in terms of a CEO role, for example, that the chair has "general supervision" over the organization. If the organization is large enough to have a staff CEO, avoid having a treasurer unless demanded by law or standard setters. If a treasurer is a must, let the CEO also play that role. Consider having the CEO be secretary as well. There is no power in these roles when they are properly construed, so the board loses nothing but ambiguity.

- *Committees*. If the bylaws are under the control of the board, there is no reason any committee needs to be included. The bylaws can all be dealt with in board policies. If, however, the bylaws are under the control of a membership, the membership can enshrine in bylaws whatever mechanisms it wishes. Of course, the board is the primary mechanism, but the membership may want to define a nominating committee with which it will select board members. I would caution against going as far as American savings and loan institutions in establishing a special committee as a shadow board.

- *Staff*. Bylaws are for the membership and board, not for staff. All material relating to staff can be omitted.

- *Legal review*. The bylaws constitute a legal document. Legal counsel should review any substantive changes. It is best that legal counsel not *write* bylaws, but only review the board's product. Attorneys are qualified to opine on the legality and risk exposure of bylaws, but are not qualified to determine how the board wishes to be.

Policy Contributors

Several board policies have been used to illustrate points in the text. The policies are not reproduced as examples of ideal content or specificity, but as actual products of real governing bodies. Because they are subject to revision and repeal, I do not claim that any of these policies will be in effect at the time of publication. Policies from the various sources have been converted to a common format for convenience of reading, but language and organization have been preserved.

Hundreds of policies were made available to me by organizations using the Policy Governance model or some adaptation thereof. I am grateful to all the organizations that so graciously allowed me to reprint their documents. Unfortunately, space allowed only a few to be used in this text, here listed by policy title.

"Asset Protection." An Executive Limitations policy of the College of Medical Laboratory Technologists of Ontario. *Exhibit 5.5.*

"Board Job Contributions." A Board Process policy of Ramsey Action Programs, St. Paul, Minnesota. *Exhibit 7.5.*

"Board Meetings." A Board Process policy of the Cincinnati–Hamilton County Community Action Agency, Cincinnati, Ohio. *Exhibit 7.4.*

"Board Members' Code of Conduct I." A Board Process policy of Glendale Elementary School District No. 40, Glendale, Arizona. *Exhibit 7.3.*

"City Manager Job Description." A Board-Executive Relationship policy of the City Council of Burnsville, Minnesota. *Exhibit 6.2.*

"Committee Principles." A Board Process policy of the Bissell Centre, Edmonton, Alberta. *Exhibit 8.2.*

"Communication and Support to the Board." An Executive Limitations policy of People Services to the Developmentally Disabled (People, Inc.), Williamsville, New York. *Exhibit 5.4.*

"Culture Conducive to the Needs of the College Community." An Ends policy of the Algonquin Students' Association, Nepean, Ontario. *Exhibit 4.3.*

"Delegation to the President." A Board-Executive Relationship policy of Garden City Community College, Garden City, Kansas. *Exhibit 6.1.*

"Diving Industry Image." An Executive Limitations policy of the Diving Equipment and Marketing Association, Anaheim, California. *Exhibit 5.6.*

"Financial Condition." An Executive Limitations policy of the Voyageur Outward Bound School, Minnetonka, Minnesota. *Exhibit 5.1.*

"Financial Planning." An Executive Limitations policy of the City Council of Bryan, Texas. *Exhibit 5.2.*

"Governing Style." A Board Process policy of the Ohio College of Podiatric Medicine, Cleveland. *Exhibit 7.2.*

"Mission." An Ends policy of the Law Society of Manitoba, Winnipeg. *Exhibit 4.4.*

"Mission." An Ends policy of the Ohio State Board of Education, Columbus. *Exhibit 4.1.*

"Monitoring Executive Performance." A Board-Executive Relationship policy of Summit Pointe, Battle Creek, Michigan. *Exhibit 6.3.*

"Officer Responsibilities." A Board Process policy of Planned Parenthood of Metropolitan Washington, Washington, D.C. *Exhibit 8.1.*

"Ownership." A Board Process policy of Canadian Mental Health Association, Winnipeg Region, Winnipeg, Manitoba. *Exhibit 7.1.*

"Purpose of MIBOR." An Ends policy of the Metropolitan Indianapolis Board of Realtors, Indianapolis, Indiana. *Exhibit 4.2.*

"Staff Treatment." An Executive Limitations policy of the Tennessee Managed Care Network, Nashville. *Exhibit 5.3.*

References

Ackoff, R. *Creating the Corporate Future.* New York: Wiley, 1981.

Albee, E. *Who's Afraid of Virginia Woolf?* New York: Atheneum, 1962.

Anthony, R. N. "Can Nonprofit Organizations Be Well Managed?" In D. Borst and P. J. Montana (eds.), *Managing Nonprofit Organizations.* New York: AMACOM, 1977.

Argenti, J. *Your Organization: What Is It For? Challenging Traditional Organizational Aims.* London: McGraw-Hill Europe, 1993.

Baker, H. H., Jr. "Replace Congress with a 'Citizen Legislature.'" *Chicago Tribune,* June 16, 1989, sec. 1, p. 27.

Barth, N. "Clear Policy Statements Can Free You to Act Creatively." *Board Leadership,* 1992, no. 1, p. 8.

Blumenthal, L. "Nonprofits Awakening to Need for Effective Boards." *Nonprofit Times,* 1988, *2,* 5–20.

Brudney, J. L., and Murray, V. "The Nature and Impact of Changes in Boards of Directors of Canadian Not-for-Profit Organizations." Unpublished paper, 1996.

Carver, J. "The Director's Employment Contract as a Tool for Improved Governance." *Journal of Mental Health Administration,* 1979a, *6,* 14–25.

Carver, J. "Profitability: Useful Fiction for Nonprofit Enterprise." *Administration in Mental Health,* 1979b, 7(1), 3–20.

Carver, J. *Business Leadership on Nonprofit Boards.* Board Monograph Series, no. 12. Washington, D.C.: National Association of Corporate Directors, 1980a.

Carver, J. "Toward a Technology of Governance." Unpublished paper, 1980b.

Carver, J. "Is America Ready for Self-Governance: The Third Sector." In D. Nachmias and A. Greer (eds.), *The Crisis of Authority: Citizen Boards and the Governance of Public and Private Agencies.* Milwaukee: Urban Research Center, University of Wisconsin, 1981a.

Carver, J. "The Market Surrogate Obligation of Public Sector Boards." *Journal of Mental Health Administration,* 1981b, *8,* 42–45.

Carver, J. "Toward More Effective Library Boards." *Focus on Indiana Libraries,* 1981c, *35*(7/8), 8–11.

Carver, J. "Improving Board Control and Effectiveness: The Problems of Non-Profit Governance." Three-part series for the *Non-Profit Administrator's Guide,* 1982: *1*(2), 14–16; *1*(3), 9–16; *1*(4), 7–11.

Carver, J. "Leadership Through Boards, Councils, and Commissions: Creating the Future Through Better Governance." Paper presented at the annual meeting of the National Association of Community Leadership Organizations, Cleveland, Ohio, Sept. 19, 1983.

Carver, J. "Consulting with Boards of Human Service Agencies: Leverage for Organizational Effectiveness." *Consultation,* 1984a, *3*(3), 27–39.

Carver, J. "Professional Challenges for an Emerging Community: The Challenge to Nonprofit Governance." Paper presented at the annual meeting of the Nonprofit Management Association, San Francisco, June 6–10, 1984b.

Carver, J. "Redesigning Governance in the Cities." *Florida Municipal Record,* 1984c, *58,* 2–4.

Carver, J. *Strategic Leadership: New Principles for Boards, Councils, and Commissions.* San Francisco: Public Management Institute, 1985a. Audiotape.

Carver, J. *A Tested, Fresh Approach to Designing the Board's Job.* Milwaukee, Wis.: Family Service America, 1985b. Audiotape.

Carver, J. "Women on Governing Boards." Unpublished paper, 1985c.

Carver, J. "Boards as Cost Centers." Unpublished paper, 1986a.

Carver, J. *Eighteen Principles for Effective Leadership by the Board of Directors: An Introduction to the Technology of Governance for Nonprofit Organizations.* Untitled monograph series. Berkeley, Calif.: Center for Community Futures, 1986b.

Carver, J. *Nonprofit and Governmental Boards: New Design for Leadership.* Atlanta: Georgia Power Company, 1986c. Videotape.

Carver, J. *Governing Parks and Recreation: Board Strategic Leadership in a New Light.* Alexandria, Va.: National Recreation and Park Association, 1987. Videotape.

Carver, J. "Re-Inventing the Governing Board." *Access,* 1988a, *1*(1), 4–8.

Carver, J. "Vision, Values, and the Trivia Trap." *Florida Focus,* 1988b, *1*(2), 1–5.

Carver, J. "A Model for Strategic Leadership." *Hospital Trustee,* 1989a, *13*(4), 10–12.

Carver, J. *Re-Inventing the Board: Strategic Leadership for Public and Nonprofit Governance.* Athens: University of Georgia, 1989b. National video teleconference.

Carver, J. "Economic Development and Inter-Board Leadership." *Economic Development Review,* 1990a, *8*(3), 24–28.

Carver, J. "Governing Parks and Recreation." *Parks and Recreation,* 1990b, *8*(3), 24–28.

Carver, J. "The CEO and the Renegade Board Member." *Nonprofit World,* 1991a, *9*(6), 14–17.

Carver, J. "Recommendations to the West Virginia Legislative Oversight Commission on Education Accountability." Unpublished paper written under contract to the West Virginia legislature, 1991b.

Carver, J. "Redefining the Board's Role in Fiscal Planning." *Nonprofit Management and Leadership,* 1991c, *2*(2), 177–192.

Carver, J. "Creating a Single Voice: The Prerequisite to Board Leadership." *Board Leadership,* 1992a, no. 2, pp. 1–5.

Carver, J. *Empowering Boards for Leadership: Redefining Excellence in Governance.* San Francisco: Jossey-Bass, 1992b. Audiotape.

Carver, J. "A Few Tips for the Chairperson." *Board Leadership,* 1992c, no. 3, p. 6.

Carver, J. "First Things First: An Imaginative Exercise for Revitalizing Your Mission." *Board Leadership,* 1992d, no. 1, pp. 1–5.

Carver, J. "The Founding Parent Syndrome: Governing in the CEO's Shadow." *Nonprofit World,* 1992e, *10*(5), 14–16.

Carver, J. "Just How Long Should Board Meetings Be?" *Board Leadership,* 1992f, no. 1, p. 6.

Carver, J. "Partnership for Public Service: Accountability in the Social Service Delivery System." Unpublished paper written under contract to the Ontario Ministry of Community and Social Services, 1992g.

Carver, J. "Time to Junk the Old Formula for Boards." *Chronicle of Philanthropy,* 1992h, *4*(22), 36–37.

Carver, J. "When Customers Are Owners: The Confusion of Dual Board Hats." *Nonprofit World,* 1992i, *10*(4), 11–15.

Carver, J. *Board Leadership: A Bimonthly Workshop with John Carver.* Special board self-evaluation issue, no. 10, 1993a.

Carver, J. *Board Leadership: A Bimonthly Workshop with John Carver.* Special fiduciary issue, no. 6, 1993b.

Carver, J. *John Carver on Board Governance.* San Francisco: Jossey-Bass, 1993c. Videotape.

Carver, J. *Reinventing Governance: Enabling a Revolution in Leadership for Community College Boards.* Washington, D.C.: Association of Community College Trustees, 1993d. Videotape.

Carver, J. "When Board Members Are the Only Staff in Sight." *Board Leadership,* 1993e, no. 9, pp. 6–7.

Carver, J. "New Means to an End." *Times Educational Supplement,* July 1, 1994a, 6.

Carver, J. "One Board Fails to Follow Its Own Monitoring Policy and Courts Fiscal Disaster." *Board Leadership,* 1994b, no. 14, pp. 3–5.

Carver, J. "Protecting Board Integrity from the Renegade Board Member." *Board Leadership,* 1994c, no. 13, pp. 1–8.

Carver, J. "Protecting Governance from Law, Funders, and Accreditors." *Board Leadership,* 1994d, no. 11, pp. 1–5.

Carver, J. "Board Accountability in the Modern Charity." *Solicitors' Journal,* spring 1995a.

Carver, J. *Board Leadership: A Bimonthly Workshop with John Carver.* Special ownership issue, no. 18, 1995b.

Carver, J. "Ends and Means: Nurturing the Relationship Between a Congregation and Its Governing Body." *Practice of Ministry in Canada,* Feb. 1995c, *12*(1), 17–19.

Carver, J. "Policies 'R' Us." *Board Leadership,* 1995d, no. 20, pp. 1–8.

Carver, J. "Shaping up Your Bylaws." *Board Leadership,* 1995e, no. 20, pp. 4–6.

Carver, J. "What Happens to Conventional Documents Under Policy Governance?" *Board Leadership,* 1995f, no. 21, pp. 1–6.

Carver, J. "Who Is in Charge? Is Your Organization Too Staff-Driven? Too Volunteer-Driven?" *Board Leadership,* 1995g, no. 22, pp. 4–6.

Carver, J. *Board Leadership: A Bimonthly Workshop with John Carver.* Special CEO evaluation issue, no. 26, 1996a.

Carver, J. *The Chairperson's Role as Servant-Leader to the Board.* The Carver-Guide Series on Effective Board Governance, no. 3. San Francisco: Jossey-Bass, 1996b.

Carver, J. *Creating a Mission That Makes a Difference.* The CarverGuide Series on Effective Board Governance, no. 6. San Francisco: Jossey-Bass, 1996c.

Carver, J. "Families of Boards I: Federations." *Board Leadership,* 1996d, no. 25, pp. 1–6.

Carver, J. "Families of Boards II: Federations." *Board Leadership,* 1996e, no. 27, pp. 1–8.

Carver, J. *Planning Better Board Meetings.* The CarverGuide Series on Effective Board Governance, no. 5. San Francisco: Jossey-Bass, 1996f.

Carver, J. "Policy Governance Views Citizens as Owners." *Nation's Cities Weekly,* Jan. 29, 1996g, p. 5.

Carver, J. "Recruiting Leaders: What to Look for in New Board Members." *Board Leadership,* 1996h, no. 23, pp. 1–8.

Carver, J. *Three Steps to Fiduciary Responsibility.* The CarverGuide Series on Effective Board Governance, no. 3. San Francisco: Jossey-Bass, 1996i.

Carver, J. "When Bad Governance Is Required." *Board Leadership,* 1996j, no. 24, pp. 1–8.

Carver, J., and Carver, M. M. *Basic Principles of Policy Governance.* The CarverGuide Series on Effective Board Governance, no. 1. San Francisco: Jossey-Bass, 1996a.

Carver, J., and Carver, M. M. *Your Roles and Responsibilities as a Board Member.* The CarverGuide Series on Effective Board Governance, no. 2. San Francisco: Jossey-Bass, 1996b.

Carver, J., and Carver, M. M. *Reinventing Your Board: A Step-by-Step Guide to Implementing Policy Governance.* San Francisco: Jossey-Bass, 1997.

Carver, J., and Clemow, T. "Redeeming the Church Board." Unpublished paper, 1990.

Carver, J., and Mayhew, M. *A New Vision of Board Leadership: Governing the Community College.* Washington, D.C.: Association of Community College Trustees, 1994.

Chait, R. P., and Taylor, B. E. "Charting the Territory of Nonprofit Boards." *Harvard Business Review,* 1989, *129,* 44–54.

Crosby, P. B. *Quality Is Free.* New York: McGraw-Hill, 1979.

Crosby, P. B. *Quality Without Tears.* New York: McGraw-Hill, 1984.

Davis, S. M. *Managing Corporate Culture.* New York: Ballinger, 1984.

Deming, W. E. *Out of Crisis.* Cambridge: Center for Advanced Engineering Study, Massachusetts Institute of Technology, 1986.

Drucker, P. F. *The Effective Executive.* New York: HarperCollins, 1967.

Drucker, P. F. *Management: Tasks, Responsibilities, Practices.* New York: HarperCollins, 1974.

Drucker, P. F. "Managing the Public Service Institution." In D. Borst and P. J. Montana (eds.), *Managing Nonprofit Organizations.* New York: AMACOM, 1977.

Drucker, P. F. "Managing the 'Third Sector.'" *Wall Street Journal,* Oct. 3, 1978, p. 26.

Drucker, P. F. "What Business Can Learn from Nonprofits." *Harvard Business Review,* July–Aug. 1989, *89*(4), 88–93.

Ewell, C. M. "How Hospital Governing Boards Differ from Their Corporate Counterparts." *Trustee,* Dec. 1986, pp. 24–25.

Felton, E. "The Politics of Influence Peddling." *Insight,* Sept. 18, 1989, 22–23.

Ferguson, M. Untitled paper presented at the World Future Society, Toronto, July 1980.

Fram, E. H. "Nonprofit Boards: They're Going Corporate." *Nonprofit World,* 1986, *4*(6), 20–36.

Fram, E. H. *Policy vs. Paper Clips: Selling the Corporate Model to Your Nonprofit Board.* Milwaukee, Wis.: Family Service America, 1988.

Geneen, H. S. "Why Directors Can't Protect the Shareholders." *Fortune,* 1984, *110,* 28–29.

Gregory, T. W. "How to Implement Policy Governance." *Trustee Quarterly,* 1996a, no. 1, pp. 5–6.

Gregory, T. W. "What Is Policy Governance?" *Trustee Quarterly,* 1996b, no. 1, pp. 3–4.

Guy, J. "Good Investment Decisions Are Policy Driven." *Board Leadership,* 1992, no. 4, p. 8.

Guy, J. "Making Decisions: The Role of Governance." *Journal of Financial Planning,* 1995, *8*(1), 34–38.

Haskins, C. P. "A Foundation Board Looks at Itself." *Foundation News,* Mar.–Apr. 1972, *13*(2).

Houle, C. O. *Governing Boards: Their Nature and Nurture.* San Francisco: Jossey-Bass, 1989.

Imai, M. *Kaizen.* New York: Random House, 1986.

Juran, J. M., and Louden, J. K. *The Corporate Director.* New York: American Management Association, 1966.

Kiernan, M. "Your Guy in Washington: Members of Congress May Be More Useful Than You Think." *U.S. News & World Report,* 1989, *107*(6), 54–56.

Kirk, W. A. *Nonprofit Organization Governance: A Challenge in Turbulent Times.* New York: Carlton Press, 1986.

Koontz, H. *The Board of Directors and Effective Management.* New York: McGraw-Hill, 1967.

Lorsch, J. W. *Pawns or Potentates: The Reality of America's Corporate Boards.* Boston: Harvard Business School, 1989.

Louden, J. K. *The Effective Director in Action.* New York: AMACOM, 1975.

McConkey, D. *MBO for Nonprofit Organizations.* New York: AMACOM, 1975.

McGowan, R. A. "An Integrated Approach to Board Development." *Health Care Management Review,* 1987, *12*(3), 29–30.

Mueller, R. K. *Board Life: Realities of Being a Corporate Director.* New York: AMACOM, 1974.

Mueller, R. K. *The Incompleat Board: The Unfolding of Corporate Governance.* Lexington, Mass.: Heath, 1981.

Murray, V. "Is Carver's Model Really the One Best Way?" *Front & Centre,* Sept. 1994, p. 11.

Nader, R. Cited in M. Kiernan, "Your Guy in Washington: Members of Congress May Be More Useful Than You Think." *U.S. News & World Report,* 1989, *107*(6), 54.

Nason, J. W. *Foundation Trusteeship: Service in the Public Interest.* New York: Foundation Center, 1989.

National School Boards Association. Untitled advertising flyer. Alexandria, Va.: National School Boards Association, n.d.

Neu, C. H., Jr., and Sumek, L. J. "Municipal Governance Challenge of the 1980s." *Florida Municipal Record,* 1983, *56,* 11–22.

O'Connell, B. *The Board Member's Book.* New York: Foundation Center, 1985.

Odiorne, G. S. *Management and the Activity Trap*. New York: HarperCollins, 1974.

Peters, T. J. *Thriving on Chaos: Handbook for a Management Revolution*. New York: Knopf, 1988.

Peters, T. J., and Waterman, R. H. *In Search of Excellence: Lessons from America's Best-Run Companies*. New York: HarperCollins, 1982.

Price, W. S. *Manual on Governance and Policy Planning for Board Members*. Silver Spring, Md.: Wolfgang S. Price Associates, 1977.

Reddin, W. J. *Effective Management by Objectives: The 3-D Method of MBO*. New York: McGraw-Hill, 1971.

Royer, G. "Proactive About What?" *American School Board Journal*, 1996a, *183*(6), 34–39.

Royer, G. *School Board Leadership 2000: The Things Staff Didn't Tell You at Orientation*. Houston, Tex.: Brockton, 1996b.

Skinner, W. "The Productivity Paradox." *Harvard Business Review*, 1986, *64*, 55–59.

Smith, C. J. "Eight Colleges Implement Policy Governance." *Trustee Quarterly*, 1996, no. 1, pp. 8–10.

Smith, D. K. "Making Change Stick." *Leader to Leader*, 1996, no. 2, pp. 24–29.

Smith, E. E. "Management's Least-Used Asset: The Board of Directors." In *The Dynamics of Management*. AMA Management Report, no. 14. New York: American Management Association, 1958. Cited by H. Koontz, *The Board of Directors and Effective Management*. New York: McGraw-Hill, 1967.

Sternberg, E. *Just Business: Business Ethics in Action*. New York: Little, Brown, 1994.

Swanson, A. "Who's in Charge Here? Board of Directors and Staff—The Division of Responsibility." *Nonprofit World*, 1986, *4*(4), 14–18.

Waterman, R. H., Jr. *The Renewal Factor: How the Best Get and Keep the Competitive Edge*. New York: Bantam Books, 1988.

Witt, J. A. *Building a Better Hospital Board*. Ann Arbor, Mich.: Health Administration Press, 1987.

Index